International Affairs 1939-

HODDER AND STOUGHTON
LONDON SYDNEY AUCKLAND TORONTO

International Affairs 1939–1979

R N RUNDLE

The cover illustration, of a soldier looking out over the Suez Canal, is reproduced by permission of the Keystone Press Agency Ltd.

British Library Cataloguing in Publication Data

Rundle, R.N.
  International affairs 1939–1979.
  1. History, Modern – 20th century
  I. Title
  909.82   D421

ISBN 0 340 23709 0

First published 1981

Filmset, printed and bound in Great Britain for Hodder and Stoughton Educational, a division of Hodder and Stoughton Ltd, Mill Road, Dunton Green, Sevenoaks, Kent, by Hazell Watson & Viney Ltd, Aylesbury, Bucks

Acknowledgements
The author and publishers wish to thank the following for granting permission to reproduce the illustrations in this book: the Society for Cultural Relations with the USSR, pages 2 and 3; John Topham Picture Library, pages 8, 13, 27, 32, 33, 39, 41, 42, 44, 66, 68, 104, 107, 108, 110, 126, 128, 129, 138, 139, 142, 155, 157, 167, 175, 179, 185 and 196; Popperfoto, pages 9, 17, 46, 47, 97, 101, 147, 161, 171, 174 and 182; Keystone Press Agency Ltd, pages 21, 31, 144, 165, 189 and 195; Archives Documentation Française, pages 28, 58 © Photo CCE, and 63 (both photographs); United Nations, pages 43, 44 and 45; the Imperial War Museum, page 31; Shell UK Ltd, page 79; the Sunday Times, page 82, photograph by Donald McCullin; Camera Press Ltd, pages 118, photograph by Donald McCullin/ILN, and 119, photograph by David Terry; Oxfam, page 131; Associated Press Ltd, page 201.

Sources of extracts
The Second World War, Winston S Churchill (Cassell and Co Ltd), pages 21, 34
The Public Papers of the Secretaries-General of the United Nations, selected and edited with commentary by Andrew W Cordier and Max Harrelson
(Columbia University Press, New York, 1977), pages 40, 45, 149, 202.
The Discovery of India, Jawarhal Nehru (Meridian Books Ltd, London), pages 124, 126.
Full Circle: Memoirs, Sir Anthony Eden (Cassell and Co, 1960), page 138.
Philippe Devillers and Jean Lacouture: Histoire de Vietnam (translated by Alexander Lieven and Adam Roberts, Pall Mall Press, 1969), page 115.

CONTENTS

MAPS

PROLOGUE:
The Decline of European Influence

In 1939 Western Europe, with its great industrial wealth, vast overseas empires, superior technology and military supremacy, exerted over the continents of Asia and Africa a powerful influence which was out of all proportion to its size and population. The United States, insulated by the Pacific and Atlantic Oceans, seemed largely content with this state of affairs, provided its traditional guardianship of the western hemisphere was not disputed. The Soviet Union had an uneasy relationship with its neighbours, being feared for its great size and potential power, yet itself fearful of attack by either Nazi Germany or Japan. China, the victim of its failure to modernise, was torn by civil war and partitioned by Japan.

The Second World War weakened Europe and left it in 1945 a hostage to the United States and the Soviet Union, which had emerged from the conflict as superpowers. Since neither dared to withdraw from Europe lest the other filled the power vacuum, Europe became divided into two mutually hostile blocs, with Western Europe dependent for its survival upon the United States, and Eastern Europe subordinate to the policies of the Soviet Union. North America and Western Europe formed a military partnership when they joined the North Atlantic Treaty Organisation in 1949. The communist countries of Eastern Europe and the Soviet Union formed the rival Warsaw Pact in 1955 in reply. The rival military alliance systems were a great source of international tension, and a factor in the Cold War developing between the two superpowers.

Europe's ties with the rest of the world were transformed by the political and economic upheavals associated firstly with the war, and secondly, after 1945, with decolonisation and the emergence of the so-called 'Third World' of under-developed nations. As the countries of Western Europe gradually came to terms with their diminished status by forming the European Economic Community, so the prospect of war between them, for centuries one of the major themes in European history, receded. At the same time Europe was relegated to become part of a network of trade relationships, in which crippling economic pressure could be brought to bear upon it by the Third World countries (though at considerable cost to themselves). Thus in 1973, and again in 1979, the world economy was thrown into turmoil when OPEC, the Organisation of Petroleum Exporting Countries, increased the price of oil. The energy crisis enabled OPEC to influence the foreign policies of the United States and other Western countries, by threatening to cut back on oil production, if the actions of these powers did not reflect the interests of OPEC members.

After 1970 the global nature of superpower diplomacy was further complicated by the emergence of the People's Republic of China as a superpower in its own right, thereby threatening to disturb the equilibrium which had been precariously established between the Soviet Union and the United States. The potential of these latter two nations to destroy each other in a nuclear war and in the process wreak havoc upon the rest of the world, together with the explosive social and economic problems of the Third World, form a sombre backcloth to contemporary international affairs.

CHAPTER ONE:
The Second World War, from the Attack on Poland to Pearl Harbour

At daybreak on Friday 1 September 1939, five German armies invaded Poland. Part of Kuchler's Third Army advanced south westwards from East Prussia to meet the German Fourth Army pushing eastwards from Pomerania, while the other part, Guderian's panzer divisions, drove south in a great out-flanking threat to Brest Litovsk. Meanwhile, from Silesia, three armies commanded by von Rundstedt swept towards Warsaw.

In the air the *Luftwaffe* (the German air force) swiftly won complete supremacy, and was able to attack Polish troop formations with little opposition. The Poles were dismayed by the sustained ferocity and speed of the German onslaught, in which long-ranging armoured columns wrought havoc with their lines of communication. The Polish armies, outnumbered and outmanoeuvred by better-equipped opponents, were experiencing a new form of 'lightning warfare', *blitzkrieg*, employed for the first time by the Germans with brilliant and terrifying success.

German troops crossed the river Vistula on 5 September, thus sealing the Polish Corridor and linking East Prussia with the rest of Germany. They reached the outskirts of Warsaw four days later, while Brest Litovsk was captured by Guderian's panzer divisions on 14 September. When the Soviet Union invaded eastern Poland, occupying Lwow on 22 September, Poland's cause was hopeless. Warsaw, ruthlessly bombed

Russian tanks move into Poland.

by the *Luftwaffe*, held out until 27 September, but on 6 October the last Polish troops ceased fighting.

Poland was doomed from the start of the war, for its long frontiers were impossible to defend adequately. Moreover, Britain and France, which declared war on Germany on 3 September, did not come to Poland's aid, while the Soviet Union joined forces with Germany to obtain a share of Poland's territory. After the initial German break-through the Polish armies were never allowed time to regroup, while courage and cavalry were no match for armoured divisions exploiting a new concept of warfare. After the first week's fighting only energetic military intervention by France and Britain could have saved Poland, and this was not to be. Poland's allies made no move against Germany's weakly defended frontier in the west, and the war was three months old before the British army suffered its first casualty. In the meantime, Poland, the first victim of the German *blitzkrieg*, had been divided between Germany and Russia.

Although ultimately victorious, the Russians suffered many setbacks in the Winter War. Here, armoured cars, trucks and tanks have been abandoned in confusion on the Suomussalmi front.

The Russo-Finnish War (30 November 1939– 13 March 1940)

While the Russo-German attack upon Poland was in progress, the Soviet Union compelled the governments of Estonia, Latvia and Lithuania to enter into agreements whereby it secured bases in their territories. The German government raised no objections to these moves, since the Nazi-Soviet Pact of August 1939 had placed Finland and the Baltic states within the Russian sphere of influence.

In October the Finnish government was asked to cede territory and bases to Russia, since Stalin was worried about the defence of Leningrad, Russia's second largest city with a population only slightly less than that of Finland. Leningrad, which was only twenty miles from the Finnish frontier, was vulnerable to an attack either from the direction of the Gulf of Finland, or through southern Finland. As Finland was not strong enough to repel a German attack, Stalin demanded guarantees of Russian security from invasion. These involved pushing back the Finnish frontier on the Karelian Isthmus, the cession of Hankö (allowing Russia to control the Gulf of Finland) and territory on the Rybachiy Peninsula in the far north, which would guarantee Russia control of the Petsamo Fiord.

The Finns rejected Stalin's requests, and both sides prepared for war. Having belonged to the Russian Empire from 1809 to 1917, the Finns feared that they would lose their independence if they surrendered any territory. The Russians recalled that during the Civil War (1918–20) the Finnish government had connived at British and German forces operating from its territory against the Bolsheviks. Stalin also suspected that a German attempt to destroy Russian communism might not be an unwelcome prospect to the Finnish government. Above all else, however, he was determined to make Leningrad less vulnerable to attack.

On 30 November Russian troops invaded Finland, and the *Winter War* began. For two months the Finns put up a successful resistance which won the admiration of the rest of Europe, but in

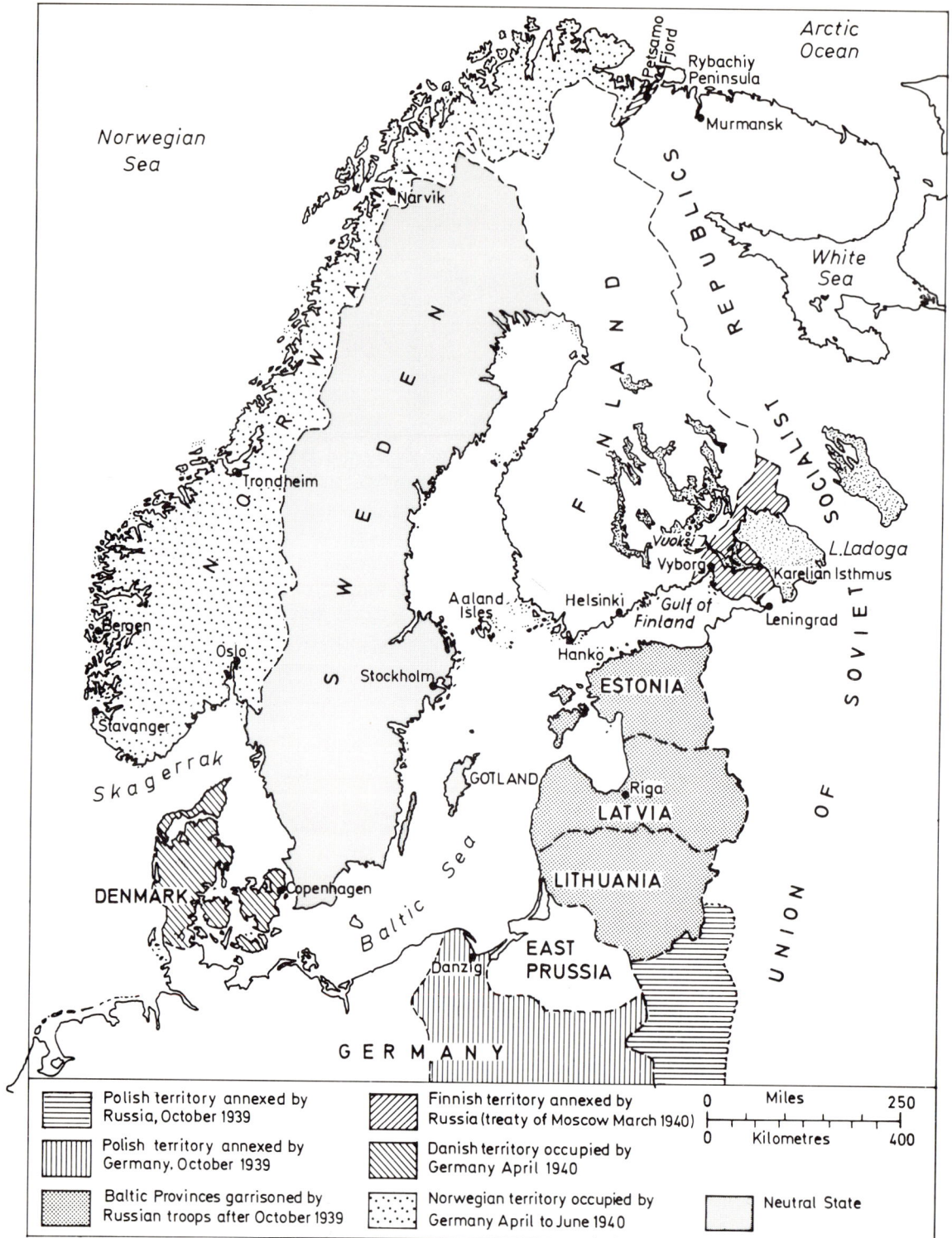

Map labels:

Arctic Ocean

Norwegian Sea

Petsamo Fjord · Rybachiy Peninsula · Murmansk

White Sea

Narvik

REPUBLICS

SOCIALIST

Trondheim

F I N L A N D

L. Ladoga

Vuoksi · Vyborg · Karelian Isthmus

Aaland Isles · Helsinki · *Gulf of Finland* · Leningrad

Bergen · Oslo · Hanko

Stavanger

Stockholm

ESTONIA

GOTLAND

Riga

LATVIA

Skagerrak

Baltic Sea

LITHUANIA

DENMARK · Copenhagen

Danzig · EAST PRUSSIA

G E R M A N Y

UNION OF SOVIET

S W E D E N

N O R W A Y

Legend:

Polish territory annexed by Russia, October 1939	Finnish territory annexed by Russia (treaty of Moscow March 1940)
Polish territory annexed by Germany, October 1939	Danish territory occupied by Germany April 1940
Baltic Provinces garrisoned by Russian troops after October 1939	Norwegian territory occupied by Germany April to June 1940
	Neutral State

Miles 0 — 250
Kilometres 0 — 400

1   *The Baltic States, 1939–40*

February 1940 the Red Army broke through their defences, and in March the Treaty of Moscow ended the war. Finland ceded a tenth of its territory, including Vyborg, its second largest city, the industrial area on the river Vuoksi, and half the Rybachiy Peninsula. Stalin thereby secured the guarantees he wanted, but at the cost of provoking the Finns to join the German attack upon the Soviet Union in 1941.

The German occupation of Norway

The British government had considered the idea of helping the Finns, although such action would have involved the risk of war with the Soviet Union, with unpredictable consequences. Perhaps fortunately for Britain, the collapse of Finnish resistance reprieved the Cabinet from making a decision. Nevertheless, prompted by Winston Churchill, who was anxious for a new theatre of war to be opened up in Scandinavia, it decided to intervene in Norway.

Norway's geographical position and long coastline involved it in the strategic planning of both the British and German High Commands. British possession of Narvik would have deprived Germany of its supplies of iron ore from Sweden, and assisted the Royal Navy in its task of closing to enemy warships the North Sea exit to the Atlantic. Until February 1940 Hitler considered Norway's neutrality to be, on balance, more advantageous to Germany than the seizure of bases, provided this neutrality was respected by Britain.

In February 1940 a British destroyer rescued 300 captured British seamen from the *Graf Spee's* supply ship, the *Altmark*, which was intercepted in Norwegian waters as it was returning home to Germany. The *Altmark* incident resolved Hitler's indecision over Norway, and invasion plans were rapidly drawn up. British intentions to occupy Narvik were frustrated by a daring and unexpected German seaborne invasion of Norway, when a force of 10,000 troops captured the ports of Narvik and Trondheim in April 1940. Simultaneously Denmark was occupied by German troops, with hardly a shot fired.

Although British troops landed near Narvik in the middle of April and captured the port six weeks later, they were withdrawn at the beginning of June, when the British and French armies faced disaster at Dunkirk in northern France.

The Battle for France 1940

In Western Europe Poland's defeat was followed by a six months' lull in the fighting. The *phoney war*, as it was called, ended abruptly on 10 May 1940, when German armies invaded the Low Countries and France. The Hague and Rotterdam were attacked at dawn by airborne troops, while German armoured columns swept across the border. Rotterdam was ruthlessly bombed with heavy loss of civilian life, and the Dutch government, alarmed by the *Luftwaffe's* threat to Holland's crowded and defenceless cities, surrendered after only five days' fighting.

Belgium, too, was thrown into confusion by aerial attacks on its towns and airfields. German paratroops attacked defensive positions along the Albert Canal, and the seemingly impregnable fortress of Eben-Emaul was put out of action. Refugees crowded the roads, and alarm and despondency spread rapidly as fifth columnists (enemy agents among the civilian population) were suspected everywhere. Belgium resisted for two weeks before surrendering unconditionally on 28 May.

The decisive blow, however, was being delivered further south. Massed in the mountainous, heavily wooded area of the Ardennes, was a convoy of tanks, lorries, motorised troops and infantry which stretched back almost 100 miles into Germany. Seven panzer divisions advanced swiftly, penetrating the lightly held French defences (for no attack was expected in this sector) and reaching the river Meuse, near Sedan, within forty-eight hours.

With the support of dive bombers which acted as heavy artillery, bridgeheads were established across the Meuse by nightfall. By 18 May German armour had captured St Quentin, half-way to the Channel, which was reached on 20 May. In ten days, therefore, German motorised units

FINLAND

NORWAY

SWEDEN

North
Sea

Baltic
Sea

ESTONIA

LATVIA

LITHUANIA

UNION OF
SOVIET
SOCIALIST
REPUBLICS
(concluded
non-aggression
pact with
Germany in
Aug 1939)

IRELAND

DENMARK

GREAT
BRITAIN

Atlantic
Ocean

HOLLAND

BELGIUM

GERMANY

E. PRUSSIA

POLAND

CZECHOSLOVAKIA

FRANCE

SWITZERLAND

HUNGARY

RUMANIA

Black
Sea

YUGOSLAVIA

PORTUGAL

SPAIN

CORSICA

ITALY

BULGARIA

ALBANIA

GREECE

TURKEY

GIBRALTAR

SARDINIA

Mediterranean Sea

SICILY

CRETE

Axis powers in 1938	Seized by Germany Sept 1939	Bessarabia: occupied by USSR June 1940
Annexed by Germany 1938-39	Occupied by USSR 1939	Vichy French territory 1940
Occupied by Hungary 1938-39	Annexed by USSR 1940	Awarded to Hungary August 1940
Annexed by Italy April 1939	Occupied by Germany 1940	Became Germany's Allies April-June 1941

Conquered by Germany and its Allies April-June 1941

Neutral States

German protectorate

Miles   0 — 500
Kilometres   0 — 800

2   *The Second World War in Europe, 1939–41*

had advanced 240 miles, cutting off the main British and French armies which were trapped near Dunkirk.

By a combination of luck, German mistakes and the efforts of the Royal Navy, the greater part of the Allied armies was rescued. To his enemies' surprise, Hitler ordered the panzers to halt, anxious to conserve his tanks for the next stage of the battle for France. Mindful of his experiences in the First World War, Hitler was reluctant to commit his tanks to fighting in countryside where canals, dykes and marshes severely restricted their operations, while Goering was anxious for the *Luftwaffe* to obtain its share of glory by destroying the bridgehead.

During the ten days from 26 May to 4 June, over 330,000 French and British troops were evacuated from the beaches of Dunkirk. An armada of destroyers, pleasure boats, paddle steamers and fishing boats plied across the Channel. In Britain the rescue of the British Expeditionary Force was hailed as almost a miracle – even though, as Churchill pointed out, 'Wars are

not won by evacuations.' Furthermore, the BEF had abandoned all its equipment, whose replacement would take several months. Nevertheless, the 'miracle of Dunkirk' gave Britain, protected by its Channel 'ditch', a chance of survival.

The second phase of the German offensive against France began on 5 June. Such was the disarray of the French armies that General Weygand, the French commander, faced an almost impossible task. He dispiritedly ordered his subordinates to defend the line of the rivers Somme and Aisne to the last man, which would at least save French honour. The German panzers, however, could not be checked in their advance south. When they reached the Swiss frontier the half million French troops stationed in the Maginot line were cut off, with no hope of affecting the outcome of the struggle. The Maginot Line, therefore, on whose false security the French people had relied, played virtually no part in the war, except to detain many of France's best troops who waited for an attack which never came.

Ships leaving the beaches at Dunkirk, taking troops to England.

Paris was abandoned by the French government, which declared it an Open City, so that it was saved from destruction. Winston Churchill, who replaced Neville Chamberlain as Britain's Prime Minister on the day the Battle for France began, flew to France. There, in a desperate attempt to maintain the French will to fight on, he suggested to the French government the union of Britain and France. This proposal merely divided the French cabinet, with Paul Reynaud (the French Premier) resigning when a majority of ministers declared their wish for peace. General Pétain, the First World War hero of Verdun, took his place and requested a ceasefire, ordering the French people to lay down their arms. On 22 June armistice terms were signed in the same railway carriage which was the scene of the end of the First World War. Thus Hitler secured Germany's revenge for the Treaty of Versailles (1919).

Vichy France

The surrender terms were harsh. The northern half of France was militarily occupied. The southern half was allowed to have its own government at Vichy, headed by Pétain, but it was forced to pay for the costs of the German occupation of France, while over one million French prisoners remained in captivity. In November 1942 German troops occupied the whole of France, although the Vichy government was allowed to stay in office until it collapsed in 1944.

Hitler did not, however, lay claim to the French colonies, nor did he demand the surrender of the powerful French navy. Instead it was ordered to sail to ports in French North and West Africa, where it would be immobilised. As German records make clear, Hitler did not wish to antagonise either the French navy or the colonies into going over to Britain's side.

In spite of Hitler's concessions and the instructions of Admiral Darlan (Commander of the French navy) that in no circumstances were French warships to be handed over to the enemy intact, Churchill regarded the existence of the French fleet as a menace. With most of Europe's coastline in enemy hands following Italy's entry

into the war on 10 June, Britain's naval supremacy would have been seriously challenged if the French fleet had been combined with the Italian and German navies. In Churchill's view, if the French fleet would not sail to British ports it must be destroyed where it lay, even at the risk of provoking war with Vichy France.

In July, British battleships attacked French warships lying at their moorings in Oran, Mers el Kebir and Dakar. Several French ships were sunk and others were damaged, while over one thousand French sailors were killed. At the same time French ships at Plymouth and Portsmouth were boarded by British seamen, and their crews interned. An attempt to capture the port of Dakar on the West African coast, which in enemy hands could threaten the sea route from Gibraltar to Capetown, was abandoned when the French resisted strongly. Fortunately for Britain the Vichy government did not ally with Germany. It confined its action to an air raid on Gibraltar, and to breaking off diplomatic relations with Britain. Nevertheless, the attack upon the French fleet created great bitterness in France.

Not all Frenchmen, however, agreed with Pétain's policy of collaboration with Nazi Germany. In exile, de Gaulle (a little known military figure in 1940) headed the Free French Movement, and from London broadcast to the French people that although they had lost a battle, France had not lost the war. In the course of time civilian life in Occupied France became more and more unbearable, and a strong resistance movement developed.

The Battle of Britain 1940

After the Fall of France Hitler assumed that Britain had no alternative but to come to terms with Germany. He professed that he had no desire to destroy the British Empire, which was a stabilising influence in world affairs. Hence detailed planning for *Operation Sea Lion* (the German code name for the invasion of England) only began at the beginning of August 1940, when there was little time left for an invasion before the end of the summer.

If German forces had gained a secure foothold on English soil, Britain, unaided, would have been doomed. Yet despite Germany's military superiority, the problems of invading England were immense and, in the event, proved insurmountable. The German navy could only guarantee to protect troop transports using a ten mile wide crossing, and only then if the *Luftwaffe* won complete air supremacy over the Channel. As a first step towards the projected invasion, therefore, Hitler ordered the *Luftwaffe* to destroy the Royal Air Force. Goering allocated one month to this task, which he code-named *Operation Eagle*.

When the Battle of Britain began the German air force had 1900 bombers and 1100 fighter aircraft. Fighter Command in Britain possessed approximately 1000 fighters, and had to cope with the problem of repelling attacks at times and in places chosen by the enemy. Fighter Command, however, had two important advantages. The first was radar, an early warning system whereby the approach of enemy aircraft could be detected even before they had crossed the French coastline. The second advantage was that most aerial combats were over England or the vicinity of the coast, so that British pilots who safely baled out lived to fight again, while their opponents' fate was a prisoner-of-war camp.

At first the *Luftwaffe* directed its attacks against the radar stations. Fortunately for Fighter Command, these were almost immediately discontinued, since the stations were difficult to destroy and their importance was not sufficiently appreciated by the Germans. Thereafter attacks were concentrated on airfields and aircraft factories. Though German losses were greater than those of the British during this stage of the Battle of Britain, Fighter Command's losses in pilots exceeded the output of training squadrons and could not have been sustained for a very long period.

At this critical stage in the battle the *Luftwaffe* switched its attention to bombing London. This was in retaliation for an RAF raid on Berlin, which Goering had assured Hitler would never happen. Hitler also hoped that by placing civilians in the front line the population would be terrorised into submission. Thirdly, Goering was convinced that Fighter Command was nearing the limit of its resources, and by drawing the RAF into battle in ever greater numbers to defend London he would succeed in destroying it. German losses in daylight raids on the capital were unacceptably high, however, and the *Luftwaffe* increasingly turned to bombing at night. Although the *Blitz* destroyed the centres of a score of British cities, Fighter Command survived.

Without air supremacy invasion was impossible and Hitler abandoned *Operation Sea Lion*. Despite having failed to conquer Britain, he was convinced that he had nothing to fear. His attention was now focussed upon the Soviet Union which, if left free to consolidate its armed forces, could threaten the security of the Third Reich.

North Africa and the Balkans

On 10 June, when France's defeat was inevitable, Italy entered the war. To most neutral observers Mussolini's decision almost certainly meant the collapse of British power in North Africa and the Mediterranean, since Egypt and the Suez Canal (a vital lifeline of the British Empire) were only guarded against 250,000 Italian troops by a tiny army commanded by General Wavell. Italian and German air power made the Mediterranean dangerous for British vessels, so that reinforcements could only reach Egypt by a roundabout voyage down the west coast of Africa, up the east coast, and through the Red Sea to the Suez Canal.

An Italian invasion of southern France made little headway, but in East Africa the British could not prevent Italian forces from seizing British Somaliland in August. In North Africa, however, General Graziani's army delayed its advance until mid-September, when it established fortified positions at Sidi Barrani. There it remained on the defensive while Italian forces invaded Greece in October. Meanwhile, the British government, alarmed by the Italian threat to the Suez Canal and Middle East oil supplies, rushed out reinforcements to Wavell's army.

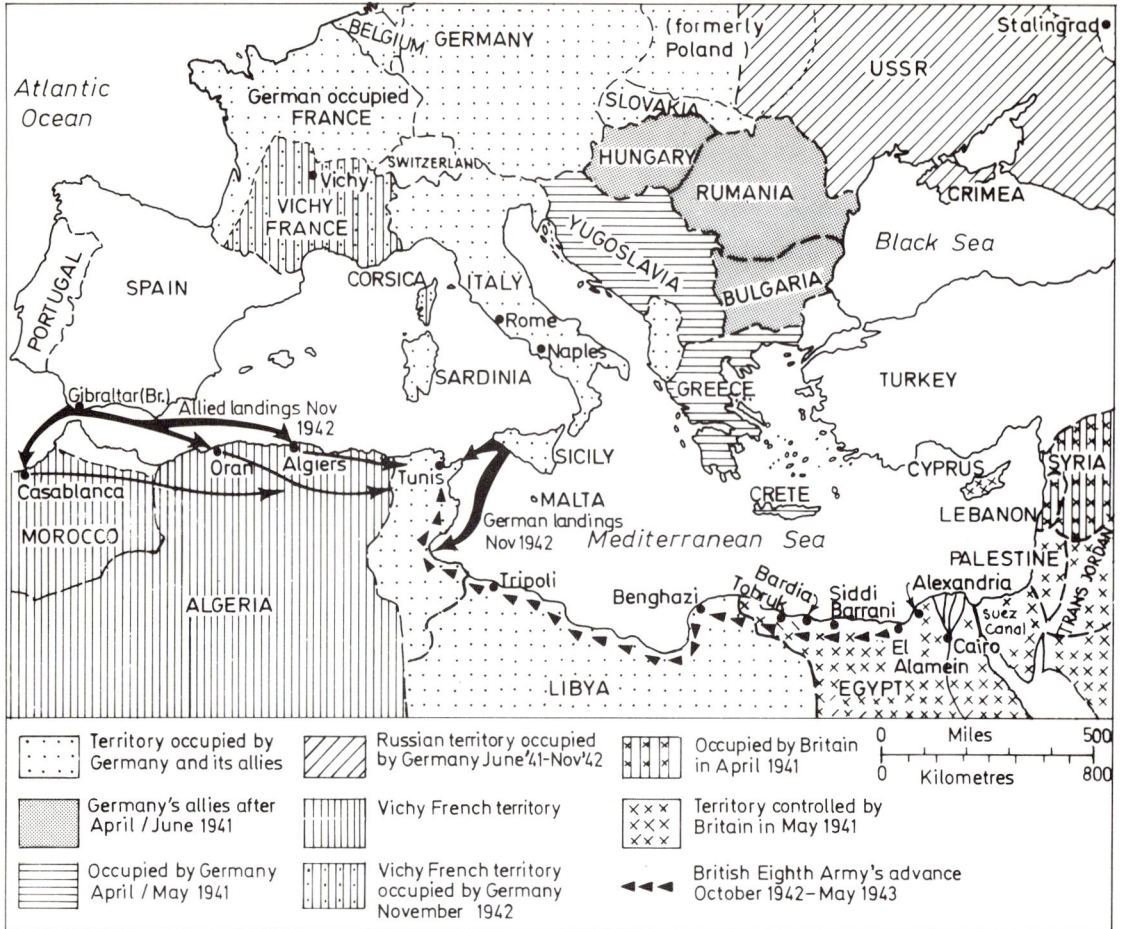

3   The War in Europe and North Africa, November 1940 to November 1942

Wavell ordered a limited offensive against the Italians in early December, and to his surprise achieved an overwhelming victory, capturing Sidi Barrani and 40,000 prisoners. The remnants of the Italian army retreated to Bardia. There they were encircled and captured by British and Australian troops, who went on to occupy Tobruk in late January. When Benghazi fell a few days later, the way seemed clear for the conquest of Tripoli, the last Italian foothold in North Africa.

The jubilant British troops were halted by Churchill's decision to assist the Greeks, in the hope of forming a league of Balkan states which would act as a base for launching an attack upon southern Germany. The Greeks were reluctant to accept British aid lest it provoke German intervention, but Churchill prevailed, and in March 1941 50,000 British troops landed at Salonika.

Hitler's reaction was swift and decisive. German forces invaded Greece and Yugoslavia, routing the British army which was hurriedly evacuated to Crete. In May, however, the island was attacked by German airborne troops, and the demoralised British forces were overwhelmed. Only 16,000 British and Greek troops were rescued from this second 'Dunkirk', at a heavy cost to the Royal Navy.

The British paid dearly for squandering the opportunity to drive the Italians out of North Africa. Hitler decided to help his Italian ally, and in February 1941 a German army, called the *Afrika Korps* and commanded by Rommel, arrived in Tripoli. In April the British army was driven back to the Egyptian frontier and Wavell was replaced by General Auchinleck, whose army was reinforced with as many tanks and troops as could be spared. The *Afrika Korps* was driven back to Libya, but Rommel launched a powerful counter-attack, forcing the British Eighth Army back to Tobruk. There a temporary stalemate developed, as the war suddenly assumed new dimensions. In June Hitler attacked the Soviet Union.

Barbarossa: the German invasion of Russia

There were several reasons for Hitler's decision to attack Russia. For many years he had dreamed of the destruction of communism and the seizure of 'living space' (*Lebensraum*) in Eastern Europe. The conquest of Russia would provide the Third Reich with the foodstuffs and raw materials to make it self-sufficient, and Germany's domination of Europe would then be complete.

Guerrilla warfare played an important part in the fight against the German invaders. A Russian soldier makes use of the cover afforded by his horse.

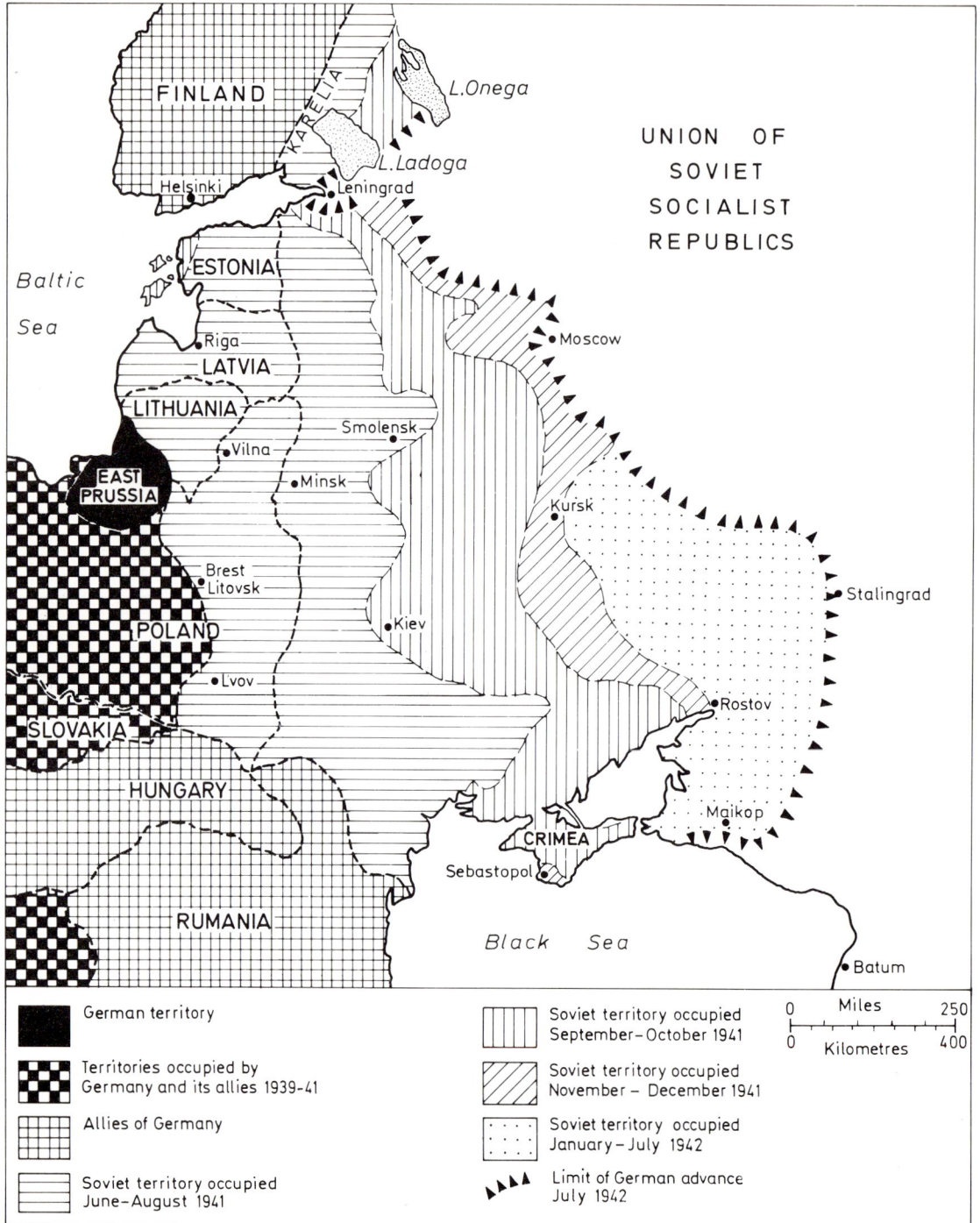

4   *The Barbarossa campaign: the German invasion of Russia, 1941–42*

Once Russia had been defeated, Hitler was confident that Britain would agree to a compromise peace settlement. Since Britain was powerless to intervene in Europe there appeared to be no risk of Germany becoming involved in a war on two fronts, which Hitler's diplomacy had skilfully avoided. Moreover, Germany's astonishing military successes against Poland, France, and the Low Countries, had removed Germany's need to keep the terms of the Nazi-Soviet Pact.

Stalin was desperately anxious to strengthen Russia's frontier before the threatened German attack could take place. After the annexation of the eastern part of Poland, therefore, the three Baltic states, Estonia, Latvia and Lithuania, were forced to submit to Soviet demands to establish Red Army troops on their territory. Finland resisted Stalin's demands but was defeated in the Winter War, and in August 1940 the Baltic states were incorporated into the Soviet Union. Russia's southern frontier, meanwhile, was strengthened when Rumania agreed to surrender Bessarabia and northern Bukovina, which were garrisoned by Soviet troops in July 1940.

Hitler resented Russia's territorial gains and regarded Stalin as a 'cold-blooded blackmailer.' He mistakenly believed that the Red Army could be annihilated in a matter of weeks, for its performance against the Finns had not been impressive. Stalin's ruthless purges during the period 1933 to 1939 (when 35,000 officers, including a majority of those holding very senior commands, were shot or thrown into labour camps) had taken their toll of the Red Army's efficiency.

On Sunday, 22 June 1941, *Operation Barbarossa* began, as three army groups, consisting of 170 divisions, under Leeb, Bock, and von Rundstedt, drove their way into Russia. Their objectives were Leningrad, Moscow, and Kiev respectively. The Red Army was taken completely by surprise, for Stalin had believed up to the last minute that his policy of appeasing Germany was succeeding. He even ignored as unreliable, detailed information provided by a spy about the planned invasion of Russia, including the date and the time of attack.

In the next six months the Red Army suffered a series of disastrous defeats. Bock's army in the centre captured Brest Litovsk, and by the end of June the Russian army defending Minsk had been isolated in three pockets of resistance, which were eliminated by the infantry following the panzer forces. Smolensk was captured in mid-July, when 300,000 Russian troops were taken prisoner. Soon afterwards a further 600,000 Russians were trapped by the German drive to Kiev, while in the north the long siege of Leningrad began in September.

By October, however, a combination of poor roads, mud and snow was slowing down the progress of the battle-fatigued German troops. Some scattered units reached the outskirts of Moscow during early December, but the limits of the German advance in 1941 had been reached. Even more serious from Hitler's point of view was the fact that, although two thirds of Russia's military strength at the beginning of the campaign had been eliminated, the Red Army had not been decisively defeated. Marshal Zhukov's counter offensive in December was an ominous reminder of the vast reserves of manpower upon which the Soviet war machine could draw. Nevertheless, by the end of 1941, German armies had occupied nearly all European Russia, containing two thirds of Russia's heavy industry and forty per cent of its population.

The United States enters the war

Since 1937 Japan had been busy with the conquest of China, so that, in the autumn of 1941, the United States was the only great power not at war. Most Americans had no desire for war against Germany, and President Roosevelt, who realised that his country's security would ultimately be threatened by Nazi aggression, had been unable to overcome this attitude. Congress resolutely refused to repeal the Neutrality Act of 1935 which prohibited the export of munitions to countries at war. Only with difficulty was it persuaded to amend the act to permit the sale of arms on a 'cash and carry' basis, a decision which clearly favoured Britain and France since Germany was blockaded by the Royal Navy.

After the Fall of France it was clear that Britain could not win the war unaided, but Roosevelt dared not outpace public opinion in his efforts to provide all aid to Britain short of war, especially as he had decided to stand as a candidate for the Presidency for a third time. Nevertheless, in September 1940, Congress allowed the transfer of fifty First World War destroyers to Britain, in exchange for ninety-nine year leases on bases in the Caribbean. After his re-election Roosevelt instituted a massive programme of rearmament, not only because he was concerned over the threat of war in the Far East, but also to make available the large quantities of munitions required by Britain. Thus American industry was geared to war production several months before the outbreak of war with Japan.

By the end of 1940, however, Britain was desperately short of cash, and unless the Neutrality Act was amended again the flow of arms from the United States to Britain would cease for lack of payments. In a series of compelling speeches Roosevelt argued that if your neighbour's house was on fire, common sense dictated that you should lend him your hose to put it out; you would not ask to be paid for it first. Eventually, in March 1941, Congress agreed to an ingenious scheme whereby the government lent, or leased, arms to Britain, and the United States became the 'great arsenal of democracy'. In November 1941 the Neutrality Act was finally repealed.

If Hitler had been seeking war with the United States he now had sufficient reason. The United States had already extended its territorial waters to a 300 mile wide belt around its coasts, within which American warships had instructions to fire at sight on German submarines. Furthermore, Greenland and Iceland had officially been placed under American protection, thus freeing ships of the Royal Navy for duties elsewhere. The peaceful existence of the United States, however, was shattered not by the war in Europe, but by developments on the other side of the world.

Hitler's invasion of the Soviet Union had momentous consequences in the Far East, where Japan became free to follow an expansionist policy without fear of Russian intervention. Japan was presented with an ideal opportunity either to attack the Soviet Union (its traditional enemy), or to seize the virtually defenceless

possessions of Britain, France, and Holland in the East Indies. Both the Anti-Comintern Pact of 1937 and the Tripartite Pact (September 1940), whereby Germany, Italy and Japan promised to assist each other if attacked by a great power not already in the war, suggested that Japan should invade Siberia, whose territory and mineral resources it had long coveted. A combination of economic and strategic considerations, however, in which Japan's Non-Aggression Pact with Russia (April 1941) played only a minor role, dictated a move in the south.

The Japanese conquest of China was progressing slowly, for Chinese resistance was sustained by aid from the United States, which supported an 'open door' trade policy in China. In July 1940 Japan had announced the creation of the Greater East Asian Co-Prosperity Sphere, inviting all the countries of South-East Asia to join. The Dutch East Indies refused to participate, however, and the Japanese government realised that its economic and political ambitions in this area could only be fulfilled by war, or by the threat of war.

In August 1940 Britain and France reluctantly agreed to Japanese demands for bases in northern Indochina, from which China's supply lines could be bombed. One year later Vichy France conceded bases in southern Indochina, which brought the British naval base of Singapore within range of Japanese bombers. This mounting evidence of Japan's aggressive intentions provoked a stern reaction from the United States. Japanese assets in America were frozen, and all oil exports to Japan were prohibited. Britain and Holland immediately followed America's lead, but far from deterring Japan, this action drove it into war.

Over ninety per cent of Japan's oil supplies were imported from the United States and the Dutch East Indies. Without oil Japan could not wage war, and its economy would be ruined. In order to remain a major power Japan had no choice but to seize its own oil supplies. Furthermore, by 1942 Japan's oil stocks would be so low that military action would be ruled out. This was the background against which Admiral Yamamoto, Commander-in-chief of the Imperial Japanese Navy, drew up his daring plan of a sudden attack upon the United States fleet at Pearl Harbour, in Hawaii, over 3000 miles from Japan.

Japan could not hope to equal the industrial and military strength of the United States, and its strategy, therefore, was based upon rapidly winning an empire which it would be so costly to defeat that a compromise peace settlement would be preferable. To achieve this aim, any potential threat to the success of the operation had to be eliminated. This meant the destruction of the United States navy in the Pacific. On 7 December 1941 Japanese aircraft from six aircraft carriers attacked the American naval base at Pearl Harbour. Complete surprise was achieved, and of the eight battleships lying at their moorings, four were sunk, and the remainder seriously damaged. Only two aircraft carriers escaped because they were on manoeuvres, and in seventy minutes Japan won complete naval supremacy in the Pacific.

When the news reached London the British government immediately declared war on Japan, and Hitler decided to assist Japan by declaring war on the United States. In this way the Grand Alliance of the United States, the Soviet Union and Britain was formed. Its immediate prospects of victory, however, were distant, for at the end of 1941, fascism controlled all Western Europe apart from the British Isles and the neutral countries, Sweden and Switzerland. In Russia Hitler's armies stood before the gates of Moscow and Leningrad, while in the Far East Japanese forces were soon to achieve an astonishing series of victories.

Churchill rejoiced at the United States' entry into the war, for he felt certain it spelled the eventual defeat of Nazi Germany. He wrote:

No American will think it wrong of me if I proclaim that to have the United States at our side was to me the greatest joy. How long the war would last or in what fashion it would end no man could tell, nor did I at this moment care. Hitler's fate was sealed. Mussolini's fate was sealed. No doubt it would take a long time. I expected terrible forfeits in the East; but all this would be merely a passing phase. United we could subdue everybody else in the world. Many disasters, immeasurable cost and tribulation lay ahead, but there was no more doubt about the end.

The bombing of Pearl Harbour.

The Japanese conquest of South East Asia

The day after the Japanese attack on Pearl Harbour the two British battleships in Far Eastern waters, the *Prince of Wales* and the *Repulse*, were sunk by Japanese bombers as they tried to intercept enemy troop transports *en route* to Malaya. The British government was preoccupied with the war in Europe, and, with ships and aircraft in short supply, was not prepared to send reinforcements to the Far East. Churchill was aware that he was taking a calculated risk, but in his desire for a victory in North Africa, he declared his readiness to pay any forfeits in the Far East. They were to be far heavier than he imagined.

Japanese troops invaded Hong Kong (which fell on Christmas Day 1941), the Philippines and Malaya, where the British were driven remorselessly southwards and forced to retreat to the island fortress of Singapore. Singapore, however, offered neither respite nor security, for its fortifications had been designed to repel a seaborne attack only. The Japanese quickly forced their way across the mile-wide stretch of water separating it from the mainland of Malaya, and two weeks later, in February 1942, the mighty naval base, the 'Gibraltar of the Far East', was in their hands. The loss of Singapore was a major disaster for Britain, and its capture the greatest triumph in Japan's history. By May 1942 the Japanese had seized the Dutch East Indies and the Philippines, driven the British out of Burma, and cut the Burma Road, China's vital supply route. Thus in a campaign lasting five months the Japanese armies had conquered an immense area, rich in oil and raw materials.

Hasty preparations were made for the defence of India and Australia. American troops under General MacArthur joined Australians hurriedly transferred from the Middle East, and in May 1942 the Japanese suffered their first setback. They encountered the American fleet in the battle of the Coral Sea, fought at long range by carrier-based aircraft from fleets which never saw each other. In June an American fleet inflicted heavy losses upon the Japanese navy at the battle of Midway, sinking five aircraft carriers for the loss of two of their own. The battles of the Coral Sea and Midway checked the long run of Japanese victories, and preserved Australia from invasion.

The Battle of the Atlantic

The battles for naval supremacy in the Pacific were swift and decisive, whereas the Battle of the Atlantic was a grim war of attrition which, in June 1942, had been in progress for over two years.

The German navy was not fully prepared for war in 1939, but it was still a formidable force, skilfully deployed by Admiral Raeder. During the last few days of peace, the pocket battleships *Graf Spee* and *Deutschland* slipped unobserved into the Atlantic, where they were to operate as surface raiders. German U-boats were stationed in British coastal waters and the Atlantic approaches, where they gained early successes. A German submarine sank the aircraft carrier *Courageous*, and in October U-boat Forty-Seven sank the battleship *Royal Oak* at its moorings in Scapa Flow. Meanwhile, magnetic mines sown in coastal waters accounted for many smaller vessels. Britain's only consolation was the

Map

U S S R

MONGOLIA

MANCHURIA
(Manchukuo) Vladivostok

SAKHALIN   KAMCHATKA

Kurile Is.

Aleutian Is.

C H I N A

KOREA
Seoul

JAPAN

Tokyo

Pacific
Ocean

Nanking
Shanghai

Chungking

Nagasaki Hiroshima

Okinawa

Midway
Is.

INDIA

Burma Rd

TAIWAN
(Formosa)

Marianas
Is.

Wake
Is.

BURMA

Hanoi

Hong
Kong

Rangoon

THAI FRENCH
LAND INDO-CHINA

PHILIPPINE
IS.

Guam
Is.

Marshall
Is.

Saigon

Caroline Is.

MALAYA

SARAWAK   CELEBES

Gilbert
Is.

Sing
apore BORNEO

NEW
GUINEA

SUMATRA

DUTCH EAST INDIES

PAPUA

Solomon
Is.

Ellice
Is.

JAVA

Guadalcanal

Darwin

New
Hebrides

Fiji
Is.

Coral
Sea

New
Caledonia

Indian
Ocean

AUSTRALIA

Brisbane

Perth

Adelaide

Melbourne

Auckland

NEW
ZEALAND

Wellington

TASMANIA

Dunedin

	Japan		Occupied by Japan up to Dec 1941		Conquests after attack on Pearl Harbour	++++	Limit of Japanese expansion	0 Miles 1000
								0 Kilometres 1600

5 *Japanese conquests after the attack on Pearl Harbour*

destruction of the *Graf Spee* in December, which scuttled itself in the River Plate in Uruguay, after a battle with British warships.

British merchant shipping losses in 1940 amounted to more than two million tons, but they doubled in 1941, when German submarines were able to operate from French and Norwegian bases, which greatly extended their range. Immediately after Germany's declaration of war on the United States U-boat commanders found rich pickings in American coastal waters. In 1942 U-boat commanders developed 'wolf pack' tactics in order to attack convoys escorted by destroyers. 'Wolf packs' were formed by one U-boat shadowing a convoy, and using its wireless to 'home-in' other U-boats until a strong force had been collected. Attacks on convoys were made at night when the U-boats could surface with little danger of their low silhouettes being detected in the darkness.

In the summer of 1943, however, the U-boat menace was dramatically overcome. Convoys were now escorted for the entire Atlantic crossing. Long range aircraft patrolled large expanses of the ocean, forcing the U-boats to remain under the surface for long periods, where they were far less effective. A new type of radar, which could detect U-boats without them being aware of it, gave escort vessels a keen advantage. The Allied victory in the Battle of the Atlantic assured the survival of Britain and enabled a procession of convoys from the New World to transport American troops, supplies and equipment to Britain, in preparation for the Allied assault upon Occupied Europe.

The Allied victory in North Africa

Meanwhile, the turning point in the North African campaign had been reached. In June 1942 Rommel's *Afrika Korps* launched its second great offensive, capturing Tobruk and chasing the British Eighth Army across 300 miles of desert to El Alamein, only sixty miles from Alexandria. Its capture would have endangered Britain's position in the Middle East, as well as making the loss of Egypt almost certain.

Rommel's advance was checked by General Auchinleck at the first battle of El Alamein, but when he refused to advance prematurely he was replaced by General Montgomery. Another seven weeks passed before Montgomery was satisfied with his own preparations. The second battle of El Alamein began on 23 October, and after eleven days of heavy fighting the *Afrika Korps*, greatly outnumbered in men, tanks and aircraft, began to retreat.

In November Anglo-American and Free French forces landed in Morocco and Algeria, behind Rommel's supply lines, in an operation code-named *Torch*. Admiral Darlan, who commanded the Vichy French forces, issued instructions that the Allies were to be offered no resistance. Nevertheless, hopes of an Allied victory in North Africa before the end of the year, faded when German troops occupied Vichy France and German reinforcements poured into

Tunisia; it was not until May 1943 that the German and Italian armies surrendered. The Allies were then in possession of the entire southern shore of the Mediterranean Sea.

The Stalingrad campaign 1942–43

In June 1942, the *Wehrmacht* resumed its offensive against a Red Army desperately short of equipment. In a *blitzkrieg* campaign Kleist's panzers captured Maikop after a six weeks' headlong advance, bringing German troops within striking distance of the Caucasian oilfields, and von Manstein's army completed the German occupation of the Crimea.

Meanwhile, Hitler had defined the capture of Stalingrad as the army's most important objective. In July the Sixth German army commanded by von Paulus crossed the river Don, and by early August reached the outskirts of Stalingrad. Throughout the next three months the Germans desperately tried to capture the city before the dreaded Russian winter arrived, but they met bitter resistance. Factories and warehouses were turned into strongpoints and the battle raged street by street, building by building, in countless hand-to-hand encounters. Finally, by mid-October, the German advance had been halted.

The Sixth Army's failure to capture Stalingrad placed it in a perilous situation, from which Hitler forbade retreat. The Russians prepared an offensive to encircle the demoralised German forces and on 19 November Marshal Zhukov unleashed a series of attacks along a front of 130 miles. After four days' fighting the Sixth Army was trapped. An attempt by von Manstein's army to relieve von Paulus was driven back in December, and in January 1943 Hitler instructed Kleist's forces in the Caucasus to retreat, before their escape route was cut off by the collapse of the Stalingrad front. Finally, in February, von Paulus and 90,000 men surrendered. Over 200,000 German soldiers lost their lives in the struggle for Stalingrad; the graveyard of a German army and one of the decisive battles of the Second World War. It proved that the German armies in Russia were not invincible and it forced them to retreat.

The Eastern front 1943–44

The Russian winter offensive halted in March 1943, when the spring thaw made troop movements almost impossible, and the Germans made preparations for another offensive on Russian soil. In July nearly half a million troops attacked near Kursk, but they failed to capture as many prisoners as they had expected, and began to retreat before Russian counter-attacks.

By now the Red Army was superior both numerically and in equipment, since Hitler had been forced to withdraw troops from Russia in order to strengthen 'Fortress Europe', which was threatened by an Allied invasion. The output of Russian armaments factories, hurriedly rebuilt behind the Ural Mountains at the start of the war, had reached impressive proportions. The Allies also supplied tanks, aircraft and machinery through the ports of Vladivostock, Murmansk and Archangel.

The Russians advanced steadily, establishing bridgeheads across the river Dnieper in October, and trapping a German army in the Crimea in November. Moscow was freed from the threat of capture as the front line was pushed back nearly 300 miles from the Russian capital, and in January 1944, Leningrad was relieved after a terrible siege which had lasted over 900 days. By this time the Red Army had won the initiative, which it was to keep until the end of the war.

The invasion of Sicily

Meanwhile, the Allied assault upon Occupied Europe had begun. Stalin had long been urging the Allies to open up a second front in order to relieve the pressure on the Russian front. The Allies themselves feared that, unless they carried the war to the European mainland, Stalin might come to terms with Hitler as he had done in 1939. The Americans were in favour of landings in southern France rather than Italy. In August 1942, however, the commando raid by Canadian troops on Dieppe (in which sixty per cent of the attackers became casualties), proved that any attempt to invade Europe needed favourable conditions and careful planning.

At the Casablanca Conference in January 1943 Roosevelt agreed to Churchill's plan for the invasion of Italy, 'the soft underbelly of Hitler's Europe'. Allied possession of the Italian mainland would cut Axis★ communication in the Mediterranean, and would provide airfields for bombing the Rumanian oilfields. It would also provide a springboard for the invasion of southern France or the Balkan peninsula, thereby compelling Germany to station troops in these threatened areas.

Allied forces landed in Sicily in July 1943 and captured the island after six weeks' fighting. Many Italians now turned against Mussolini's leadership and a new government was formed under Marshal Badoglio, who wished to negotiate armistice terms with the Allies. But Hitler, fearful lest the Italians should decide to surrender, rushed German troops into Italy – not only to reinforce the Italian army, but also, if necessary, to occupy the country.

There was to be no easy conquest of Italy, however, for Badoglio was unable to prevent the German occupation of his country, and the Allies lacked the strength to enforce surrender terms. They were also divided over their Italian strategy. Churchill believed that the speedy capture of Rome was the best possible preparation for the projected invasion of 'Fortress Europe'. Roosevelt argued that the Italian campaign was a sideshow and was reluctant to commit resources which he felt should be reserved for a direct cross-Channel invasion, or for the war in the Pacific against Japan. The stubborn resistance of General Kesselring's army also slowed down the Allied advance up the Italian mainland, thereby strengthening the American view that priority should be given to the Normandy landings. As a result, twelve months passed before the Allies reached the Pisa-Rimini line, and conquered territory which Hitler had originally been prepared to surrender when Mussolini was overthrown.

★ When Italy and Germany became allies in 1936 Hitler suggested that the link between Rome and Berlin would be an Axis (or imaginary line) 'around which the rest of Europe would revolve'. Henceforward Italy and Germany were known as the 'Axis Powers'. They were joined by Japan in 1937.

The bomber offensive against Germany 1943–5

The aerial bombardment of Germany was intended to destroy civilian morale and industrial production. Throughout 1943 and 1944 Bomber Command pounded German cities by night, while American 'Flying Fortresses' and 'Liberators' carried out daylight precision bombing raids on strategic targets. In 1943 the first thousand bomber raid devastated Cologne, and in a series of raids Hamburg was almost completely destroyed, with over 42,000 inhabitants killed. Between November 1943 and March 1944 over nine thousand planes attacked Berlin. By this time, however, RAF Bomber Command losses were unacceptably high, and after the disastrous attack on Nuremberg in March 1944, when ninety-five out of 795 planes were shot down, it abandoned its strategy of mass raids on distant targets. The Americans had also reached similar conclusions, following crippling losses in their daylight attacks upon the ball-bearing works at Schweinfurt, in October 1943.

The results of the bombing offensive bore no relation to its cost. Inadequate aiming methods made it impossible to hit small targets such as

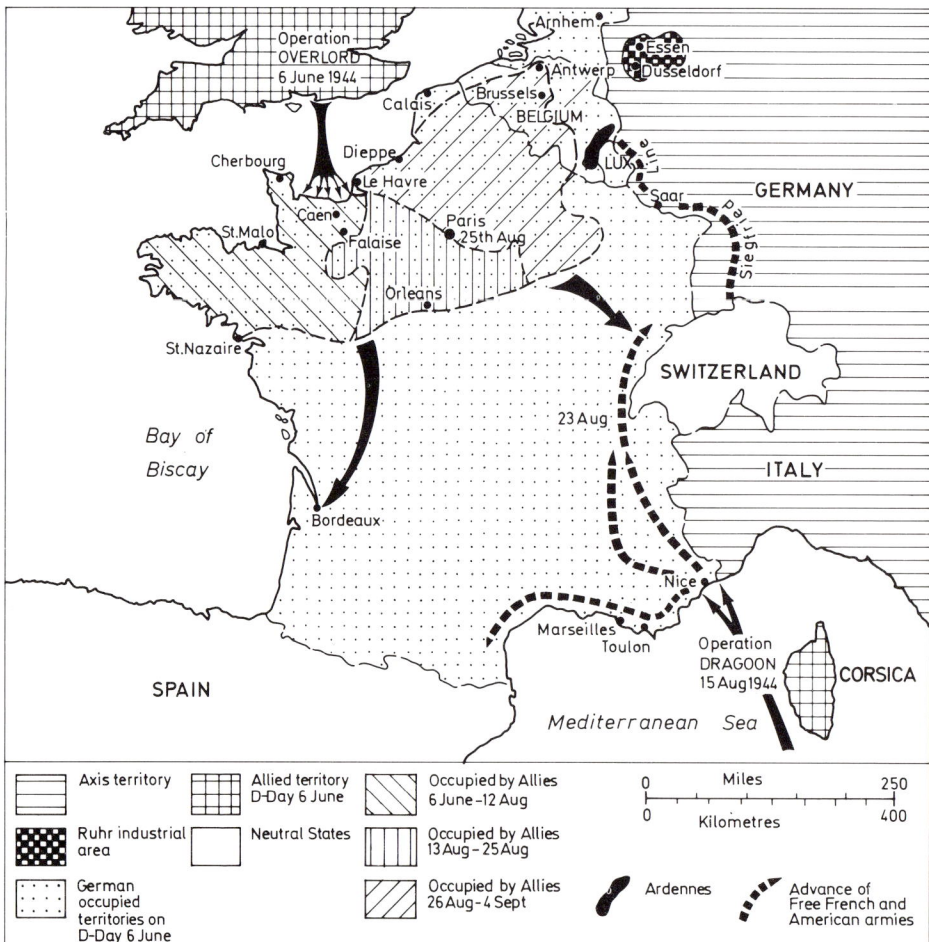

6 *The Allied invasion of France, June to September 1944*

factories with any degree of accuracy. Strategic industries were dispersed, and Albert Speer, Hitler's Minister of Armaments and War Production, performed wonders in reorganising industrial production. The German economy was not seriously disrupted by the bombing; indeed, the output of armaments significantly increased during 1943.

The bomber offensive, far from winning the war (as its chief architect, 'Bomber Harris', expected), made the German people even more determined to resist. After the war, argument raged over the morality of area bombing which, because it was indiscriminate, made civilians front-line targets. While it is true that it was Hitler's decision to destroy Coventry which set the precedent, over 590,000 German civilians died as a result of Allied air raids, compared with only 60,000 civilians killed during German air attacks upon Britain. The most controversial raid was the RAF attack on Dresden in February 1945, when nearly 100,000 people died in the firestorm that was created.

Operation Overlord: the invasion of Normandy 6 June 1944

The invasion of Normandy was not only the Allies' most hazardous venture of the entire war, but also the most important. For Germany, the only chance of avoiding defeat was to drive the invaders back into the sea, before they had time to establish a secure bridgehead. Hitler was confident that the Atlantic Wall, the immensely strong system of defences constructed from the Pas de Calais along the entire French coastline, was impregnable. For the Allies the consequences of failure would have been calamitous. With invasion no longer a threat, Hitler would have been able to withdraw substantial forces from Western Europe, thus giving him an opportunity to win a decisive victory against the Russians. Moreover, given time, the new weapons developed by German scientists, such as electro-U-boats, jet aircraft and long range rockets like the V1 (a pilotless aircraft nicknamed the *doodlebug* by the British) and the

A Mulberry harbour at Arromanches, showing the pontoons supporting the 'road' that enabled vehicles and supplies to be brought ashore (see page 28).

supersonic V2, might easily have tipped the balance of the war in Germany's favour. At the very least, the war would have been prolonged several years.

The Allied landings in Normandy between Caen and Cherbourg on 6 June 1944 (D Day) took the Germans by surprise, for Field Marshal von Rundstedt, the German commander in Western Europe, believed that the invasion would take place in the Calais area and had stationed his best troops there. The sheer weight of the assault threw the Germans into confusion. On the first day alone 130,000 men were landed, while the overwhelming air supremacy of the Allies enabled them to destroy communication centres and to slow down the German reactions in the vital first few days of the invasion. Thus the German army failed to drive the invaders into the sea.

American troops captured Cherbourg at the end of June, though its port installations were destroyed by the German troops before they evacuated the town. Supplies still had to be landed by means of the pre-fabricated *Mulberry* harbours, or floating platforms, which had been towed across the Channel, and linked up to form artificial harbours. A pipe line under the ocean (PLUTO) maintained the supply of petrol to the Allied armies, without which their advance would have come to a halt.

The liberation of France

In July 1944, American forces under General Patton broke through the German front south of Cherbourg, and trapped part of two German armies in the 'Falaise pocket'. Paris was liberated on 25 August, and General Charles de Gaulle

A joyful event in the war: the liberation of Paris.

made a triumphant entry into the capital, where he assumed control of the new government. On 1 September American troops crossed the river Marne at Verdun, within striking distance of the Saar industrial area, and less than one hundred miles from the Rhine.

Meanwhile, a combined American and Free French army had landed in southern France. After capturing the port of Marseilles, it advanced rapidly northwards up the Rhône valley where it linked up with American armies near the German-Swiss frontier. By mid-September all France, with the exception of Lorraine, had been liberated. Most of Belgium had also been freed by Canadian and British troops commanded by General Montgomery, and Brussels and Antwerp were in Allied hands.

Allied hopes of victory before the end of the year, however, soon receded. The Germans retreated to the powerful Siegfried Line of defences stretching from Switzerland to the Dutch frontier, and the momentum of the Allied advance slowed down. Moreover, the German armies succeeded in inflicting two serious reverses upon the Allies, at Arnhem and in the Ardennes.

The battle of Arnhem

Montgomery and Patton wanted to make a sudden breakthrough into the Ruhr, whose capture would cripple the German war effort and bring peace nearer. General Eisenhower, however, who was in overall control, refused to depart from his policy of advancing on a broad front. Nevertheless, he agreed to Montgomery's daring plan of an airborne assault behind the German lines, at Arnhem. An Allied Airborne Army was given the task of capturing vital bridges across the Rhine at Arnhem, Nijmegen, and Eindhoven, in order to clear the way for armoured spearheads to advance into the heart of Germany. Arnhem, however, was an Allied disaster, since the British troops were unable to fight their way to the Rhine bridges and link up with the encircled paratroops, who were compelled to surrender after several days of bitter fighting.

The German offensive in the Ardennes

When the Allies resumed their advance in the late autumn they met stubborn resistance. In mid-December they were taken completely by surprise by General von Rundstedt's ferocious counter-attack in the Ardennes: a rugged, wooded area considered by the Allied commanders to be unsuitable for tank warfare. Assisted by a spell of bad weather which grounded Allied reconnaissance aircraft, the German armies advanced fifty miles along a broad front before they were eventually halted. The 'Battle of the Bulge' lasted until the end of January 1945, when the Germans were forced back to their original lines.

The Warsaw uprising

The Red Army renewed its offensive along an 800-mile front stretching from Finland to the Balkans in June 1944, and in a five weeks' advance swept deep into Poland. As Russian troops neared the suburbs of Warsaw, the Polish resistance movement in the capital rose in revolt against the German overlords. The Poles expected Russian help, but none was forthcoming, as the Russian advance was halted. When it was resumed several weeks later the Polish resistance, which might have disputed Soviet control of Poland, had ceased to exist.

The surrender of the Balkan countries and Finland

In the meantime, the Red Army was winning major victories in the Balkans. With the capture of Bucharest at the end of August, Rumania surrendered, and Bulgaria soon followed its example by sueing for peace. The German armies now escaped from the Balkans as quickly as they could, to avoid capture. Greece was evacuated in early October, so that British troops were able to land there unopposed, but by the end of December they were causing international tension by supporting the recognised Greek government against Greek communists. In

Yugoslavia Marshal Tito's partisans captured Belgrade, and liberated their country, while far in the north the Finns were forced to surrender and Russian troops occupied the Baltic states.

The onset of winter brought a lull in the fighting, but in February 1945 the Red Army captured Budapest, the capital of Hungary, and Austria surrendered two months later when Vienna was occupied. Thus by the spring of 1945 Marshal Zhukov's armies were poised along the river Oder for the final assault upon Berlin.

In late April Russian troops fought their way into the suburbs of Berlin. On 30 April, two days after Mussolini had been captured and killed by Italian partisans, Hitler committed suicide in his bunker, with Russian troops a few blocks away. Hitler's last acts were to marry his mistress, Eva Braun, who died with him, and to appoint Admiral Doenitz as his successor. On 7 May Doenitz agreed that Germany would surrender unconditionally, and the war in Europe was over at last.

The end of the war in Europe

In March 1945 American forces crossed the Rhine near Coblenz, and Montgomery's troops established another bridgehead across the river 150 miles downstream. They met little resistance, for most Germans realised that defeat was inevitable and preferred their country to be occupied by British and American troops, rather than by the Red Army. By 11 April the Americans had reached the River Elbe, where they halted.

The Americans and the Russians were now almost equidistant from Berlin. Churchill, who suspected the Russians of wanting to dominate post-war Eastern Europe, urged Eisenhower to resume his advance. The Supreme Commander of Allied Armies in Western Europe refused, however, to indulge in a 'race for Berlin', to satisfy what Americans regarded as Churchill's groundless suspicions of Stalin's intentions.

There were a number of important reasons for Eisenhower's decision. Berlin lay in the promised Russian sector of post-war Germany, and Stalin had made it clear that he regarded Berlin as a Red Army prize. Secondly, Eisenhower believed that the river Elbe would serve as a clear demarcation line between American and Russian troops. Thirdly, Roosevelt died on 12 April 1945, and Harry Truman became President of the United States. Truman was optimistic that the Americans and Russians could agree on their approach to post-war problems in Europe, and he had no wish to damage Russian-American relations over Berlin.

The War against Japan

The American naval victories in the battles of the Coral Sea and at Midway Island had marked the turning point of the war in the Pacific and heralded Japan's eventual defeat. The American conquest of Guadalcanal in February 1943, and the capture of New Guinea (an area the size of Germany) by the end of the year, safeguarded Australia from invasion.

Vast distances were involved in the Pacific theatre of war, and the Americans relied upon their naval superiority to destroy enemy lines of communication and protect their own. The American strategy was to capture key Japanese positions, and to by-pass territories held by the enemy once they had been neutralised by their inclusion in American-controlled areas. These tactics were known as 'island-hopping', and by the summer of 1944 the Americans had brought Superfortress bombers within range of the Japanese mainland.

The Japanese navy suffered crippling losses when it tried in vain to prevent American forces landing on the island of Leyte, in the Philippines, in October 1944. The Japanese defenders fought with such determination, however, that although Manila, the capital, was freed early in 1945, the conquest of the Philippines was not completed until July. Thus General MacArthur, who commanded the American troops in the Pacific, fulfilled his promise to return, made when the islands had been seized by the Japanese. The loss of the Philippines was a serious blow to Japan, since the American navy was able to disrupt the transport of oil and other raw materials from Malaya and the former Dutch East Indies to Japan.

Meanwhile, the capture of Iwo Jima in March, and Okinawa in June, brought American forces to within 350 miles of the Japanese mainland. Its cities, ports and industrial areas were now subjected to incessant bombing, while large areas of Tokyo were also devastated by fire raids similar to those which had destroyed the town of Dresden in Germany. In the so-called 'forgotten war', British, Indian, and American troops succeeded in re-opening the Burma Road, the vital supply route to Chiang Kai-shek's Nationalist armies in China, and drove the Japanese out of Burma in May 1945.

Japan surrenders

By now the Japanese were doomed to defeat, but the enormous casualties which would result from an invasion of Japan itself appalled the Americans. This was the dilemma which the United States government, with the agreement of the British government, resolved by its decision to drop atomic bombs on two Japanese cities.

Leaflets warning of the atomic attack were dropped several days previously, in the hope that Japan would surrender first. When the Japanese government failed to respond, a single Superfortress bomber, *Enola Gay*, flew so high that it was beyond the reach of Japanese fighters and

The shoeless body of a Japanese soldier is totally disregarded by American troops on their way to Manila.

A view of Hiroshima. Attempts to re-build seem to emphasise the destruction.

anti-aircraft fire, and dropped an atomic bomb on Hiroshima on 6 August 1945. It flattened twenty square kilometres of the city, and killed an estimated 70,000 people. Many more died later of radiation sickness, the new disease caused by atomic explosions.

Russia declared war on Japan immediately, and invaded Manchuria. This was because Stalin, realising that the United States possessed a weapon of such terrible destructiveness that it would soon compel Japan to surrender, wanted the right for the Soviet Union to be represented at the eventual peace settlement with Japan.

The Japanese did not accept an ultimatum to surrender, so that a second atomic bomb was dropped, this time on Nagasaki, on 9 August. Five days later the Emperor Hirohito agreed to unconditional surrender terms, which were signed on board the American battleship *Missouri*, anchored in Tokyo Bay.

CHAPTER THREE:
Allied Wartime Cooperation and the Peace Settlements

Anglo-Russian military cooperation began in June 1941, when Germany attacked the Soviet Union. Churchill promised Stalin that Britain would help Russia to overcome Nazi Germany, but it was not until May 1942 that a formal twenty year alliance was signed. The delay was caused chiefly by Britain's reluctance to recognise Russia's seizure of Polish territory and the Baltic states. The United States became Russia's ally after the attack on Pearl Harbour, though Russia did not take part in the war against Japan until nearly four years later.

The 1943 conferences

At the very beginning of the war Churchill began to correspond with President Roosevelt, anticipating the time when Britain and the United States would become allies. Out of this correspondence was born the idea of wartime conferences attended by the Allied leaders.

At the Casablanca meeting in January 1943 Roosevelt and Churchill agreed that Germany should be forced to surrender unconditionally. Some people have argued that this only served

Chiang Kai-Shek, President Roosevelt and Winston Churchill at the Casablanca Conference.

to prolong the war by ensuring that the German people had nothing to lose by fighting to the bitter end, but the Allied leaders wished to avoid making the mistake of 1918.★ Churchill declared that:

The term 'unconditional surrender' does not mean that the German people will be enslaved or destroyed. It means the Allies will not be bound to them at the moment of surrender by any pact of obligation. . . . No such arguments will be admitted by us as were used by Germany after the last war, saying that they surrendered in consequence of President Wilson's 'Fourteen Points'. Unconditional surrender means that the victors have a free hand.

Three more top level meetings took place later in the same year. At Quebec in August, Churchill and Roosevelt discussed in secret the progress being made on the development of the atomic bomb. In November they flew to Cairo, where they were joined by the Chinese Nationalist leader, Chiang Kai-shek, for talks on the Far East situation. From Cairo the two Western leaders went to Teheran, in Persia, where they met Stalin. The 'Big Three' reviewed the whole course of the war, and decided upon May 1944 as the projected date for the opening of a second front in Europe. Two other important decisions were taken. Stalin promised that Russia would enter the war against Japan after Germany had been defeated, while there was general agreement that the Curzon Line† should become the future Russo-Polish frontier. This restored to Russia the territory ceded to Poland in 1921 by the Treaty of Riga.

★ The First World War ended when an armistice, or ceasefire, was agreed. After the war, many Germans bitterly objected to the harsh terms of the peace treaty of Versailles (1919), claiming that Germany had been tricked into surrendering.

† After the First World War a Commission headed by Lord Curzon was appointed by the Paris Peace Conference (1919) to recommend a frontier between Russia and the new state of Poland. In the meantime, Polish troops seized Russian territory to the east of the line chosen by Curzon, which Poland refused to give up when peace was eventually restored.

The growing antagonisms between the Soviet Union and the Western allies

The Grand Alliance was nourished by the desperate need to defeat the Axis Powers. Although the internal strains of the Alliance were concealed from the rest of the world for the greater part of the war, they were nevertheless very real. Growing evidence of the disunity between the Americans, Russians, and British emerged even before victory over Germany had been achieved. Hitler therefore nursed the hope that his country would be saved at the last minute by the outbreak of war between the Soviet Union and its two Western allies.

Stalin distrusted both his powerful allies, and regarded all Western Europe as basically hostile towards the Soviet Union. He remarked to Churchill, in February 1945:

Russians cannot forget what happened in December 1939, during the Russo-Finnish War, when the British and the French used the League against us, and succeeded in isolating and expelling the Soviet Union from the League, and when they later mobilised against us and talked of a crusade against Russia.

Stalin also believed that Britain and France had tacitly encouraged Hitler to invade Russia, in the hope of avoiding attack themselves.

During the war Stalin criticised his colleagues for lacking a sense of urgency in mounting an assault upon Occupied Europe. As early as March 1943 he wrote to Churchill:

It is my duty to warn you in the strongest possible manner how dangerous would be from the viewpoint of our common cause further delay in the opening of the Second Front in France. This is the reason why the uncertainty concerning the contemplated Anglo-American offensive across the Channel arouses grave anxiety in me, about which I cannot be silent.

Churchill, for his part, was worried in case Stalin made a separate peace with Hitler.

Friction between the British and American leaders also arose from Churchill's suspicions that Stalin was planning to hold on to vast areas of Eastern Europe being overrun by the Red

Army from 1944 onwards. Maintaining good relations with the Soviet dictator, Churchill declared, was like trying to keep on friendly terms with a crocodile. 'You do not know whether to tickle it under the chin or to beat it over the head. When it opens its mouth you cannot tell whether it is trying to smile or preparing to eat you up.' Roosevelt, however, felt that Churchill was a landgrabber, an imperialist who planned to rebuild Britain's colonial empire. He warned the British Prime Minister that the United States was not fighting the war in order to allow Britain to cling on to its empire.

The Yalta and Potsdam agreements 1945

Allied differences, however, were largely concealed at the Yalta conference in February 1945, for although Germany's military collapse was imminent, there remained the daunting prospect of defeating Japan. Furthermore, Churchill could not afford to be too critical of Stalin's intentions, for public opinion in both the United States and Britain was full of admiration for the courageous resistance of the Russian people. Consequently, relations between the Allied war leaders were cordial. Stalin, in particular, was affable, for his bargaining position was very strong. All the capitals of Eastern Europe were in communist hands, Marshal Zhukov was closing in on Berlin, and another Russian army was less than 150 kilometres from Vienna, the Austrian capital.

The Allies reached a compromise over Germany. The Morgenthau Plan, devised in 1944 by an American Treasury official, was abandoned. Morgenthau had proposed the permanent partition of Germany into separate, small states organised on an agricultural basis. Instead, Germany was to be divided into zones of military occupation, which were to be temporary pending the final settlement with Germany. Stalin agreed reluctantly to the creation of a French zone, on condition that it was taken out of the area to be allocated to the Americans and British. The Russian zone was the largest, comprising forty per cent of Germany's territory in 1937. Berlin, which lay 175 kilometres inside the Russian zone, was also divided into four Allied sectors, with freedom of access being assumed by the Allies. Occupied Germany was to be administered by an Allied Control Commission, headed by the commanders-in-chief of the Allied armies.

It was decided to reject Stalin's suggestion that Germany should pay twenty million dollars reparations, half of which should be paid to the United States, for it would have ruined the German economy. Moreover, since much of Germany's industry lay inside the British zone, the burden of maintaining the impoverished German population would have fallen heavily upon the British tax-payer (who would, in effect, have been subsidising the Russian people). The Allies, however, agreed to the principle of reparations, and the Russians were later able to dismantle large sections of German industry, to be rebuilt on Russian soil. Nazism was to be destroyed, and war criminals were to be tried and punished. Stalin promised that free elections would be held in all the territories liberated by the Red Army.

Anglo-American relations with the Soviet Union deteriorated, however, when it became clear that Stalin had no intention of carrying out the promises he had made at Yalta. The Western Allies had done their best to safeguard Poland's independence by requesting that the communist administration, established by the Russians at Lublin, should be organised on a broader democratic basis. Stalin, however, refused to hold elections, and no non-communists were permitted to join the new government of Poland. The Lublin administration also agreed to Russia's annexation of Polish territory east of the Curzon Line. Poland was to be compensated with the southern half of East Prussia (the northern part was occupied by Russia), and German lands to the east of the rivers Oder and Neisse: comprising Danzig, part of Silesia, and much of Pomerania and Brandenburg. The Red Army assisted the Poles in expelling seven million Germans from these territories. As a result, it became unlikely that Poland's 'provisional' frontiers could be altered by any future settlement with Germany.

Churchill tried to persuade Truman that he should make a stand on the Polish issue. He suggested that both their forces should remain in occupation of German territory assigned to the Soviet Union, until Stalin had carried out the terms of the Yalta agreement. Truman, however, did not agree, since he wished to avoid giving Stalin the impression that his Western allies were combining against him. Nor did he respond to Churchill's plea that the Allies should try to occupy Berlin before the Russians could arrive. The Anglo-American armies halted on the banks of the Elbe, and awaited the arrival of the Russians.

Both Roosevelt and Truman underestimated the danger of communism sweeping through Europe. Hitherto, neither the United States nor the Soviet Union had pursued conflicting policies. Both nations were opposed to colonialism, and both possessed vast natural resources which made them self-sufficient. Moreover, it was understandable that Stalin would wish to secure some guarantee that Germany would not be able to attack Russia with impunity again. This guarantee would take the form of a cordon of friendly states on Russia's western frontier. It was only later that events proved that Stalin had moved away from the policy of 'Socialism in One Country' towards one of Russian domination of Europe. Truman was aware, too, that although the war in Europe was nearly over, the United States would have to bear the main brunt of the war against Japan. It was, therefore, important that Allied unity should be kept intact. Any postwar difficulties, he felt, could surely be resolved amicably by the Allies themselves, or by means of the United Nations Organisation which was being created.

On 2 May 1945 Russian troops entered Berlin, and five days later Germany surrendered unconditionally. Thus when Truman, Clement Attlee (the newly elected British Prime Minister), and Stalin met at Potsdam in July, the war in Europe had ended. At Potsdam the Allies agreed to follow common policies in their zones of Germany. Reparations were not to be so severe as to make necessary imports to sustain civilian life in Germany. The coal mines of the Saar were temporarily awarded to France. No time limit for the military occupation of Germany was fixed, but it was assumed by Truman and Attlee that a democratically elected government would be established in a united Germany, with which a peace treaty could be concluded. In the event, Germany remained divided and no peace treaty was signed.

The territorial settlements of the Paris Peace Conference 1947

At Potsdam a Council of Foreign Ministers was established to draft peace treaties with Germany's satellites. The first meeting took place in London in September 1945, but broke up after several months of arguments and recriminations. The Foreign Ministers left their deputies to continue the peace negotiations, and after three further meetings, in Moscow, London and Paris, agreement was reached on five separate peace treaties.

The treaties with Rumania, Bulgaria, Hungary, and Finland

The Soviet Union kept the Rumanian provinces of Bessarabia and Bukovina, which it had occupied in 1940, and Russian troops were to be stationed in Rumania until a peace settlement with Austria had been signed. Rumania also paid reparations to Russia.

Bulgaria returned Western Thrace to Greece, but kept the Southern Dobrudja, which Rumania had seized from her in 1913, and which Bulgaria, with Germany's assistance, had recovered in 1940. Hungary restored Northern Transylvania to Rumania, and Southern Slovakia to Czechoslovakia. Reparations were paid by Bulgaria to Greece and Yugoslavia, and by Hungary to Yugoslavia, Czechoslovakia, and the Soviet Union.

Finland lost a strip of territory along Lake Ladoga, together with the Karelian peninsula and the port of Petsamo, which were annexed by the Soviet Union. Thus Finland surrendered ten per cent of its territory to its powerful eastern neighbour, but managed to retain independence.

NORWAY
Oslo

FINLAND
Helsinki
Lake Ladoga
Leningrad

SWEDEN
Stockholm

ESTONIA

LATVIA

UNION OF SOVIET SOCIALIST REPUBLICS

DENMARK

LITHUANIA

North Sea

Baltic Sea

Vilna

NETHERLANDS

Berlin

POLAND
Warsaw

BELGIUM

WEST GERMANY

EAST GERMANY
Bonn

FRANCE

SAAR (returned to Germany in 1957)

Prague

CZECHOSLOVAKIA

Lvov

RUTHENIA

BESSARABIA

SWITZERLAND

Linz
Vienna

AUSTRIA

Budapest

HUNGARY

NORTHERN BUKOVINA

RUMANIA

Trieste
Venice
Fiume

ISTRIA
Zara

Belgrade

Bucharest

Black Sea

ITALY

YUGOSLAVIA

BULGARIA
Sofia

DOBRUDJA

CORSICA (It.)
Rome

Adriatic Sea

Tirana

ALBANIA

Naples

SARDINIA (Fr.)

GREECE

TURKEY

SICILY

Athens

Mediterranean Sea

CRETE

DODECANESE Is. (from Italy to Greece)

| West Germany | Territory acquired by Poland from Germany | Post-war frontier of USSR |
| East Germany | Territory lost by Italy | Territory acquired by USSR |

0 Miles 250
0 Kilometres 400

7 *Territorial changes in Europe resulting from the Second World War*

The treaty with Italy

Yugoslavia reclaimed nearly all the territory disputed with Italy since 1919, including the Adriatic islands, Istria, and the ports of Zara and Fiume, seized by Yugoslav partisans in the closing stages of the war. Italy, however, did not abandon its claims to Trieste, which was placed under the control of the United Nations. It remained a source of international tension until 1954, when the city of Trieste, inhabited by 700,000 Italians, was awarded to Italy, and the inland areas with their Slav populations were given to Yugoslavia. The Dodecanese Islands were ceded to Greece. The islands had been promised to Greece in 1919, but they had remained in Italian hands.

Italy kept Southern Tyrol, much to Austria's annoyance since it contained a significant German speaking minority, but was forced to pay indemnities to the Soviet Union and to Ethiopia, Albania, Greece and Yugoslavia, countries which had suffered from Italian aggression. Limitations were placed upon Italy's armed forces until such time as it joined the United Nations.

Italy also lost all its colonial possessions in Africa. With the exception of Ethiopia, which became independent in 1941 when it was liberated by the British, Italy's former colonies were administered by Britain on behalf of the UN Trusteeship Commission. Eventually Libya became independent in 1951, and Eritrea was joined to Ethiopia in 1952. Somaliland was restored to Italy in 1950, but won its independence ten years later.

The agreements with Czechoslovakia and Poland

Although the Paris peace treaties were not signed until October 1947, the Soviet Union signed agreements in 1945 with Czechoslovakia and Poland (both technically 'victorious' countries), which formed part of the postwar territorial settlement. Czechoslovakia transferred Ruthenia to the Soviet Union, and the district of Teschen to Poland, which also acquired from Germany the larger part of East Prussia and the territory lying east of the rivers Oder and Neisse. The latter was regarded as compensation for the loss of territory whose population, Stalin claimed, had chosen to join the Soviet Union. Britain and France, which had declared war on Germany in order to preserve Poland's frontiers, had no alternative but to accept these arrangements.

Austria

Austria, regarded as the victim of Nazi aggression in 1938, was treated leniently, and no formal reparations were exacted. The final agreement over Austria was delayed for ten years, however, as a result of the growing hostility, or Cold War, between the USSR and the Western powers. In the meantime, Austria and Vienna, like Germany and Berlin, were divided into four zones of military occupation by the great powers (the United States, Soviet Union, Britain and France). Eventually, in 1955, the Soviet Union agreed to withdraw its forces from Austria and to conclude a peace treaty. Austria retained its 1938 frontiers, and promised strict neutrality in the Cold War. Union with Germany was forbidden, as was possession of nuclear weapons. No such agreement, however, was possible over Germany, where Eastern and Western Europe met in a dangerous confrontation.

The peace settlement with Japan

When Japan surrendered, its sovereignty was limited to the mainland islands of Honshu, Hokkaido, Kyushu, and Shikoku, which were occupied by American forces commanded by General MacArthur. The Kurile Islands and the southern part of Sakhalin were occupied by Soviet troops. Korea, where Japanese troops north of the thirty-eighth parallel surrendered to the Russians, and south of that line to the Americans, was divided into two zones of military occupation. These eventually became separate states (see Chapter Ten). Formosa and the Pescadores were handed over to Nationalist China, while the Japanese colonies in the Pacific became UN Trustee Territories administered by the United

Reversal of roles at a Japanese prison camp: former guards bow as the Allied soldiers leave.

States. Under a new constitution drawn up in 1946 Japan itself became a democracy, and the Emperor a mere figurehead. War was renounced forever, and the maintenance of armed forces was prohibited.

The communist triumph in China in 1949 and the outbreak of the Korean War in 1950, led the United States to sign a peace treaty and seek friendly relations with Japan. The Treaty of San Francisco (1951) confirmed the loss of all former Japanese possessions overseas. Japan agreed to pay reparations but no final amount was fixed; the army of occupation was withdrawn, and Japan was encouraged to create a Self Defence Force. A special Security Treaty permitted the United States to maintain forces in and about Japan, which became a strategic link in America's defensive system to combat the spread of communism in South East Asia.

Although the Soviet Union attended the peace conference, Stalin refused to sign the treaty, since he objected to Japan's military alignment with the United States. Despite the resumption of diplomatic ties in 1956, Russo-Japanese relations remained unfriendly, since Japan maintained that full economic cooperation would not be possible until the Soviet Union returned the four Southern Kurile islands. These were islands to the north of Japan, seized at the end of the Second World War.

China was not invited to take part in the San Francisco conference, and did not become reconciled with Japan until 1972 when Tanaka, the Japanese premier, visited Peking and apologised for Japanese war crimes. Six years later, in August 1978, the Sino-Japanese Treaty of Peace and Friendship was signed by the two countries. This meant that the Soviet Union was isolated in East Asia, since the United States by that time had restored friendly relations with China, while maintaining its post-war alliance with Japan.

CHAPTER FOUR:
The United Nations Organisation

Statesmen can earn no greater distinction than to seek that peace which will enable the peoples to prosper in the path they have chosen, and permit men to work in happiness and security, in the free and pacified atmosphere of their own countries.

> Vincent Auriol, President of France, addressing the UN Assembly, 6 November 1951

The idea of a United Nations Organisation was born in August 1941, when Churchill and Roosevelt met on board a warship in Placentia Bay, Newfoundland, and issued the Atlantic Charter. This was a declaration of principles for establishing:

a peace which will afford to all nations the means of dwelling in safety within their own boundaries, and which will afford assurances that all men in all lands may live out their lives in freedom from fear and want.

Although the League of Nations still officially existed, there was no possibility that it would be revived after the war. Firstly, its failure had been too complete. Secondly, neither the United States, nor the Soviet Union (which had been expelled from the League in 1939) belonged to it. No post-war international peacekeeping organisation could hope to be effective unless these two nations were members.

Roosevelt and Churchill considered at first a plan for three separate Regional Councils, which would be responsible for maintaining peace in the Pacific, the western hemisphere and Europe respectively. The Regional Councils would be controlled by a Supreme World Council composed of the Big Three powers, the United States, the Soviet Union and Britain. This scheme, however, had several major defects. Britain had world-wide interests and was anxious to preserve its colonial possessions and

strengthen its Commonwealth ties, but both the United States and the Soviet Union were anti-colonial in outlook. There was a danger that such a scheme would divide the world into three distinct, competitive regions. The underlying hostility of the Soviet Union towards the Western powers, already apparent before the Second World War, became increasingly obvious during the course of the war. Finally, it presupposed a degree of 'Western' military and economic supremacy which it was unlikely that the rest of the world would tolerate for very long.

The term 'United Nations' came into official use in January 1942 when twenty-six countries signed the Declaration of the United Nations, setting out the war aims of the Allied Powers fighting Germany, Italy and Japan. As the war against Germany entered its final phase, representatives of the four great powers (the United States, the Soviet Union, Britain and China) met in October 1944 at Dumbarton Oaks, a district of Washington, USA, where they drafted preliminary details of a world-wide organisation for preserving future peace.

Disagreements over the voting procedure in the proposed Security Council were resolved a few months later at the Yalta Conference in January 1945. Also resolved was the Soviet Union's request that if the Commonwealth countries joined the UN as independent states, then its sixteen republics should also be admitted separately. The voting issue was settled by the formula that each permanent member of the Security Council would have the right to veto any decision requiring enforcement measures (thus preserving intact the great power veto). On the membership question it was agreed that the two Russian republics of the Ukraine and Byelorussia should be admitted to the UN in addition to the Soviet Union.

The General Assembly

All UN members are represented in the General Assembly, with each state having one vote, regardless of its size or importance. Unlike the procedure in the former League of Nations, where decisions could be reached only by a unanimous vote, a two thirds majority is required on important issues such as the admission or expulsion of members, while a simple majority is sufficient on less important resolutions.

The Assembly may discuss and make recommendations on any matter likely to affect world peace, and it has become a forum where world opinion can be expressed and assessed. It supervises the work of specialised agencies, such as the Universal Postal Union, and controls the activities of the Trusteeship and Economic and Social Councils, whose members it elects. The Assembly receives annual reports relating to the UN's work, controls the UN budget (apportioning the amounts to be paid by each member) and, together with the Security Council, appoints the UN Secretary General and the judges to the Court of Justice. The Assembly meets annually for about three months, or at short notice to deal with an emergency.

When the Security Council failed to achieve any semblance of unity as the Cold War developed after 1946, the Assembly steadily expanded its powers. In November 1950 it passed the 'Uniting for Peace' resolution which enabled the Assembly to recommend the use of force if the Security Council failed to act in a crisis. These powers were invoked during later crises, such as Suez in 1956, the Lebanon in 1958, and the Congo in 1960.

The Security Council

The Security Council is responsible for maintaining international peace and, under the UN Charter, can require member nations to carry out its decisions. Originally it was composed of eleven members, five permanent (the United States, Soviet Union, Britain, France and

Delegates working on the Charter at San Francisco, which was passed unanimously and came into force in October 1945.

In April 1945 delegates from fifty-one states met at San Francisco where they published the Charter, setting out the aims and framework of the United Nations Organisation. Its preamble stated the determination of the member nations to promote social progress, justice, and respect for international law and treaty obligations, to

save succeeding generations from the scourge of war, which twice in our lifetime has brought untold sorrow to mankind,

and to uphold

the dignity and worth of the human person, and the equal rights of men and women, and of nations large and small.

The United Nations has four principal organs: the General Assembly, Security Council, Secretariat and International Court of Justice, though other organs such as the Trusteeship Council and the Economic and Social Council, as well as special commissions and agencies, also play important roles.

Nationalist China★ and six non-permanent, elected for a two year period. The number was increased to fifteen in 1965, however, by the addition of four non-permanent members. Five of the ten non-permanent members were to be chosen from the Afro-Asian countries, two each from Latin America and Western Europe and one from Eastern Europe. This choice was made in order to uphold the original intention of giving representation on the Security Council to particular regions of the world or groups of states. A majority of seven (nine after 1965) enabled the Security Council to act, provided that the five permanent members were in agreement on the most important issues.

The Secretariat

The United Nations chief administrative officer is the Secretary General, a post which was described by its first holder, Trygve Lie, as 'the most impossible job in the world.'

Trygve Lie (1896–1968) was the compromise candidate in 1946, since the Soviet Union opposed the Anglo-American choice of Lester Pearson of Canada. Lie, who had been Minister for Foreign Affairs in the wartime Norwegian government-in-exile in London, had led Norway's delegation at the San Francisco Conference, and had helped to draft the UN Charter. His chief problems as Secretary General were those of securing the withdrawal of Soviet troops from Iran in May 1946, of establishing a UN peace-keeping force in Palestine in 1949, and of resolving the Korean War of 1950–3.

Trygve Lie resigned in November 1952, and was succeeded in April 1953 by Dag Hammarskjöld (1901–61), the son of a Swedish Prime Minister. Although Hammarskjöld was involved in the UN's actions over the Suez Crisis in 1956 (see Chapter Fifteen), his most difficult problem was the civil war in the Congo, where a UN peace-keeping force became involved in

★ For many years the United States used its power of veto to block the admission of Communist China to the UN, but in 1971 the People's Republic of China was admitted and took the seat on the Security Council vacated by Nationalist China.

the fighting in 1961 (see Chapter Sixteen). It was while on his way to a meeting in the Congo to arrange a ceasefire in September 1961 that Hammarskjöld was killed when his aircraft crashed in the jungle.

U Thant of Burma (1900–74), Hammarskjöld's successor, identified himself with the problems of the Third World (the under-developed nations). He declared that the three most important objectives of the UN were decolonisation, disarmament and development. His plan for a federal system of government for the Congo was accepted, and the UN force was able to leave in 1964. Unfortunately, at the same time the outbreak of communal strife between the Greek and Turkish populations in Cyprus led to the despatch of another peace-keeping force to prevent further violence on the island. U Thant's decision to withdraw the UN Emergency Force from the Suez Canal Zone, however, was almost immediately followed by the Arab-Israeli War of 1967, which resulted in heightened tension in the Middle East (see Chapter Fifteen). U Thant retired in 1971, after ten years in office.

U Thant talks to Mrs Gandhi, then Information Minister for India.

Kurt Waldheim (1918–), an Austrian diplomat, was appointed in 1972. In his efforts to publicise the problems and achievements of the UN he has visited many parts of the world, including South Africa and Namibia, whose independence was scheduled for 1979.

The International Court of Justice

The International Court of Justice is located in The Hague, and is more popularly known as the World Court. Its fifteen judges chosen from fifteen different countries, who hold office for nine years and may be re-elected, represent the major legal systems in the world. The Court gives rulings on disputes referred to it by member nations, who agree to abide by its verdict, and offers legal advice on international problems to the General Assembly and Security Council.

Trusteeship Council

An important achievement of the UN has been its success in persuading countries to bring about an end to colonial rule. The Trusteeship Council became responsible for the administration of the former League of Nations mandates (subsequently called trust territories), and its function is to ensure that they progress steadily towards independence. The Council considers annual reports of the states administering trust territories, carries out inspections of conditions in them, and makes recommendations to the General Assembly.

The Economic and Social Council, and the specialised agencies

Twenty-seven members form the Economic and Social Council, which coordinates the economic, social, cultural and humanitarian activities of the UN. It is also responsible for the work of the various specialised agencies, the most important of which are:

FAO

The Food and Agricultural Organisation was founded in 1943 in order to improve world supplies of food. It produces statistics on food production and offers technical advice to governments on problems such as locust control, cattle disease and irrigation schemes.

WHO

Set up in 1948, the World Health Organisation keeps countries informed on the latest medical advances and advises governments on the control of epidemics, vaccination programmes and standardisation of drugs. By 1978 it had succeeded in eliminating the disease of smallpox, and was stepping up its campaign against malaria.

ILO

The International Labour Organisation dates back to 1919, when many governments were fearful of social revolution. After 1945 the ILO was affiliated to the UN, when it continued its work of giving technical advice to under-developed countries, persuading governments to guarantee decent conditions of labour and wages and combating unemployment.

IMF

The International Monetary Fund was one of two organisations created at the end of the Second World War to stabilise currencies and expand world trade by giving financial help to countries in temporary economic difficulties. Member countries contribute a quota of the funds used by the IMF in its rescue operations. When in difficulty over its balance of payments, a member country may purchase from the IMF the foreign exchange it needs, using its own currency. Once its trading position has become healthy again, that country is expected to repurchase the excess of its own currency over its quota.

The IMF works closely with the World Bank, which encourages foreign investment in member states and arranges loans to governments.

UNESCO The aim of the United Nations Scientific and Cultural Organisation is to increase international understanding by promoting the exchange of scientific and other useful information.

UNICEF The United Nations International Children's Emergency Fund was founded in 1946 by the UN General Assembly to provide relief for mothers and children affected by the Second World War. Today UNICEF works in the developing world and most of its programmes are long-term operations closely related to the national development plans of individual countries.

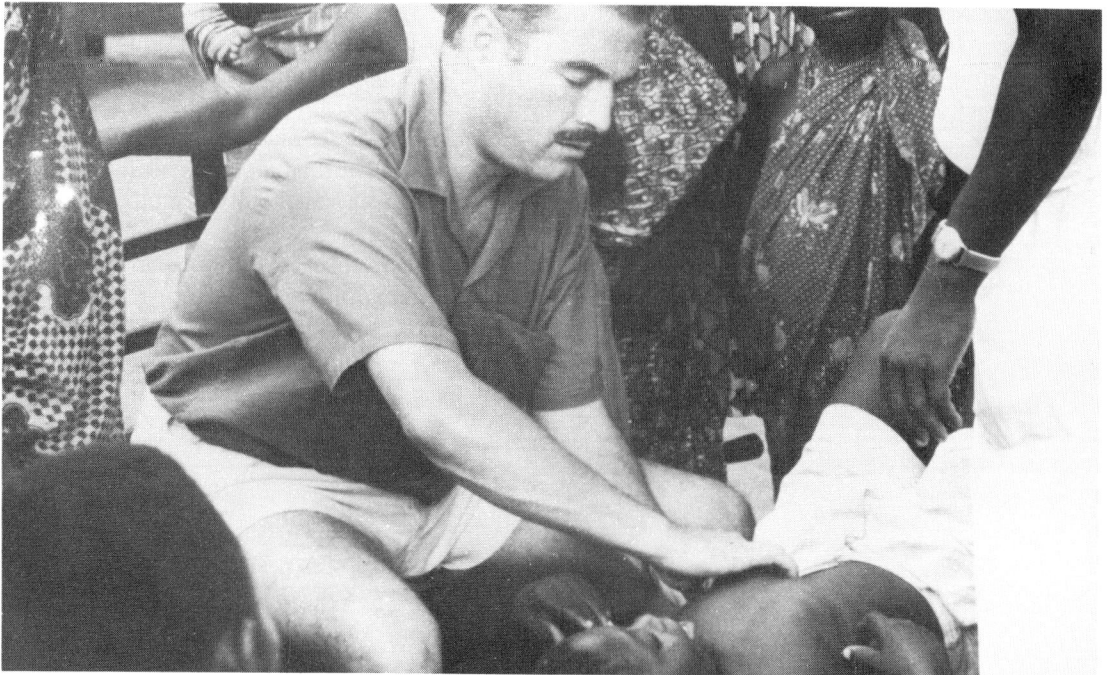

The changing role of the UN in world affairs

In its early years the UN reflected the interests of the rich, industrialised nations of the Western world. As the new nations of Africa and Asia emerged from the dissolution of the European empires there has been a great increase in UN membership since 1960 and the balance of power in the General Assembly has shifted. The Western countries often find themselves in a minority when the votes on UN resolutions are counted. The so-called non-aligned countries have exploited the rivalry between the superpowers and their respective allies, in order to win economic aid and to focus attention on their problems.

At the same time there is a danger that the importance of the Assembly will be undermined by the admission of very small or very poor countries (micro-states, or 'mini' states). These

A WHO malaria expert in Togo carries out tests on a patient. Villagers are trained to carry on the project.

countries enjoy equal voting rights with the great powers, but lack both the economic and military strength to support resolutions passed by the Assembly.

It is not easy, therefore, to assess the effectiveness of the United Nations Organisation. Since 1945 it has mediated in over one hundred disputes, and on various occasions it has restored peace to troubled areas. Yet world tensions have remained, and little progress towards world disarmament has been achieved under UN auspices. To regard this as the failure of the UN to achieve its primary aims, however, would be less than fair. The UN does not have the military forces at its command, as was first envisaged, to compel nations to reach peaceful solutions to their quarrels; it has to rely upon the goodwill of nations, which is not always forthcoming.

If the United Nations Organisation has not lived up to the expectations of its founders, it has, nevertheless, a vital role to play in world affairs. This can best be described in the words of U Thant, when he addressed a special meeting of the UN staff on the twenty-fifth anniversary of the United Nations:

Our powers are less; we act by persuading, by enlightening, by promoting peace, understanding, generosity and tolerance. But, basically, we are part of the same old process of good government which consists in denouncing and redressing injustices, abusive powers and harmful divisions, and in ensuring the good things expected by the people. He concluded by saying: *We must look far into the future and warn nations of problems that may lie in store for humanity.*

Mankind must hope that nations and governments will take heed of the advice.

The United Nations building in New York. In the foreground is a statue donated by the Soviet Union: 'Let us beat swords into ploughshares.'

CHAPTER FIVE:
*The German Question and the
Onset of the Cold War*

The immediate consequences of Germany's defeat

For Germany the cost of the war was horrifying. Most major cities were masses of rubble, with thousands of people living in cellars, or seeking shelter in the remains of railway stations and public buildings. An American newspaper correspondent wrote: 'Berlin can now be regarded only as a geographical location heaped with mountainous mounds of debris.' Transport,

A former official of Buchenwald concentration camp, Hans Schmidt, hears the death sentence passed upon him. He is stretcher-bound owing to a recent operation.

communications and banking had all broken down. In the British sector of Germany, only 1000 kilometres of railway were in working order. There was neither central nor local government, since Nazi officials had either gone into hiding, been captured, or had committed suicide. Industry was at a virtual standstill, with coal production in the Ruhr less than three per cent of its pre-war total. The population of the cities had been increased by hundreds of thousands of refugees who had escaped from the paths of the advancing Russian armies. Several million Germans had also been expelled from Czechoslovakia, Poland, Hungary, Rumania and Yugoslavia as part of a deliberate policy to rid these countries of their German minorities.

Thousands of Nazi suspects were rounded up and thrown into internment camps. In the American zone all Germans over eighteen years old had to answer a questionnaire. Those discovered to have been Nazis were tried by military courts, whose penalties could range from death to exclusion from all jobs except that of manual labourer. This process was very slow, however, and de-nazification was soon handed over to the civilian authorities. Altogether, some 600,000 Germans were found guilty. Most were fined, and only a few thousand were found unfit for public office.

At Nuremberg twenty-one leading Nazis were tried for war crimes and crimes against humanity. The tribunal was composed of judges and prosecutors appointed by the governments of the United States, Britain, France, and the Soviet Union. Twelve Nazis, including Hermann Goering, Von Ribbentrop, Julian Streicher, and Generals Keitel and Jodl, were condemned to death by hanging. Three were sentenced to life imprisonment, three others to lesser terms of imprisonment and three were acquitted.

As a result of the Nuremberg Trials the German people and the rest of the world learned the full extent of the crimes committed by the German leaders, arising in part from Hitler's determination to exterminate all the Jews in Europe. Survivors from the death camps related how Jews and other 'undesirables' such as gypsies and mentally disabled people had been herded into concentration camps like Dachau, Buchenwald, Belsen and Ravensbruck. There many thousands were killed, or died as a result of ill-treatment.

The horrific progress towards 'the final solution of the Jewish problem' had been speeded up when Germany invaded the Soviet Union and the Baltic states. As the German armies advanced they had been followed by *Einsatzgruppen*, SS 'killer groups', whose purpose was to execute Jews living in the conquered areas. As shooting proved too cumbersome a method of dealing with the large numbers of people involved, extermination camps were established in Poland, where an estimated six million Jews were gassed. The most notorious extermination camps were at Auschwitz, Chelmno, Belzec, Maidanek, Sobibor and Treblinka. These names became by-words for inhumanity. There was no intention, however, of incriminating the whole German people as accomplices, for if the Allies had at one time trusted Hitler, it was unreasonable to condemn the German people for having done so.

The problem of Germany and the start of the Cold War

The arrangements made at Potsdam scarcely concealed the growing quarrel between the Soviet Union and its allies, which within two years led to a state of Cold War between them. The Allies had agreed that the four occupied zones of Germany should be administered from Berlin according to a common policy laid down by the Council of Ministers. Their meetings

The horrific sight which greeted the Allies when they came to liberate one of the concentration camps.

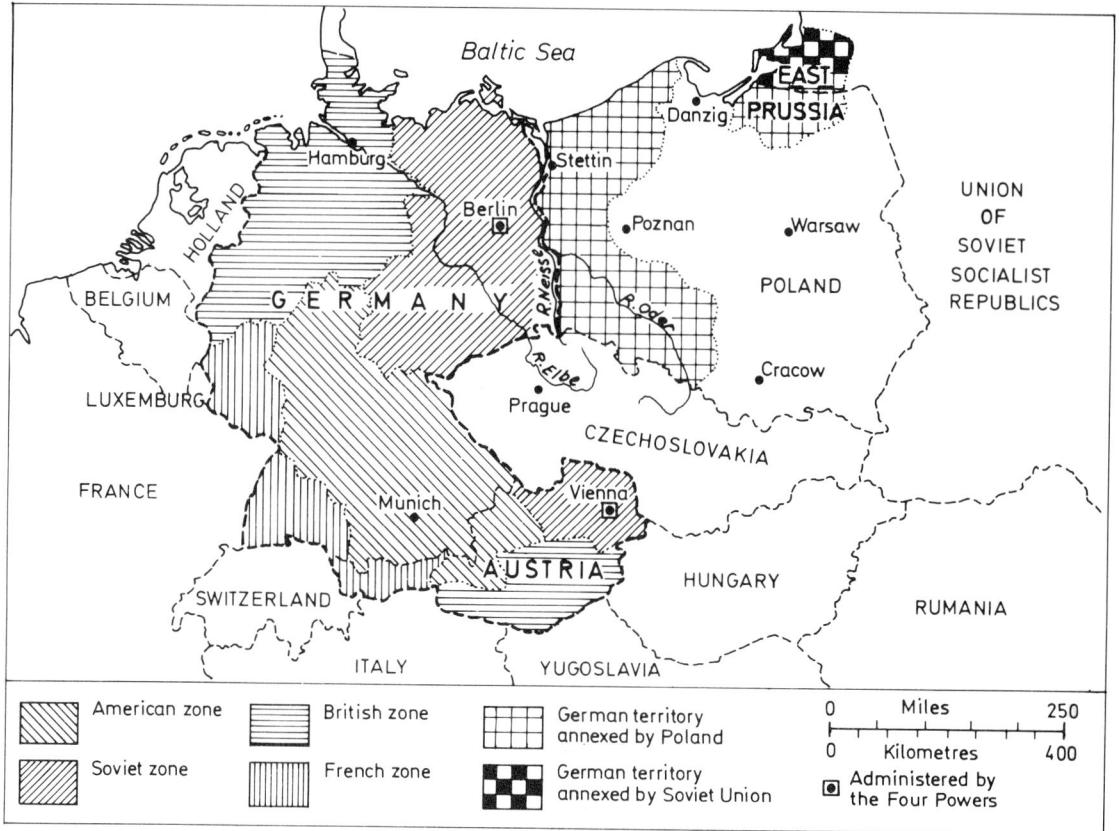

8   *The division of Germany and Austria in 1945*

however, degenerated into interminable wrangling over matters of detail and propaganda speeches. Likewise, the Allied Control Commission, headed by the four commanders-in-chief, could not function as intended. Agreement had to be unanimous, and it was soon obvious that the Soviet representative was not interested in allowing progress to be made towards the development of a prosperous, reunited and independent Germany.

From the beginning, therefore, the Eastern and Western zones developed along divergent lines. In the Russian zone the foundations of a communist society were laid. The large estates of the Junkers were destroyed by limiting land ownership to 250 acres, and blocking bank accounts of over 300 marks, so that private fortunes, however acquired, were confiscated by the State. Four political parties were set up, to

act as 'shells' to be taken over by the Communist Party at a later date.

In the Western zones ten *Länder*, or states, were restored for administrative convenience. In each a minister-president was appointed. Political parties were organised, and in January 1946 elections to local councils were held in the American zone. Wider measures of self-government soon followed. On 1 January 1947 the American and British zones were joined for economic purposes, since the artificial division of Germany into separate zones, in conjunction with the systematic dismantling of industry in the Russian zone, was impeding economic progress. In May the Anglo-American and French zones were amalgamated into the so-called Bizonia. These measures were bitterly attacked by Stalin as violations of the Yalta and Potsdam Agreements.

Marshall Aid

By 1947 Europe was split into two armed camps, and Churchill spoke of an 'Iron Curtain', dividing the democratic countries of Western Europe from the communist satellite states of Eastern Europe. In February 1947 the United States government recognised the communist threat to Western Europe by the announcement of what came to be known as the Truman Doctrine. When the British government informed the United States that it could no longer afford to maintain troops in Greece, where they were attempting to put down a communist revolt, Truman declared that the United States would support the 'free peoples of the world in their struggle against communism.'

Financial support for this policy followed in June, with the offer of Marshall Aid. Communist successes in the French and Italian elections convinced the American government that the extreme weakness of the Western European economies was a serious danger, for it provided conditions in which communism might flourish. General Marshall, the American Secretary of State, said that the United States would give financial aid to any European country (with the exception of Spain, which had a fascist government under General Franco), providing only that the receiving government cooperated in promoting the recovery of Europe as a whole. The governments of sixteen Western European countries gratefully accepted the offer, and formed themselves into the Organisation for European Economic Cooperation (OEEC) in April 1948. In the next five years 13,000 million dollars of American aid were injected into Western Europe, saving it from economic collapse and setting it on the path to unprecedented prosperity. Stalin, however, forbade the communist governments of Eastern Europe to accept, even though some, notably the Czechoslovak government, wished to do so.

Dollar aid to Western Europe more than anything else saved it from communism. Unfortunately, but unavoidably, Marshall Aid also reinforced the division between Western and Eastern Europe. Stalin claimed that it was a bribe to induce governments to join a coalition of states hostile to the Soviet Union and its partners. The United States was, in his opinion, substituting economic imperialism for political imperialism. Stalin also denounced dollar aid as part of a calculated plan to revive Germany as a strong power which could, once again, become a threat to the Soviet Union.

The impasse over Germany

Stalin realised that there was no hope of uniting Germany under a subservient communist regime until American forces had left Europe. He therefore proposed that the Allies should withdraw all troops from the occupied zones as a pre-condition for Germany unity. This solution, however, would have left the Red Army poised upon the eastern frontier of Germany, opposed only by the weak forces of France and Britain. Germany might then have followed the pattern of Eastern European countries by succumbing to a Soviet-inspired communist dictatorship. Not surprisingly, the Western allies refused to consider Stalin's request seriously. Henceforward, Stalin was determined to obstruct any measures aimed at promoting the political and economic recovery of Germany.

The Western allies were in a dilemma. They had occupied Germany as conquerors rather than liberators, and no government relished the prospect of a strong, united Germany. France, in particular, dared not agree to any proposals which would have led to the economic recovery of Germany before the rest of Western Europe, since that would have given Germany economic supremacy in Europe. Yet the recovery of Western Europe was closely bound up with the economic recovery of Germany. Secondly, only a prosperous Western Europe could withstand the military threat from the Soviet Union. Gradually, therefore, Western Europe's fear of the Soviet Union became greater than its fear of a revived and powerful Germany.

In 1948, after the Council of Foreign Ministers at a meeting in London had failed to reach agreement over Germany, the Western allies embarked upon a policy which resulted in the creation of the Federal Republic of West Germany. With the consent of the Foreign Ministers of the Benelux countries (Belgium, the Netherlands and Luxemburg), the three Western zones of Germany were merged into an economic union and arrangements were made for a constitution to be drawn up. In June 1948 a single currency for the Western sectors was introduced, as a major step towards the establishment of a government for West Germany. The Soviet Union responded with an attempt to drive the Western allies from Berlin.

The Berlin blockade

The presence of American, French and British troops in West Berlin was a constant source of irritation to the Russians. West Berlin constituted an isolated area of Western democratic influence deep inside the Russian zone of Germany. Apart from enabling thousands of discontented East Germans to escape from communist rule, it stood as a symbol for the future reunification of Germany.

The Berlin blockade did not begin suddenly. Throughout 1947 the Russians made efforts to drive the Allies from Berlin by restricting access to the city. Trains from the Western sectors of Germany would be diverted into sidings, and roadblocks created long queues of military vehicles trying to enter the city. Aircraft using the air corridors into Berlin were harassed by Soviet military aircraft. On 24 June 1948, however, all land routes into West Berlin were closed by Soviet troops.

Berlin thus became the centre of a Cold War confrontation, since the Allies refused to surrender their rights in the city. It seemed impossible that West Berlin could be supplied by air with the 4000 tons of foodstuffs and raw materials it needed daily, but by April 1949 two new airfields had been constructed, and a daily average of 8000 tons of supplies was being flown into the beleaguered city.

The blockade was lifted in May 1949, when Stalin conceded that the Allies could not be forced to leave against their will. From the Russian viewpoint the blockade had become coun-

ter-productive. The intensification of the Cold War had brought about the formation of the North Atlantic Treaty Organisation (see Chapter Six), when twelve Western countries combined to resist a communist attack in Europe. Moreover, the blockade was raising the morale of the West Berliners, and was forcing West Germany into closer political ties with Western Europe.

The creation of two Germanys

The Federal Republic of West Germany was proclaimed in May 1949, with its capital at Bonn. (For obvious reasons Berlin could not be chosen.) West Berlin became a city state, with its own constitution, but was regarded as part of the Federal Republic, whose implied authority extended over East Germany. Most German politicians were reluctant to consider any constitutional arrangements which recognised, or resulted in, the division of Germany, lest they came to be regarded as traitors. The idea that East Germany would one day be reunited with West Germany was an important factor in East-West tension.

The new constitution provided for a lower chamber (the *Bundestag*), elected every four years by direct universal suffrage, and an upper chamber (or *Bundesrat*), composed of delegates from the state governments. The President of the Federal Republic was to be chosen by a special assembly, but the Chancellor, in whom real power was vested, was chosen by the lower chamber, and responsible to it. Foreign trade and affairs, reparations, and control of the Ruhr industrial area and rearmament were initially kept in Allied hands. A civilian Allied High Commission replaced the military Control Commission, but the military occupation remained in force for the time being.

In September 1950 the state of war between Germany and the Western allies officially came to an end, and reparations ceased. In 1952 the Allied High Commission was abolished, and West Germany was declared to be a free and equal member of the community of nations. In May 1955 it became an independent sovereign state. In the meantime, the German Democratic Republic had been created in October 1949. Like its Western counterpart, East Germany declared that the reunification of Germany was one of its primary objectives. Otto Grotewohl, a Social Democrat who had joined the communist united front, was its first Chancellor.

The recovery of West Germany under Adenauer's chancellorship

Under the chancellorship of Konrad Adenauer (1949–63) West Germany achieved rapid economic growth and became fully integrated, economically and militarily, into Western Europe. Konrad Adenauer (1876–1967) had a long and active life in politics, from which he retired reluctantly at the age of eighty-seven. A leader of the Roman Catholic Centre party in Weimar Germany, he was Mayor of Cologne from 1917 to 1933, when he was dismissed by Goering for opposition to the Nazis and spent some time in

Adenauer re-visits his old cell in concentration camp.

a concentration camp. After the war Adenauer founded the Christian Democrat party, and was elected Chancellor of West Germany in August 1949.

Adenauer believed in strong, benevolent rule. He outlawed the extremist Socialist Reich party, which was neo-Nazi in outlook and later, in 1956, the Communist party. As Chancellor, he was determined not to repeat the mistakes of the Weimar Republic. His greatest achievements were to provide a long period of political stability, and to reconcile West Germany with its former enemies in Western Europe. In 1955 West Germany joined the North Atlantic Treaty Organisation and, one year later, became a founder member of the European Economic Community, or Common Market (see Chapter Six). Adenauer developed a strong friendship with President de Gaulle of France, and played an important part in ending the enmity which had existed between their two countries since 1870.

West Germany's 'economic miracle'

The transformation of West Germany within a few years of the end of the Second World War, from a landscape with ruins into one of the most prosperous countries in the world, was a remarkable achievement. Underlying it was the hard work of the Germany people, and their determination to rebuild their country's prosperity out of the chaotic conditions which existed in 1945. A second factor was industrial modernisation. Large portions of German industry had been completely destroyed during the war but, financed by dollar aid under the Marshall Plan, it was restored and re-equipped with the most up-to-date machinery.

Thirdly, political stability, enterprising leadership and an absence of industrial strife all promoted economic recovery. Workers were readily accepted on to boards of management, and they were encouraged to hold shares in the major industries so that West Germany should become a model 'property owning democracy'. Wage bargaining was simplified by the existence of only sixteen trade unions.

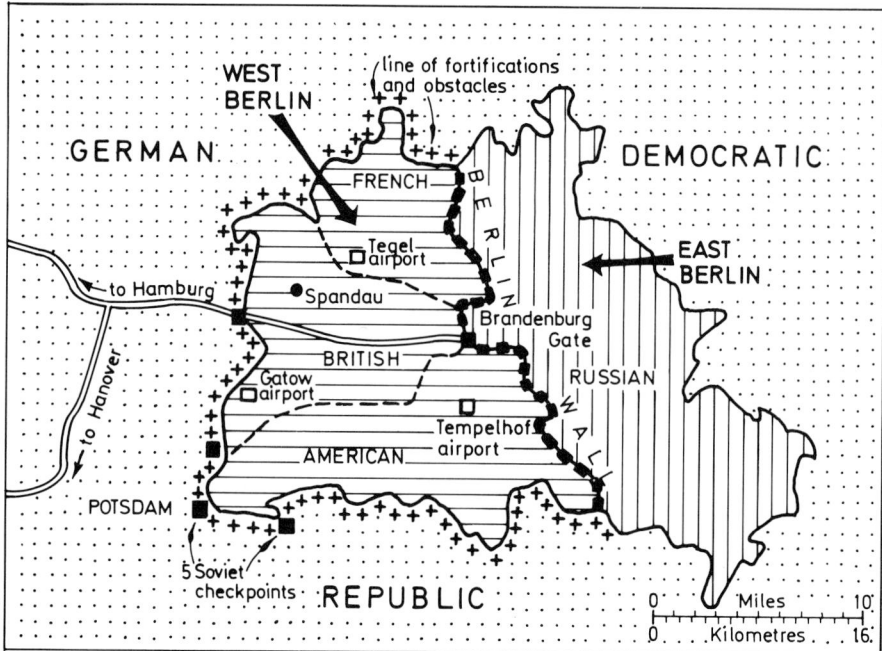

9   *Berlin*

The second Berlin crisis 1958

West Germany's material prosperity contrasted favourably with the less spectacular progress of East Germany, and each year the country attracted thousands of refugees fleeing from communist rule. Although the frontier between the two countries was effectively sealed, it was relatively easy for discontented East Germans to travel to West Berlin, and from there escape into West Germany. Since the end of the war over three million East Germans had voted with their feet, depriving East Germany of skilled workers, as well as being a poor advertisement for socialism.

Furthermore, it was conceivable that West Germany's new-found confidence, together with its membership of NATO, might encourage moves towards reunification. It was in an effort to reduce this risk, by neutralising a potential flashpoint in East-West relations, that the Soviet Union tried once again to drive the Western Allies from West Berlin.

In November 1958 Nikita Khrushchev, the Soviet Premier, demanded that all foreign troops should be withdrawn from Berlin, since the Potsdam agreement was clearly no longer in operation. Access to the city would be controlled by the East German government. Unless the Western Allies complied with these demands, Khrushchev threatened that the Soviet Union would make a separate peace with East Germany.

The Americans refused to make any concessions, however, and the issue was eventually relegated to a fruitless meeting in Vienna in June 1961, attended by Khrushchev and the American President, John F. Kennedy. In August, however, construction began on the Berlin Wall, which completely sealed off the Eastern sector from the rest of the city. The Wall was yet another reminder that the Soviet Union was not prepared to allow any changes in the map of Eastern Europe.

The two Germanys become reconciled

Adenauer's government refused to acknowledge the legal existence of East Germany, nor would it accept diplomatic links with any country which recognised East Germany (the so-called Hallstein doctrine). During the chancellorship of Dr Kurt Kiesinger (1966–69), however, this policy was modified cautiously when German trade missions were established in Rumania and Yugoslavia.

By the late 1960s the stalemate over Germany had acquired an air of permanence and Willi Brandt, Chancellor of West Germany from 1969 to 1974, was able to adopt a much more flexible policy, setting out to improve West Germany's relations with its neighbours in Eastern Europe. This meant accepting the Polish-German frontier, and recognising East Germany.

In 1970, Brandt visited Moscow twice in order to assure the Soviet government that his intentions did not constitute a threat to Soviet interests. West Germany then signed treaties with Poland and the Soviet Union, and agreed that the Oder-Neisse frontier between Poland and East Germany should be permanent. A compromise solution to the problem of Berlin was reached in September 1971, when the Western Allies agreed that their sectors did not form part of West Germany, while the Soviet Union promised that communications between West Berlin and West Germany would be unimpeded.

The success of Willi Brandt's *Ostpolitik* ('Eastern policy') earned him the Nobel Peace Prize, and led, in 1972, to the Treaty of Berlin. This established good neighbourly relations between East and West Germany, based on a recognition of their equal rights. In September 1973 the two Germanys were admitted into the United Nations as sovereign states. Thus German unity, forged in war in 1871 and destroyed by war in 1945, was officially renounced. The past was buried, if not forgotten, and the hope grew that Europe's peace could now be strengthened.

CHAPTER SIX:
Western Europe from Diversity to Unity

By conquest and annexation, Hitler imposed upon Europe a degree of political and economic unity greater than any which had existed since the collapse of the Napoleonic Empire in 1815. Occupied Europe was liberated only after the United States came to the assistance of the Soviet Union and Britain. Thus for the second time in the twentieth century the United States intervened in Europe to rescue it from the consequences of its national rivalries.

After 1945 a number of statesmen, disillusioned with the nationalism which had been a major cause of two world wars, proposed the creation of a united Europe, which would make war between European countries impossible. They looked for a lead to the British government, which had supported several wartime projects for European unity. In 1940 the exiled governments of Poland and Czechoslovakia agreed in London that their countries should form a confederation after the war. So too did those of Yugoslavia and Greece. Just before the Fall of France in 1940 Churchill had proposed the union of Britain and France, together with their empires. Furthermore, in a famous speech at Zürich, Switzerland in 1946, Churchill spoke of the need to build a 'kind of United States of Europe'. Although Churchill was no longer Prime Minister, his prestige was so great that his words stirred the hopes of many Europeans.

Britain, however, for many years proved to be a luke-warm supporter of the idea of European unity, and unwilling to become part of a European confederation. There were several important reasons for this attitude. Clement Attlee's Labour government (1945–51) was preoccupied with the tasks of constructing the Welfare State and granting independence to India. Britain had strong links with the Commonwealth (see Chapter Eight) and a large overseas empire, which successive governments did not wish to weaken or abandon. Also valued was the special relationship with the United States, resulting from the wartime Grand Alliance. Britain's democratic institutions had survived intact the severe test of a long war, whereas those of continental Europe had never appeared very stable. Nor had the British population suffered the humiliation and defeat which had been the recent fate of most European countries. Instead, it had emerged from the struggle victorious, full of national pride for its achievement in resisting Nazi tyranny. The British as a whole took the view that, having helped to save Europe, there was little advantage to be gained from joining it more closely.

Benelux

The first moves towards the union of Western Europe were inspired by its weaknesses. It was fear of a revived Germany, and the realisation that the Soviet Union was rapidly consolidating its military control over Eastern Europe, which prompted the efforts to unite Western Europe. As early as October 1944 the governments of Belgium, the Netherlands and Luxemburg had agreed to form a free trade area. In 1948 this became a reality when the Benelux customs union was set up.

The Western Union

The French government, too, faced the age-old problem of its relationship with the German nation, in 1945 divided and helpless in defeat but potentially very powerful. In March 1947 the French and British governments signed the Treaty of Dunkirk, and entered into a fifty-year alliance, whereby each country promised to help the other if either was attacked by Germany. In the following year this alliance was expanded into the Western Union by the Brussels Treaty, when the Benelux countries joined France and Britain. This time, however, the member states promised aid against any armed attack, so that it was also aimed against the Soviet Union, with which both France and Britain had a legally valid military alliance.

Unaided, however, the Western Union could not hope to resist a determined communist attack, a danger which seemed very real in the late 1940s. The communist revolt in Greece and the establishment of communist governments in all the East European states overrun by the Red Army (see Chapter Nine), together with the growing rift between the Western Allies and the Soviet Union over the future of Germany, all seemed ominous evidence of Stalin's determination to expand Soviet influence in Europe. Only the vast industrial resources of the United States and its monopoly of atomic weapons could counter-balance the military power of the Soviet Union and its satellites.

The Truman Doctrine

The precise nature of Stalin's intentions towards a virtually defenceless Western Europe, however, can only be a matter for speculation, as in March 1947 the United States government reversed the policy of withdrawing its armed forces from Europe. When the British government informed the United States in February 1947 that it could no longer afford to give military help to the Greek government, President Truman persuaded Congress to vote the huge sum of 400 million dollars to enable him to give military and economic aid, not only to Greece, but also to Turkey, which felt itself threatened by the Soviet Union. In March Truman announced that the United States would not only take over Britain's commitments in Greece, but would also 'support free peoples who are resisting subjugation by armed minorities or by outside pressures', and . . . 'assist free peoples to work out their own destinies in their own ways'. This was the famous Truman Doctrine. Combined with Marshall Aid (see page 49) it showed that the United States would not repeat the mistake it had made after the First World War, of retreating into isolation.

The North Atlantic Treaty Organisation

Tension between the United States and the Soviet Union was further heightened by Allied preparations to merge their occupation zones in Germany, a process which culminated in the creation of the Federal Republic of West Germany in September 1949. During the Berlin Blockade (June 1948 to May 1949) the Russians tried unsuccessfully to drive the Allies from Berlin, before this became an accomplished fact.

This was the Cold War background against which the North Atlantic Treaty Organisation was formed in April 1949. Twelve countries—the United States, Canada, France, Britain, Italy, Portugal, Iceland, Denmark, Norway and Benelux—joined this mutual defence alliance. The treaty provisions stated that an attack upon any one of these countries would be regarded as an attack upon all, though each country was free to decide what assistance it would give to the country attacked. NATO was expanded in February 1952 when Turkey and Greece joined.

The Council of Europe

NATO was prompted by the urgent need of the countries of Western Europe to combine against the powerful military threat of the Soviet Union and its communist partners. The Council of Europe, formed in May 1949, was an attempt to integrate the countries of Western Europe into a close community, in the hope of eliminating the possibility of war between its members.

In 1948 several hundred supporters of the idea of a united Europe met at an unofficial congress at the Hague, and drafted a constitution for the Council of Europe. The governments of ten countries—Denmark, Norway, Sweden, Ireland, Britain, Benelux, France and Italy—agreed to cooperate to safeguard their common heritage, and to promote economic and social progress. They also promised to respect fundamental human rights in their treatment of individuals.

The machinery of the Council of Europe consisted of a Consultative Assembly or European Parliament, composed of 147 delegates chosen from the national parliaments, and a Council of Ministers. Though membership of the Council of Europe rose to eighteen, it lacked any authority to act over the heads of the member governments, and its aims were far too vague for it to become the means of uniting Europe. Today, although it encourages the growth of a more European outlook, its achievements have been largely limited to such matters as the organisation of a European Conservation Year in 1970, and to the championship of human rights.

The European Coal and Steel Community

The failure to make the Council of Europe a supra-national organisation capable of binding all the countries of Western Europe into a single community, resulted in a more limited, practical approach to the problem. By 1950 it was recognised that a strong, prosperous Western Europe could never be built without the economic recovery and full participation of West Germany. Even so, such a prospect was very alarming to many people, particularly in France and the Benelux countries.

In May 1950 Jean Monnet, the architect of a four year plan for French industry and agriculture, persuaded Robert Schumann, the French Foreign Minister, to propose a scheme to the Council of Europe. According to this plan, the entire coal and steel production of France and

West Germany, and of any other interested country, would be placed under the control of a High Authority acting independently of national governments. The union of the French and West German coal and steel industries would make future war between the two countries impossible.

Despite the refusal of the British government to participate, the governments of France, West Germany, Benelux and Italy agreed to form the European Coal and Steel Community. In April 1951 nine representatives of these countries met in Luxemburg and formed the High Authority, whose decisions rapidly transformed the economies of the six member nations. Although the coal industry contracted due to the competition of cheap oil, steel production doubled in the period 1952–66. The most profitable coal mines were modernised, uneconomic pits were shut down and over 200,000 redundant coal miners were assisted, by generous resettlement and retraining grants, to find productive jobs in other industries.

The European Coal and Steel Community was a remarkable success, and its foundation marked a decisive stage in the progress towards the economic integration of Western Europe. The same six members of the ECSC became the founder members of the European Economic Community, or Common Market, in 1957.

The European Defence Community

The security of Western Europe since the end of the Second World War had been largely assured by the United States' monopoly of atomic weapons. This situation was altered in October 1949, when Russia exploded an atomic bomb. Although the array of countries in NATO was impressive on paper, it was doubtful whether the alliance could have prevented communist forces from overrunning Western Europe in a conventional war. Yet NATO requests for greater American military involvement in Western Europe fell upon deaf ears. The United States was heavily committed in the Korean War which began in 1950 (see Chapter Ten), and it therefore insisted that Western Europe should assume greater responsibility for its own defence. The obvious solution appeared to be to rearm West Germany.

The French, haunted by the spectre of German militarism, were dismayed by this suggestion, and many other Europeans shared their misgivings. Most West Germans, disillusioned by their recent experience of militarism, did not relish the prospect. Furthermore, rearming West Germany was a provocative action when a majority of its population had not abandoned the hope of future German reunification.

To overcome some of these difficulties the French proposed in October 1951 the formation of a European army which would include contingents from West Germany. The army would be under the civilian control of a European Government. Its budget would be voted by a European Parliament. The officers and men would wear a common uniform and their allegiance would be to the European Community, not the governments of their individual countries. In May 1952 West Germany, Benelux and Italy agreed to join France in the establishment of a European Defence Community, which would become a kind of United States of Europe.

Britain, soon to become the third country to possess the atomic bomb, refused to join, though it was prepared to be closely associated with the EDC. After much debate the French Parliament, disconcerted by Britain's decision, rejected the treaty in August 1954, for it was not prepared to agree to any scheme for West German rearmament unless Britain participated in it.

John Foster Dulles, the American Secretary of State, had already issued clear warnings that if the EDC treaty was not ratified, the United States would have to review its policy towards Western Europe. A crisis was only averted when Sir Anthony Eden, the British Foreign Secretary, and Dulles agreed upon an alternative plan. They proposed that West Germany should be admitted into the Western Union. West Germany would be allowed limited conventional rearmament, but would be forbidden to manufacture atomic weapons. In October the new alliance, re-named the Western European

Union, came into being. The rearmament of West Germany and its admission to NATO in 1955 were proof of the determination of the governments which belonged to the ECSC, to continue their search for a closer association with one another, despite their failure to agree upon a European Defence Community.

The European Economic Community (EEC)

Encouraged by the success of the Coal and Steel Community, the Dutch suggested that instead of enlarging the Community's scope to include other forms of energy, such as electricity and atomic power, the ECSC countries should form a free trade area.

In June 1955, the Foreign Ministers of the Six met at Messina in Sicily to consider the Dutch proposal. They approved the scheme, and also recommended that the six governments should adopt identical policies for social policy, transport and energy. Henri Spaak was appointed chairman of the planning committee, and Britain was invited to join the discussions.

At this stage the Six were still anxious that Britain should belong to the Community, but the British government did not think that a multi-national European organisation would be a success, particularly if Britain remained outside it. It preferred instead to develop the concept of a multi-racial Commonwealth, whose members enjoyed preferential treatment in their trade with one another. Furthermore, the British Parliament was not prepared to surrender any of its authority to a European Commission.

During the negotiations leading up to the Treaty of Rome Britain suggested that Western Europe should form a free trade area, but without the common tariff on external trade. This scheme would have enabled Britain to freely import foodstuffs and raw materials from the Commonwealth. It would have completely altered the character of the Community, however, whose intended development was full political union of the member countries. Britain's proposal was therefore rejected.

The Treaty of Rome 1957

After two years' hard bargaining, representatives of the six countries signed the Treaty of Rome in March 1957, setting up a customs union, or European Economic Community (EEC), which came into being on 1 January 1958. The Six agreed to abolish by stages all tariffs on trade between the member states, and to adopt a common tariff and trade policy towards non-member countries. Common agricultural and transport policies were to be developed, and there was to be free movement of workers, capital and services within the Community.

The machinery of the EEC

The machinery of the EEC consists of a European Commission of nine members, a Council of Ministers, a European Parliament (not to be confused with the Consultative Assembly of the Council of Europe) and a Court of Justice.

The Commission is responsible for implementing the Treaty of Rome. It is responsible only to the Community, for it works with the Council of Ministers. The Commission undertakes the day to day administration of the Community and initiates new legislation, on which the Council of Ministers makes the final decision. Its regulations are enforced by the law courts.

The Council of Ministers formulates EEC policy. Its membership can change according to the subject under discussion, but each country is represented by at least one minister who is usually a senior civil servant. Unanimous voting is generally required, so that each government can protect its vital interests by vetoing unwelcome legislation. Progress towards political union of the EEC members, therefore, has been slow. The Werner Plan for monetary union of the Six, put forward in June 1970, was rejected by governments reluctant to surrender powers to determine national levels of inflation and unemployment and to control their balance of payments.

The signing of the Treaty of Rome, 25th March, 1957, by the heads of state and ministers of foreign affairs of the Six.

The powers of the European Parliament are limited. Its delegates were nominated by the EEC governments until June 1979, when the first direct elections to the European Parliament took place. They are consulted by the Commission about its policies and can, by a two thirds majority vote, dismiss the Commission *en bloc*. But lacking executive powers, the European Parliament is little more than a forum for discussion.

The Court of Justice interprets the Treaty of Rome. It can fine individuals, firms and governments for infringements of the Community's laws and regulations, and during its existence it has steadily created a body of European law.

Euratom

Euratom (the European Atomic Energy Community) was established at the same time as the EEC, in an effort to reduce Western Europe's dependence upon Arab oil. Demand for fuel was rising rapidly, and the closure of the Suez Canal in 1956 during the second Arab-Israeli war had demonstrated Western Europe's vulnerability to an interruption of its oil supplies.

Agreements were reached with the United States, Canada and Britain for the sharing of information on nuclear research, but Euratom was not a success. Britain remained outside the European Community until 1973, and was reluctant to disclose knowledge which might have very important military and industrial implications. France was keen to develop its own nuclear capability; under de Gaulle's leadership it had visions of the EEC developing into a third world-power bloc, on terms of equality with the United States and the Soviet Union. Cooperation between the members of Eratom, therefore, was very limited.

The European Free Trade Area (EFTA)

Although the British government was at first doubtful about the long term prospects of the EEC, it tried to insure the British economy against any adverse effects of the Community's trade policies by forming a rival free trade area. By the Treaty of Stockholm (January 1960) Britain, Norway, Sweden, Denmark, Portugal, Austria and Switzerland formed the European Free Trade Area (EFTA), or 'Outer Seven'.

The EFTA members were free to trade with outside countries on whatever terms they wished, but they agreed to reduce tariffs on internal trade to bring them into line with those of the EEC. In this way any future merger with the EEC would be facilitated. At the same time they agreed that none would join the EEC without the consent of the others. Finland became closely associated with EFTA, and Iceland joined in 1970 when EFTA, with a population of 100 millions, was responsible for fourteen per cent of the world's trade.

The enlargement of the EEC

The Treaty of Rome provided for other countries to become full or associated members of the EEC. Non-European states could become associates so the Dutch overseas possessions and the French colonies in Africa joined on this basis. As they became independent their relationship with the Community was re-defined by the Yaoundé Convention, signed in 1963. Apart from several African nations, Greece (1962), Turkey (1964) and Malta (1971) also became associated members.

In 1961 Britain, Ireland and Denmark applied for full membership of the EEC. Although Britain's admission was strongly favoured by West Germany and the Benelux countries, the application was vetoed by President de Gaulle, who disliked Britain's special relationship with the United States. In 1962, while the application was being considered, the United States supplied Britain with Polaris nuclear missiles on the understanding that its nuclear strike capability would become part of NATO's armoury. This meant that Britain could not join an exclusively European force, and it convinced de Gaulle that Britain was not sufficiently European in outlook to justify full membership.

ICELAND (joined EFTA in 1970)

SWEDEN

FINLAND

NORWAY

North Sea

USSR

DENMARK (5)

IRELAND (3·1)

GREAT BRITAIN (56)

HOLLAND (3·6)

BELGIUM

EAST GERMANY

POLAND

Atlantic Ocean

WEST GERMANY (61·8)

LUX

CZECHOSLOVAKIA

FRANCE (52·7)

SWITZERLAND

AUSTRIA

HUNGARY

RUMANIA

PORTUGAL (8·7)

SPAIN (35·5)

YUGOSLAVIA

BULGARIA

ITALY (55·8)

ALBANIA

GREECE (9)

Mediterranean   Sea

MOROCCO   ALGERIA   TUNISIA

| EEC in 1958 | Assoc. members of the EEC |
| Joined EEC in 1973 | EFTA members 1960 | Applications for membership pending in 1979 | (35·5) Population in millions 1979 |

Miles 0 ———————— 500
Kilometres 0 ———————— 800

10   *The growth of the European Economic Community*

In May 1967 Britain re-applied. Once again France's opposition halted discussions, but de Gaulle's resignation in 1969 cleared the way for Britain's entry. President Pompidou, de Gaulle's successor, withdrew the French veto and in June 1970 the British Prime Minister Edward Heath renewed Britain's application.

Formal terms of entry were agreed in Brussels in July 1971 and Britain, along with Ireland and Denmark, joined the Community on 1 January 1973. Norway, which had also applied for membership, rejected the terms after a referendum. Thus the Six became the Nine, with a total population of 256 millions. British industrialists welcomed the benefits of easier access to a very large and rich market, responsible for forty per cent of the world's trade. Although Harold Wilson, who headed the two Labour administrations elected in 1974, renegotiated Britain's membership terms, the long debate had been finally settled; in the referendum of June 1975 there was a two to one majority in favour of continued membership.

The EEC became the most powerful trading bloc in the world, but as the Soviet military threat receded during the 1960s and 1970s the momentum towards political union slowed to a virtual standstill. With the resurgence of nationalism the ideal of supra-nationalism lost much of its appeal. Closer economic cooperation was welcomed, but the individual EEC governments seemed increasingly determined to retain sovereignty over their own affairs. If the Community was not to stagnate, France, West Germany and Britain had to learn to work together in greater harmony, in order that the collective interests of all its members might be effectively promoted.

The sudden collapse of France in June 1940 was hardly surprising in view of the defeatist attitude of the French High Command. During the previous two decades France's guarantees of security from an attack by Germany had disappeared as, stage by stage, the Versailles treaty was overthrown. Finally, having loyally followed the British policy of appeasing Hitler by sacrificing Czechoslovakia in 1938–9, the French placed their faith in the defensive strength of the Maginot Line of fortifications. When the German armies failed to oblige by making a frontal assault upon it (invading France via Belgium as the easier alternative), the French generals had no answer to the German *blitzkrieg* tactics. Lacking a natural barrier such as the English Channel with which to buy time and a leader capable of rallying it, the French government yielded to the inevitable by signing an armistice.

With the Fall of France the Third Republic came to an end. The new government for Unoccupied France formed by the aged Marshal Pétain (the hero of the First World War) withdrew to Vichy where it would be free from the pressures of the Paris populace, in order to quietly await the end of the war. The evacuation of British troops from Dunkirk, regarded by some Frenchmen as a betrayal of their country, seemed an admission that further resistance to Germany on the part of either France or Britain was useless.

The Vichy government reflected the confused state of the French people. Some, weary of the political aimlessness and bitter class conflicts which had divided French society for over twenty years, actually welcomed the collapse of the Republic in the hope that it would lead to a national revival. Few agreed with the proposal of Pierre Laval (Vichy Prime Minister after April 1942) for a Franco-German alliance, yet the strength and authority of the Nazi regime was admired by the fascist leagues and by the right wing *Action Française*. This group believed that Europe owed its salvation from communist revolution to the establishment of fascist governments in Germany, Italy and Spain. Others believed that collaboration with the enemy was necessary if France was to be a prosperous part of German Occupied Europe.

French resistance

Organised civilian resistance to Germany was slow to develop. The French Empire obeyed the instructions of the legally constituted Vichy government, and few people responded to General de Gaulle when he appealed to Frenchmen to continue the fight against Nazi Germany.

Charles de Gaulle (1890–1970) had escaped to England in June 1940, where he formed the Free French Movement, and claimed the status of head of a French government-in-exile. Meanwhile, in France itself, resistance grew as the harsh realities of German occupation became clear. Thousands of French families were expelled from Alsace and Lorraine and resettled in France. During the latter stages of the war when Germany was desperately short of skilled manpower, thousands of Frenchmen were deported to Germany in order to work in factories and mines. Some of the French prisoners-of-war still in captivity were released in exchange.

The turning point in the development of the French Resistance movement, however, was Germany's invasion of Russia, after which Britain had a powerful ally and a German victory no longer seemed inevitable. Moreover, it transformed the attitude of the French Communist party from one of silent acceptance of the German occupation to one of active hostility.

The *maquis*, so-called after resistance bands in Corsica, sabotaged transport and communications, organised escape routes for Allied pilots shot down over enemy occupied territory, acted as an espionage network and assassinated important German officials. The Germans retaliated by shooting hostages as a deterrent, the most horrific reprisals occurring in June 1944 when ninety-nine civilians from Tulle and the entire population of the village of Oradour-sur-Glane were massacred by SS troops, as they were on their way to the Normandy front.

Although the Resistance movement played a minor part in Germany's defeat, it nevertheless tied down thousands of troops for police duties who would otherwise have been available to fight in the front line. By providing intelligence and sabotaging the enemy's war effort it performed a valuable service to the Allies, while after D-Day the *maquis* harassed German troop movements, and liberated several *dèpartements* unaided. The cost, however, was heavy, and several thousand heroic French men and women paid for their resistance with their lives.

The establishment of the Fourth Republic

When Paris was liberated in August 1944 de Gaulle formed a provisional government. Its authority was readily accepted, although several thousand people were summarily executed by local Resistance groups for collaborating with the enemy. In the state treason trials which followed the liberation of France, nearly 100,000 people were punished by imprisonment or loss of civic rights, and 800 offenders, including Pierre Laval, were executed. Marshal Pétain was spared this fate in view of his age, but was sentenced to imprisonment for the rest of his life.

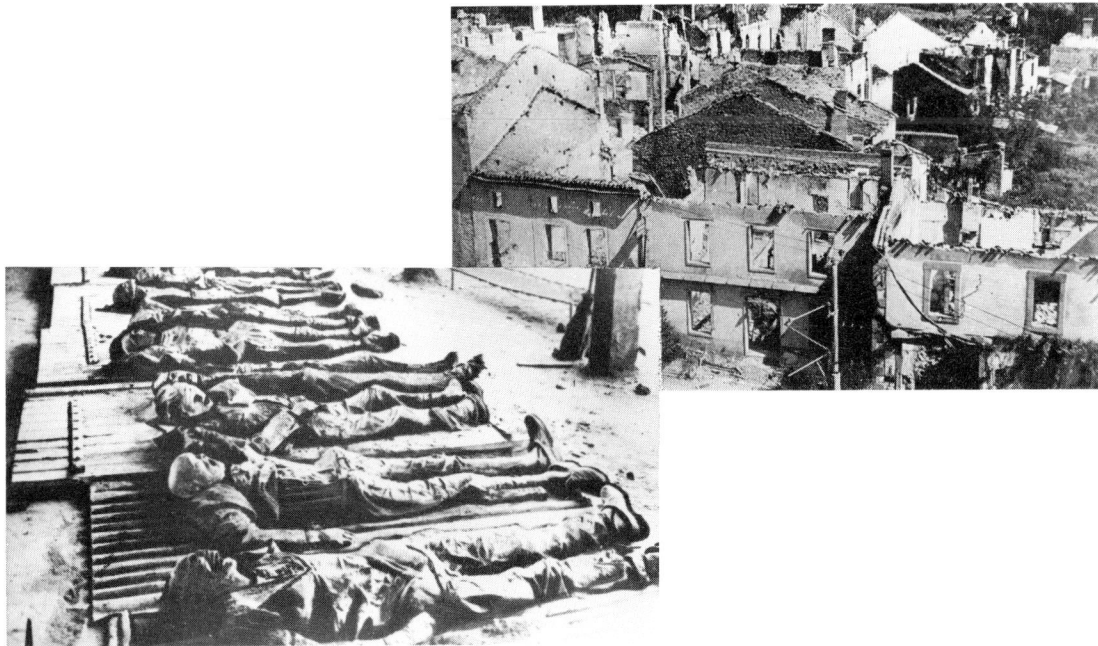

Oradour-sur-Glane: bodies that were exhumed after the massacre, and an aerial view of the ruined village.

Immediately after taking office, de Gaulle announced that as soon as the war was over and French prisoners-of-war and conscripted workers had been repatriated, the nation would decide upon a fresh form of government. Accordingly, elections were held in October 1945 to an assembly which confirmed de Gaulle's appointment as Provisional President, and began its task of drafting a constitution.

De Gaulle wanted a strong presidency, in order to ensure that France would not suffer from the weak, short-lived coalition governments which had been a feature of French political life before the war. The Communists and Socialists who dominated the assembly, however, suspected de Gaulle of having ambitions to become a military style dictator, and they proceeded to draw up a constitution in which the assembly held the balance of power.

De Gaulle, confident that his wartime leadership had made him indispensable, resigned in protest in January 1946, only to discover to his dismay that public opinion was unperturbed. Although the first constitution drafted was rejected by the electorate in May 1946, the second (a modified version of the first) was ratified by a narrow majority in the following October. It created a two-chamber Parliament, composed of a National Assembly and a Council of the Republic, which combined to choose a President who could hold office for seven years. The President, as Head of State, appointed the Prime Minister, but the latter depended upon the support of the deputies in the assembly. These deputies were in turn elected by a system of proportional representation in which all French men and women had the vote.

Economic recovery under the Fourth Republic

France had suffered much as a result of five years of military occupation and war, especially when large areas of the country became a battlefield during the latter stages of the fighting. Many towns lay in ruins, road and rail communications were badly damaged and half a million people had been killed.

Economic recovery was stimulated by Marshall Aid from America and by the determination of the French people to rebuild their country. Major industries such as mines, banks and the Renault car factories were nationalised, and social insurance for the whole population was introduced. Although inflation remained a severe problem, Jean Monnet, one of the architects of the European Coal and Steel Community, masterminded the modernisation and expansion of French industry, which doubled its pre-war output by 1951.

Colonial problems

During the Second World War there was an upsurge of national feeling in all the colonies belonging to the European countries. France however, unlike Britain, had special difficulties in regaining control of its overseas possessions, since much of its empire had been occupied either by the enemy or by the Allies. After 1945 many Frenchmen had mixed feelings about the value of colonies, yet national pride made it almost unthinkable that the Fourth Republic should start its existence by granting independence to the French Empire.

The need for some concessions, however, was recognised. Under the constitution of the Fourth Republic the colonies became part of a French Union, i.e. in a legal sense they ceased to be colonies and became part of France. Nevertheless, this arrangement did not satisfy the colonial peoples, for the relationship between metropolitan France and its overseas lands was unequal, with real power vested in the central government in Paris.

In 1945 Syria and Lebanon asserted their independence before France could recover control from the British. In Indochina French influence was restricted to the southern part of the country, since the Vietminh nationalists led by Ho Chi Minh, had seized the northern part. France's struggle to hold on to Indochina, which ended in failure in 1954, is described in Chapter Thirteen. In Algeria the bitter civil war which began soon after the end of the costly and protracted war in Indochina was a major cause of the collapse of the Fourth Republic.

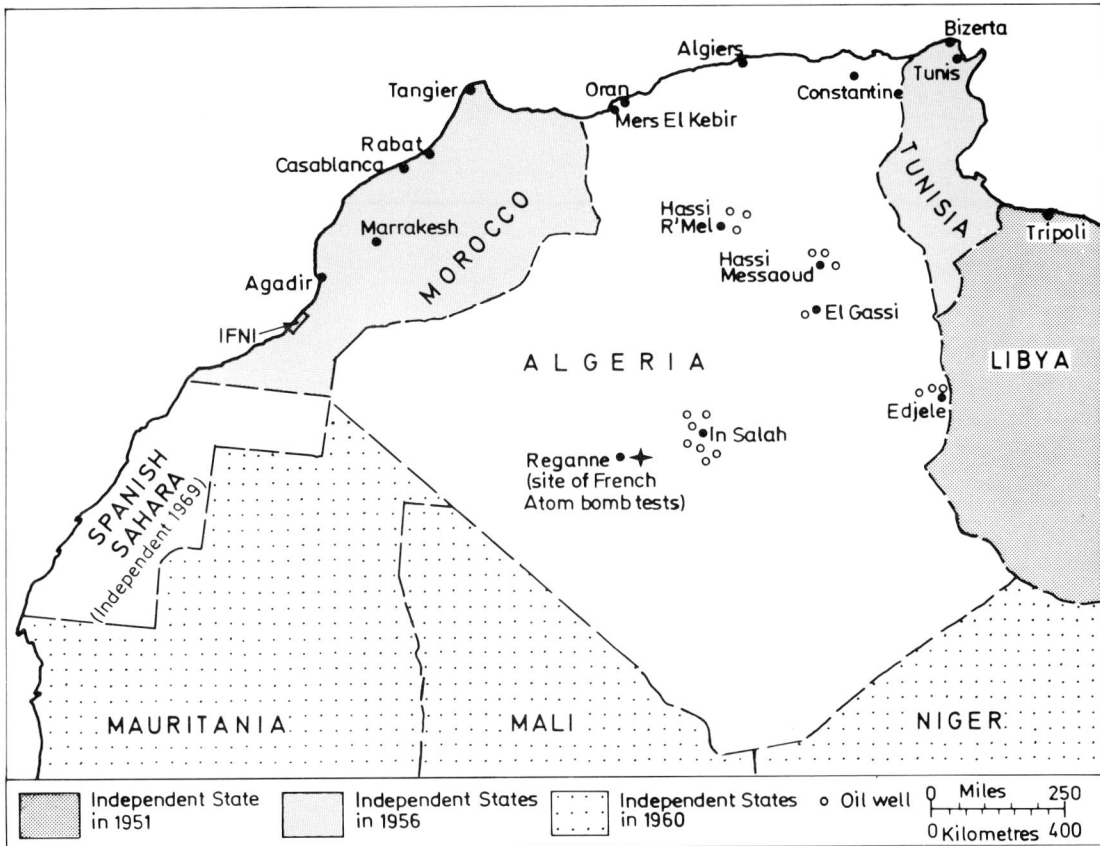

11   *North West Africa, 1960*

The Algerian war of independence 1954–62

Algeria had a population of nine million Muslims and about one million European settlers, or *colons*, half of whom were of French descent. Nationalist discontent had been stimulated by the Allied landings in North Africa in 1942, but Arab demands for self-government put forward by Messali Hadj, leader of the Algerian People's Party, and Ferhat Abbas, who drew up a Manifesto of the Algerian People in 1943, were fiercely resisted by the *colons*. Nationalist riots in Algeria at the end of the war were savagely repressed.

In 1949 Ahmed Ben Bella led a terrorist attack on Oran. Most of the leaders were arrested, but Ben Bella escaped to Cairo where, along with

Ferhat Abbas, he organised the National Liberation Front (FLN), which became strong enough to launch a revolt against French rule in November 1954. Banks, offices and police stations were attacked, and within a few months FLN terrorists were active throughout the populated areas of Algeria.

The French government was determined to hold on to Algeria, which had suddenly assumed great economic importance after the discovery of natural gas and oil in its territory. It also believed that the FLN was only sustained by Egyptian aid. In order to concentrate upon the problem of Algeria the French agreed to the nationalist demands for independence in neighbouring Morocco and Tunisia in 1956. They also asked Egypt's President Nasser to cease his support of the Algerian rebels. His refusal was one reason for the French government's collusion with the British and the Israelis in their attack on Egypt which began the Suez War in 1956 (see Chapter Fifteen).

In October 1957 Ben Bella and four other FLN leaders were interned by the French when the pilot of their chartered aircraft, in which they were flying from Morocco to Tunisia, landed at Algiers. Despite this setback, however, the FLN intensified its campaign, and successive French governments were unable to achieve victory in a savage civil war, with both sides committing terrible atrocities. Eventually, the French government decided to negotiate a settlement with the FLN.

This provoked a violent outburst from the army, which was anxious to avoid any repetition of its humiliating defeat in Indochina, and the European settlers, who were determined that Algeria should remain French. Led by General Massu, the commander of a parachutist division, the colons set up committees of public safety in Algerian towns and cities. The crisis was resolved when the French Premier Pierre Pflimlin resigned and de Gaulle was appointed Presi-

dent, for both the army and the colons were convinced that he would never agree to an independent Algeria. Events were soon to prove them wrong.

Within one year de Gaulle recognised the strength of Algerian nationalism. His announcement in September 1959 that the Algerians should be allowed to determine their own future was therefore greeted with dismay by the colons and by the army leaders. They formed a Secret Army Organisation (OAS) to prevent the transfer of power to the FLN, and several attempts were made by the OAS to assassinate de Gaulle. In April 1961 Salan and three other generals tried to seize Algeria, but were foiled by their troops, most of whom remained loyal to de Gaulle.

Meanwhile, secret talks were taking place between representatives of the FLN and the French government, and in March 1962 a settlement was agreed at Evian-les-Bains. Algeria was to become independent, but the French were to retain a nuclear testing site in the Sahara for four years, and use of the naval base at Mers-el-Kebir until 1968. Ben Bella and other interned FLN leaders were released. The OAS made a final,

Jubilant Algerians carry the new nation's flag through the streets of Oran in a parade celebrating the granting of independence.

desperate attempt to wreck the settlement by provoking further violence, but FLN reprisals forced thousands of European settlers to flee to safety in France. On 1 July the Algerians voted overwhelmingly in favour of independence, which was proclaimed by de Gaulle two days later.

Algeria since independence

The Algerian leaders quarrelled amongst themselves before Ahmed Ben Bella, strongly supported by the commander of the FLN forces, Colonel Houari Boumedienne, was elected Prime Minister in September 1962, and President in 1963. Ben Bella ruled until June 1965 when he in his turn was overthrown by Boumedienne.

Under Boumedienne (1927–78) Algeria became a socialist state, and a leader of the Third World nations. Opposed to any form of colonialism, Boumedienne helped national liberation movements in Africa by providing training facilities to guerrillas on Algerian soil. In 1973, when Algeria was host country to a conference of Arab Heads of State, Boumedienne emerged as one of the most important statesmen in the Arab world, and a leading advocate of the use of oil sanctions against those countries which continued to support Israel. In 1974 he urged the UN Assembly to devise a scheme whereby the rich nations of the world would share their wealth with the poor nations.

Algeria's relations with France were not always smooth. There was a considerable volume of trade between the two countries, and France gave valuable economic aid to its former colony. Algeria's nationalisation of the French oil companies in 1971, however, caused bad feeling between the two countries, as did France's support for Morocco over the disputed territory of the Spanish Sahara. In 1975 Boumedienne protested against Spain's decision to divide the Spanish Sahara between Morocco and Mauritania, and gave his support to the Polisario, a Saharan resistance movement which proclaimed the existence of an independent Saharan Democratic Republic.

De Gaulle and the Fifth French Republic

The crisis over Algeria was instrumental in bringing about the destruction of the Fourth French Republic and de Gaulle's return from the political wilderness, following his resignation in January 1946. Although he had formed a movement called the *Rassemblement du Peuple Français*, or Rally of the French People, it failed to win power at the polling stations, and was abandoned by its founder in 1955. De Gaulle was recalled to office in May 1958 because he seemed to be the only person capable of saving France from civil war. Regarded as a stopgap measure by his opponents, he was to remain as Head of State for eleven years.

De Gaulle secured acceptance of a new constitution which increased the powers of the President and reduced the influence of the National Assembly. In 1962 he outmanoeuvred his opponents, who wanted to restore the power of the assembly, by proposing an amendment to the constitution whereby the President would be chosen by direct popular vote. This was duly approved by a referendum of the French people.

De Gaulle's achievements were considerable. He brought to an end sixteen years of colonial warfare, and provided a long period of stable government, during which the French economy became one of the strongest in Western Europe. Abroad, France followed an independent policy, and became a nuclear power when it exploded its own atomic bomb in 1960. De Gaulle asserted French sovereignty by criticising American intervention in Vietnam, recognising communist China in 1964, developing friendly relations with the Soviet Union, and withdrawing France from the North Atlantic Treaty Organisation in 1966. In 1963 he blocked Britain's application to join the European Common Market, on the grounds that it was not sufficiently European in its outlook to justify membership of the Community.

Re-elected President in 1965, the first real test of de Gaulle's authority came with the student riots in May 1968. A cutback in public spending,

part of a package of economic measures to protect the value of the franc, led to discontent
which spread from the students to the workers,
and a full-scale confrontation with the government developed. De Gaulle broadcast a powerful
appeal to the French people, demanding a vote
of confidence on the issue of law and order. The
assembly was dissolved and in the elections
which followed, the Gaullists won an overwhelming majority.

De Gaulle, however, had outlived his popularity, and when he failed to win a vote of confidence over his proposed alteration of the
powers of the Senate in April 1969, he resigned
and retired to his country estate for the rest of
his life. It is a measure of de Gaulle's achievement
that his resignation was not followed by political
upheavals. During the 1970s France remained a
powerful economic and political force in Western European affairs.

De Gaulle during one of his famous broadcasts to the French people.

CHAPTER EIGHT:
Post-war Britain

The Second World War was accompanied by extensive changes in Britain's economic and social life. Although many of these changes were inevitable, they were accelerated by wartime regulations, whereby the population grew accustomed to a large measure of state control, and by hardships and sacrifices, which forced people to reconsider the kind of society they wished to build.

Unprecedented powers over people's lives were acquired by the government. Gas masks and identity cards were issued to all civilians, and a black-out during the hours of darkness was imposed until the end of the war against Germany. Over one million young children and their mothers were evacuated from likely targets for enemy air raids to safer parts of the country, although most of them returned home when no raids took place. Compulsory military service was introduced for all men between the ages of eighteen and fifty, except for those in reserved occupations such as coal mining and farming. Young women were also liable to be called up for non-combatant duties. Clothing, petrol and many items of food were rationed according to a strict points system, which preserved an element of choice. Customers had to give up points, or coupons, from their ration books with their purchases. Although bread was not rationed until after the end of the war typical quantities of rationed foods were four ounces (a hundred grammes) bacon, two ounces (fifty grammes) cooking fat, two ounces (fifty grammes) tea and one ounce (twenty-five grammes) cheese per person per week. Furniture and clothing were manufactured to a uniform and lower, standard, called *utility*, in order to economise on labour and materials.

Banks were compelled to lend large sums of money to the government, while income tax was raised and a new tax, purchase tax, was introduced in 1940. These measures served the twin purpose of helping to pay for the war and reducing consumer demand, so that industry could concentrate its resources on the war effort. Although most wartime innovations gradually disappeared after the war, some became permanent features of the British way of life. Post-war governments made much greater use of taxation, bank rate and interest rates for controlling the economy than pre-war governments.

Plans for post-war reconstruction

By the end of 1943 it was clear that Germany's defeat was only a matter of time, and politicians of all parties began to put forward proposals for social reform. The recommendations of the Scott Commission (1942) on the countryside were incorporated into the Town and Country Planning Acts of 1944 and 1947, which gave central and local government greater control over the development of the countryside. The New Towns Act (1946) enabled the Government to choose the sites of new towns. The first was Stevenage, while the others included Crawley, Corby and Hemel Hempstead. Under the National Parks and Countryside Act (1949) parts of the countryside were to be preserved unspoiled for the enjoyment of all.

Far-reaching changes were effected by the Education Act of 1944, piloted through parliament by R. A. Butler, the President of the Board of Education. The Act raised the status of the

Board to a Ministry, and made the local authorities responsible for providing free, compulsory, primary and secondary education for all children in their areas. The old idea of elementary education disappeared. Instead, primary schools were to offer a common curriculum up to the age of eleven. Secondary education was to be provided in three types of school: grammar schools with academic courses, technical schools with a bias towards the practical subjects and modern schools which offered a general education for the majority of children. In accordance with the Act, the school leaving age was raised to fifteen in 1947, though it was not until 1972 that it was raised to sixteen.

Allocation to secondary schools was based upon a series of tests which children took at the age of eleven. The selection process was not intended to be an examination which children passed or failed. It was soon viewed in this light, however, for although the three kinds of secondary school were intended to be equal in status, modern schools were regarded as inferior to grammar schools. Thus children who went to grammar schools were considered to have 'passed', while the rest 'failed'. Soon many people began to think that a system which segregated children at such an early age was unfair, especially as doubt was cast upon the accuracy of the selection tests. After 1960 there was a strong trend towards the development of comprehensive schools, which took children from the full range of ability and from all social classes.

The creation of the Welfare State

When the war against Germany ended it was decided that a return to normal party government should not be delayed by the continuing struggle against Japan. The Labour party's proposals for a great extension of the social services and a more equal distribution of wealth in society, appealed to the electorate. In the General Election of July 1945 the Labour party, led by Clement Attlee (1883–1967), won 393 seats and gained a majority of 149 over all other parties.

Churchill's dismissal seemed an act of ingratitude, but it reflected the mood of the people, who wanted a change after twenty years of Conservative rule.

The blueprint for the Welfare State was Sir William Beveridge's *Report on Social Insurance and Allied Services* (1942), in which he recommended that the whole population should be safeguarded against unemployment and ill-health. The first steps towards implementing Beveridge's proposals had already been taken. The hated *Means Test* had been abolished in 1941, so that family resources were no longer taken into account when claims for financial assistance were assessed. The terms 'dole' and 'workhouse', long associated with the old Poor Law, soon disappeared from popular usage. The wartime food subsidies, rationing and welfare foods for expectant mothers and young children had abolished the worst poverty, while the Family Allowances Act (1945) provided five shillings a week for every child, after the first in each family. The first allowances were drawn in 1946.

The keystone of the Welfare State was laid in 1946 with the passage of the National Insurance and National Health Service Acts. Under the first the whole adult population was compulsorily insured for unemployment and sickness benefits, pensions and death grants. It extended the scope of the 1911 act by requiring every working adult to pay weekly contributions, which were supplemented by the employer and the State. The National Health Act, the greatest achievement of the Labour government, was largely the work of Aneurin Bevan (1897–1960), who became the first Minister of Health. It entitled everyone to free medical, dental and ophthalmic treatment, while medicines, drugs, spectacles and dentures were also to be issued free of charge. Although modest charges for prescriptions and contributions towards the cost of spectacles and dental treatment had to be introduced several years later, the Act made medical care a public service instead of a matter of private enterprise. There was some abuse of the system in its early days, which added greatly to its cost, but Britain's National Health Service became the envy of many other countries and no political party has wanted to dismantle it.

Nationalisation

State ownership of the means of production and distribution had long been regarded by socialists as the best way of promoting a greater degree of social equality in society, and the Labour government interpreted its huge majority as a mandate to carry out this programme. In practice, the nationalisation of the Bank of England in 1946 made little difference to its operations, since it already existed virtually as a government department. The nationalisation of the coal industry aroused little controversy, since the mines had been run down during the war, and government aid was necessary if the industry was to become profitable. The mine owners were given generous compensation and were replaced by the Coal Board. By the Electricity Act of 1947, the generation, supply and distribution of electricity was placed in the hands of twelve area boards. Similarly, in 1948, a nationalised Gas Council was set up.

Transport was nationalised by a Civil Aviation Act (1946), and a Transport Act of 1947 which dealt with road and rail communications and the docks. During two World Wars the railways had been taken over by the State, and after the First World War the number of companies had been reduced to four. The replacement of the old-style companies like the Great Western Railway by British Rail seemed a logical step, especially as the railway companies needed considerable financial help if they were to improve their efficiency. At the same time all long distance road haulage firms, with the exception of furniture removers, were taken over by the government and merged into British Road Services.

It was the government's plan to nationalise the profitable iron and steel industry, however, which caused most controversy. Since the Conservatives were pledged to use their majority in the House of Lords to reject any steel nationalisation bill, the government introduced a measure to cut the duration of the Lords' veto from two years to one. This proposal became law in 1949 when the Parliament Act was passed. The Iron and Steel Act was duly passed in the same year, with the proviso that it would not come into operation until the electorate had pronounced its verdict on the measure. Although Labour was returned to office in 1950 with a greatly reduced majority, the nationalisation of the steel industry was short-lived, since the Conservatives reversed the decision in 1953.

The Representation of the People Act (1948)

Until 1948 a number of people had an additional vote. Some businessmen had a double vote in connection with their business addresses, and graduates of Oxford and Cambridge could vote for a candidate to represent their university as well as being able to vote in their own constituencies. The Representation of the People Act abolished the additional vote, and clearly established the principle of one vote for every adult.

Economic difficulties

While the Labour government was undertaking a varied programme of reforms, it also had to repair Britain's damaged economy. The war had transformed Britain from a major creditor, into a leading debtor nation, despite the cancellation of the larger part of the Lend-Lease repayments. When American aid ceased with the defeat of Japan the government was forced to secure a 5000 million dollar loan from Canada and the United States in order to keep the country solvent until it could earn its own living abroad.

This was not an easy matter, since the normal patterns of trade had been disrupted by the war and British industry was ill-equipped to compete in world markets. Investment in new machinery and processes had been delayed by the war, and existing plant had deteriorated as a result of a lack of proper maintenance. The modernisation of industry was bound to take some time, while raw materials had to be stockpiled before industry could expand production. In the meantime imports were costing more than Britain earned by selling goods abroad.

The government kept the home market short of consumer goods in order to boost exports and help the balance of trade. Even so, exports failed to increase fast enough, and Britain's trade deficit became serious. Wage rises for British workers meant that exports were being priced out of world markets, and even the weather conspired to add to Britain's economic difficulties, for the winter of 1946–7 was the coldest for fifty years. A blanket of snow and ice covered the country for nearly three months and a desperate fuel shortage developed. Many factories had to close down, and in February 1947 two million people were unemployed.

Sir Stafford Cripps, who succeeded Hugh Dalton as Chancellor of the Exchequer in November 1947, cut food subsidies and increased personal taxation in an effort to balance the budget. Wage increases were limited to five per cent during the period 1948–50. Despite these austerity measures, however, the government was forced to devalue the pound sterling in September 1949. Instead of the pound being worth $4.03, the rate was fixed at $2.80. Devaluation was regarded at the time as a national humiliation, but it certainly improved Britain's trading account, for although it put up the cost of imports it made British exports cheaper and therefore more competitive in world markets. Apart from 1951 and 1955 Britain achieved balance of payments surpluses during the 1950s.

By 1951, however, the government seemed to be running out of ideas, while the Korean War (see Chapter Ten) was causing inflation. The introduction of peacetime military conscription, the existence of rationing several years after the end of the war, and a housing shortage, added to Labour's difficulties and persuaded Attlee to hold a General Election in the hope of increasing his majority. Although more people voted Labour than Conservative, large Labour majorities in some constituencies were offset by narrow defeats in others. The Conservatives, who had fewer 'wasted' votes than their opponents, won 321 seats in the House of Commons, with Labour winning 295, and the Liberal party six. Thus began a long period of Conservative rule.

Conservative government 1951–64

The big trade deficit at first prevented the new government from relaxing the controls which had been a feature of Labour rule, but the Conservatives were fortunate to take office shortly before the terms of world trade swung in Britain's favour. In 1953 R. A. Butler, the Chancellor of the Exchequer, reduced income tax and purchase tax. Food subsidies were also cut, partly in order to carry out the Conservative policy of making people pay the 'true economic cost' of goods and services, and partly to meet the objections of the middle class, which felt that its tax burden was enabling lower paid workers to enjoy an artificially high standard of living.

With incomes rising steadily throughout the fifties, the nation treated itself to an enjoyable spending spree, purchasing a wide variety of consumer goods such as electrical appliances, television sets and motor cars. In 1959, Harold Macmillan was moved to tell the British people in a memorable phrase, 'You've never had it so good'. In this atmosphere of growing prosperity the Conservatives won two general elections, each time with increased parliamentary majorities; firstly in 1955 under Sir Anthony Eden (who had replaced Churchill as Prime Minister in April of the same year), and secondly in 1959 under Harold Macmillan.

The Conservatives' policy of promoting freedom of enterprise was embodied in a number of measures. In 1953 they carried out their promise to denationalise the steel industry, and also returned long distance road haulage to private ownership. Many thousands of houses were built, particularly in the early 1950s, when Harold Macmillan was Minister of Housing in Churchill's government. By the Rent Act of 1957 rents were de-controlled, thereby laying the Conservatives open to the charge of favouring landlords rather than tenants. A Resale Prices Act (1963) allowed shopkeepers to sell goods below the prices 'fixed' or 'recommended' by the manufacturers.

The need for long term planning, however, was recognised by the publication of four reports in 1963. The Buchanan Report proposed far-reaching changes in order to cope with the rapidly increasing volume of road traffic in towns and cities. The Beeching Report on the railways recommended the closure of many lines and stations in the interests of efficiency and profitability. Over the next few years the railway network was severely pruned, although the compensatory improvement in bus services, particularly in rural areas, did not take place. Two reports revealed the government's concern to improve standards in education. The Newsom Report on secondary schools recommended the raising of the school leaving age to sixteen (eventually implemented in 1972), while the Robbins Report called for the doubling of places in universities and other institutions of higher education.

Despite the fact that Britain could justly be described as an affluent society, the slow growth of the economy caused much concern. Efforts to expand production were accompanied by inflation and high wage demands, which put up manufacturing costs and made British exports less competitive abroad. On the other hand, measures designed to cut spending on consumer goods and restrict wage increases, such as a 'credit squeeze' in 1959, and Selwyn Lloyd's 'wages freeze' in 1960, were counter-productive, because they discouraged investment in industry. The government's 'stop-go' policies caused the Labour opposition to compare the running of the nation's economy under Conservative rule with a car driver who could only use the accelerator and brake.

The dilemma of trying to expand the economy without encouraging inflation was not the only major problem faced by the Conservatives. Post-war governments only slowly adjusted to Britain's new role and status in world affairs. To a large extent this may be attributed to the fact that Britain had emerged victorious from the war, and at the head of a great empire and commonwealth. Both major political parties agreed that Britain should maintain its special relationship with the United States and should also become a nuclear power, even though it could not compete on equal terms with the two superpowers. Although British scientists succeeded in developing the atomic bomb by 1952 and the hydrogen bomb in 1957, Britain had to rely upon American Polaris missiles for the means of delivering nuclear warheads.

Britain's relationship with the United States and its Commonwealth links were chiefly responsible for the failure to respond enthusiastically to the idea of European unity. Britain did not become a founder member of the European Economic Community, and its participation in the rival European Free Trade Association (see Chapter Six) was not an adequate substitute. Likewise, Sir Anthony Eden miscalculated Britain's ability to influence events when he colluded with the French and Israeli governments for a combined attack upon Egypt in 1956 (see Chapter Fifteen). The national humiliation in the Suez War marked a watershed in the nation's history; after it, no government could pretend that Britain still ranked as a major world power. At the same time, the realisation that Britain's military greatness belonged to the past facilitated the dismantling of a great empire in a way which highlighted the best features of British imperial rule.

The development of the Commonwealth

In 1945 the British Commonwealth and Empire still provoked a mixture of admiration, envy and resentment, for it covered an area of thirteen million square miles, and included about one quarter of the world's population. With the exception of Eire, all its members had been united in the war against fascism. Yet its unity was already more apparent than real and the forces of change, which had been clearly discernible since the beginning of the twentieth century, were to transform it during the next twenty-five years.

Although the most important catalysts of change were nationalism and the Second World War, the evolution from Empire to Commonwealth may be traced back to the nineteenth century, when Britain granted Dominion status to

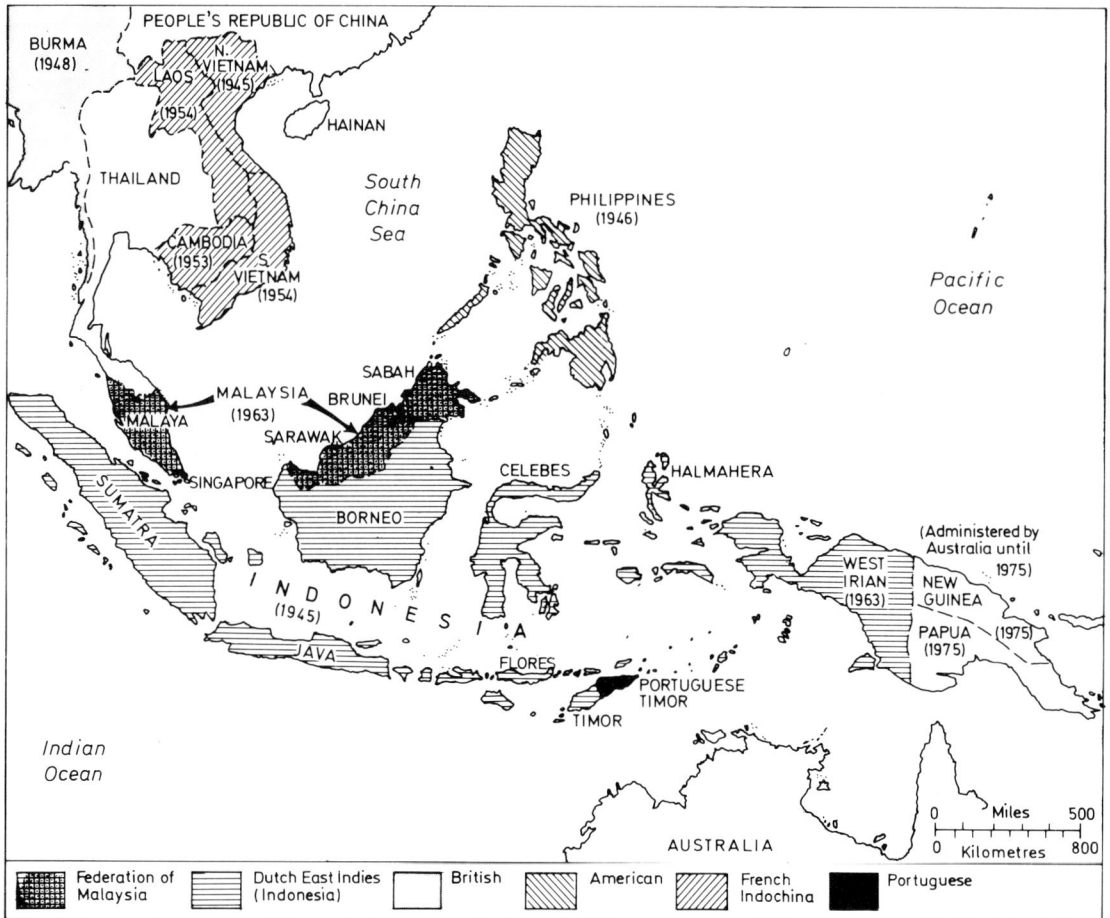

The map legend:

Pattern	Region
Federation of Malaysia	Dutch East Indies (Indonesia)	British	American	French Indochina	Portuguese

Map labels:
PEOPLE'S REPUBLIC OF CHINA
BURMA (1948)
N. VIETNAM (1945)
LAOS (1954)
HAINAN
THAILAND
South China Sea
CAMBODIA (1953)
S. VIETNAM (1954)
PHILIPPINES (1946)
Pacific Ocean
SABAH
MALAYSIA (1963)
BRUNEI
MALAYA
SARAWAK
SINGAPORE
SUMATRA
CELEBES
HALMAHERA
BORNEO
(Administered by Australia until 1975)
WEST IRIAN (1963)
NEW GUINEA
PAPUA (1975)
INDONESIA (1945)
JAVA
FLORES
PORTUGUESE TIMOR
TIMOR
Indian Ocean
AUSTRALIA
0 Miles 500
0 Kilometres 800

12   *The end of colonial rule in South East Asia*

Canada in 1867. At the turn of the century Canada's example was followed by Australia in 1901, New Zealand in 1907 and South Africa in 1909. Demands for independence from the less politically developed countries in the Empire grew stronger before the Second World War, and in the case of India and Burma, became irresistible at the end of it (see Chapter Fourteen).

Malaysia

Indian independence was rapidly achieved in 1947, but not all transitions from colonialism to self-government were accomplished so speedily.

In the case of Malaya the situation was complicated by the presence of a large Chinese minority, whose members had been encouraged by the British to come and work on the rubber plantations. During the final stages of the Japanese wartime occupation, Chinese communists attempted to seize power, but were foiled by the return of British troops in 1945. The creation of a federation of the eleven Malay States in 1948 was immediately followed by another communist rebellion, which took six years to put down.

The Malayan Emergency delayed the grant of independence until 1957, when the Federation of Malay States came into being, under the premiership of Tunku Abdul Rahman, who ruled until 1970. In 1963 Singapore, Sarawak and Sabah (formerly North Borneo) were transferred to the Federation, which then included fourteen states and was renamed Malaysia. Britain, Australia and New Zealand accepted joint responsibility for its defence.

13   *The Commonwealth in 1978* (showing dates of independence)

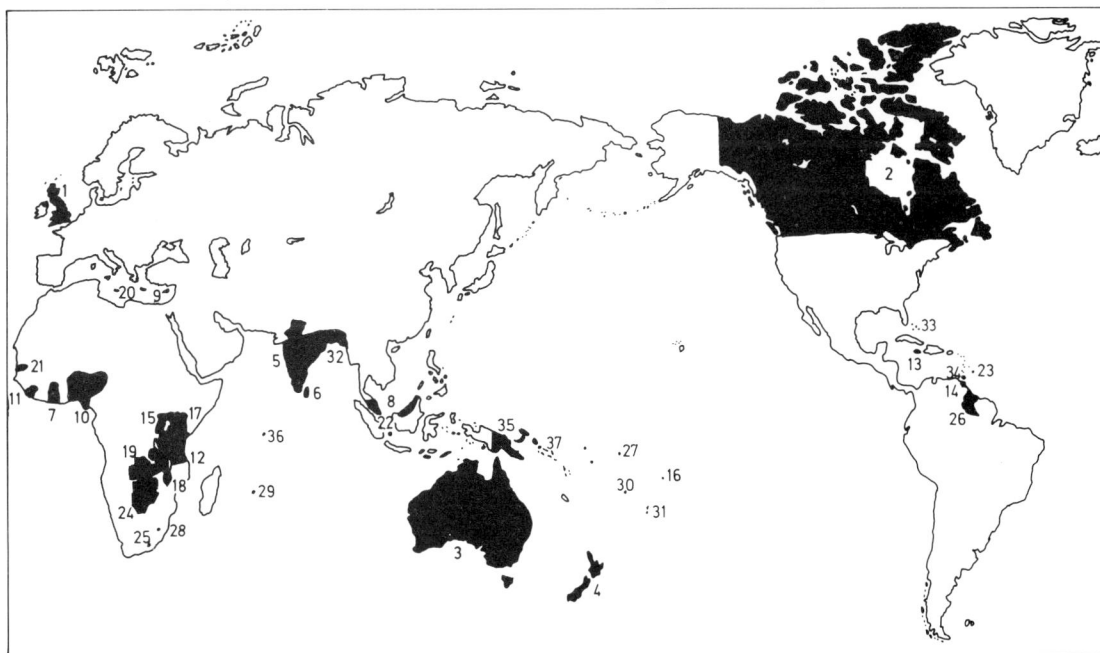

Commonwealth membership in 1978★

1		United Kingdom	18	1964	Malawi (Nyasaland)
2	1867	Canada	19	1964	Zambia (Northern Rhodesia)
3	1901	Australia	20	1964	Malta
4	1907	New Zealand	21	1965	Gambia
5	1947	India	22	1965	Singapore
6	1948	Sri Lanka (Ceylon)	23	1966	Barbados
7	1957	Ghana (Gold Coast)	24	1966	Botswana (Bechuanaland)
8	1957	Malaysia	25	1966	Lesotho (Basutoland)
9	1960	Cyprus	26	1966	Guyana (British Guinea)
10	1960	Nigeria	27	1968	Nauru
11	1961	Sierra Leone	28	1968	Swaziland
12	1961/4	Tanzania (Tanganyika)	29	1968	Mauritius
13	1962	Jamaica	30	1970	Fiji
14	1962	Trinidad and Tobago	31	1970	Tonga
15	1962	Uganda	32	1971	Bangladesh (East Pakistan)
16	1962	Western Samoa	33	1973	Bahamas
17	1963	Kenya	34	1974	Grenada
			35	1975	Papua New Guinea
			36	1976	Seychelles
			37	1978	Solomon Islands

★Burma left the Commonwealth in 1947, Eire in 1949, the Union of South Africa in 1961 and Pakistan in 1972.

These changes led to a state of undeclared war between Malaysia and Indonesia, which claimed Sarawak and Sabah. Formerly the Dutch East Indies, Indonesia had declared itself independent as soon as the Japanese military occupation came to an end, a fact which Holland reluctantly conceded in 1949. President Sukarno (1901–70), who ruled the country from 1945 until his overthrow in 1966, detested Western influence, and a peaceful settlement of the dispute between Malaysia and Indonesia was only reached after he had fallen from power. An Association of South-East Asian Nations (ASEAN) was formed in 1967, comprising Indonesia, Malaysia, the Philippines, Thailand and Singapore (which had withdrawn from the Federation of Malaysia in 1965), and British troops were evacuated from the region in 1971.

The sun sets on the British Empire

Although the Malaysian Federation was a success, Britain's attempts in other parts of the world to amalgamate colonies into larger political units proved to be disappointing failures. A Central African Federation, comprising Northern and Southern Rhodesia together with Nyasaland, was short-lived, as was the projected federation of ten West Indian islands in 1958. Both Jamaica and Trinidad feared that the other smaller, and poorer, islands would be a drain on their economies and the Federation collapsed in 1962. The West Indian islands tried to promote their prosperity by forming a Caribbean Free Trade Area in 1968.

The first British colony in Africa to achieve independence was the Gold Coast, which became Ghana in 1957. It was followed by the grant of independence in the early 1960s to all Britain's African possessions except Southern Rhodesia, where a refusal to accept the end of white supremacy led to an illegal declaration of independence in 1965. (For an account of Africa's political development see Chapters Sixteen and Seventeen.)

By 1978, when the Solomon Islands became the thirty-seventh member of the Common-wealth, the British Empire had almost vanished. A few small colonial territories, however, preferred to remain under British rule. They included Gibraltar (claimed by Spain), the Falkland Islands, which had no wish to be united with Argentina, and Hong Kong, despite its close proximity to the People's Republic of China.

The Commonwealth in 1978

Perhaps the clearest definition of the Commonwealth is that given in the Declaration of the Commonwealth Heads of Government Meeting in Singapore in 1971, when it was described as:

a voluntary association of independent, sovereign states, each responsible for its own policies, consulting and cooperating in the common interests of their people and in the promotion of international understanding and world peace.

The role of the Commonwealth is more easily defined than fulfilled. Apart from a Secretariat set up in 1965, it depends upon voluntary cooperation and personal contacts between heads of state plus individuals such as technicians, missionaries, journalists and other interested people. The member nations differ widely in race, creed, language, customs and, most important of all, wealth. These differences have eroded the feeling that the Commonwealth countries possessed much in common as a result of their association with Britain. Thus the opposition of many members to South Africa's racial policies virtually forced this country's withdrawal from the Commonwealth in 1961. Likewise, Britain's admission to the EEC in 1973 altered its relationship with the Commonwealth. Only time will prove whether the Commonwealth will flourish as an international, multi-racial organisation of states, or whether it will simply become a meaningless geographical expression.

Race relations in Britain

The existence of a multi-racial Commonwealth, of which Britain was the mother country, was brought home to the British people in the early 1960s by an influx of coloured immigrants. During the three year period 1960–62 nearly 400,000 people, mainly from the West Indies, India and Pakistan, settled in Britain. This caused a number of problems, particularly in housing, which was already in short supply, and education, since many immigrant children could speak little English. They were welcomed as they relieved labour shortages in certain sectors of the economy, but their concentration in major industrial areas such as London, Birmingham and the textile towns of Lancashire and Yorkshire, gave rise to racial prejudice. There were also fears that unless the flow of immigrants was checked, they would not be easily assimilated into British society.

In 1962, therefore, Parliament passed the Commonwealth Immigrants Act, which restricted the number of immigrants allowed into Britain each year. In 1965 and 1968 Race Relations Acts made discrimination on the grounds of race or colour illegal in the provision of goods, services, employment and housing, and a Race Relations Board was set up to investigate complaints.

A mass exodus of Kenyan Asians to Britain in 1968 led to the passage of a new Immigration Act, which imposed a quota on admissions so that immigrants could no longer enter Britain freely even if they held British passports. Thus the decision of President Amin of Uganda to expel thousands of Asians caused a sudden crisis, which was only resolved when a number of Commonwealth countries offered to share responsibility for resettling them. In order to ensure that this problem could not recur, the British government made it clear that it would refuse entry to another influx such as that from Uganda.

Economic and social development 1964–78

On the issues of immigration and Commonwealth affairs there was little difference between Conservative and Labour policies, but the Labour (socialist) government which took office in 1964, believed that a greater degree of state intervention was needed if 'thirteen wasted years' of Tory rule were to be put right.

Accordingly, Harold Wilson's government (1964–70) re-nationalised the iron and steel industry, and introduced in 1965 two new taxes, corporation tax and capital gains tax, as a means of redistributing the nation's wealth. The Rent Act was repealed in 1965, when tribunals were appointed to fix fair rents, and a Prices and Incomes Board (which had little real power or influence) was given the task of regulating wages and prices. The development of comprehensive education was speeded up, and opportunities in higher education were extended by the creation of the Open University in 1969. Other measures included the abolition of the death penalty, the lowering of the age of majority from twenty-one to eighteen years and a Road Safety Act of 1967, which authorised the police to breathalyse car drivers suspected of being under the influence of alcohol. For much of its time in office, however, the Labour government was preoccupied with the problem of managing the economy.

Although Britain's rate of economic growth during the 1960s was faster than in any decade since 1900, it did not compare favourably with that of most other industrial nations. The gradual realisation that Britain was not paying its way in the world led to a financial crisis. Foreign financiers, who were convinced that sterling would drop sharply in value, began to sell their holdings in sterling and instead, buy other currencies which appreciated in value. Despite action by the Bank of England, which borrowed large amounts of foreign currencies from the International Monetary Fund and spent some of its gold reserves in an attempt to maintain the value of the pound at its official level, the government was forced to devalue the pound sterling by fourteen per cent in 1967 (from 2·80 to 2·40 dollars to the pound). Devaluation soon produced a marked improvement in Britain's trade, and in June 1970 Harold Wilson called for a General Election. To many people's surprise, however, the Conservatives led by Edward Heath were returned to power.

The Conservatives tried to alleviate unemployment by encouraging the expansion of business and industry, and by reducing personal taxation in order to stimulate spending on consumer goods. Heath reopened the negotiations to join the EEC, since the French government was more favourably disposed towards Britain's application following President de Gaulle's resignation in 1969. Terms of entry were eventually agreed, and Britain formally joined the Common Market on 1 January 1973. To combat inflation Stage One of a statutory incomes policy was introduced in November 1972, which imposed a six months 'freeze' on pay, prices, dividends and rent. Stage Two began in the following April, when a Price Commission was set up to monitor prices, and a Pay Board to restrain wage rises.

Unfortunately, the Conservatives had no more success in curing inflation than the Socialists. The cost of most goods and services was increased by the introduction of Value Added Tax (VAT) in April 1973, while the cost of imported raw materials and foodstuffs, over which the government had no control, rose by forty-seven per cent in the same year. Moreover, the quadrupling of oil prices during the winter of 1973–4 which dislocated the economies of the entire Western world, caused a formidable balance of payments crisis in Britain.

The trade unions bitterly opposed pay restraint at a time of rapid price rises; when Stage Three of the Counter Inflation Act was introduced in November 1973, the miners, who were determined to defend their position as one of the most highly paid groups of workers, banned overtime working. A state of emergency was declared, and in January 1974 a three day working week came into operation as the government tried to make the nation's stocks of coal last through the winter. The confrontation between the government and the trade unions reached its climax when the miners went on strike. Heath appealed to the country to support his policies, but narrowly lost the General Election in February 1974.

The Labour government (1974–79), led by Harold Wilson until his resignation in March 1976 and then by James Callaghan, sought the voluntary cooperation of the trade unions in curbing wage rises as the alternative to statutory wage restraint. The Pay Board was abolished, and guidelines for unions seeking pay increases were laid down by the Trade Union Congress. Voluntary pay restraint, however, depended upon the government's success in keeping price rises within strict limits. Since the cost of living soared twenty-six per cent between June 1974 and June 1975, many unions felt it was their duty to seek larger wage increases than those recommended by the TUC. Alarmed by galloping inflation, the government introduced in August 1975 a six pounds a week limit on wage rises.

As international confidence in Britain's economy dwindled, so too did the value of the pound sterling, which had been allowed to *float* since 1972, i.e. to find its own exchange rate in the world money markets without official support from the Bank of England. The fall in Britain's gold and currency reserves forced the government to apply to the IMF for a loan of 2000 million dollars at the end of 1975. Even this was not enough to ease the pressure on the pound, which fell below the two dollar mark in March 1976. In June a group of ten of the world's wealthiest countries agreed to lend Britain up to 5300 million dollars, provided that the government strictly controlled the nation's economy. Even so, the reduction in the rate of inflation to single figures in 1978, and the pound's recovery from its low point of 1·60 dollars to over two dollars in 1979, owed more to the flow of North Sea gas and oil than to any real improvement in industrial efficiency.

The discovery of natural gas in the British sector of the North Sea in 1975 was rapidly exploited, and within two years natural gas was being pumped ashore at Easington in Humberside. By 1977 nearly all the gas consumed in Britain was supplied from seven major North Sea gas fields, and most of the old fashioned gas works on the mainland had been closed down. North Sea oil began to flow in June 1975, when the Argyll field came into operation. By 1977 ten commercial oil fields in the British sector had been verified, with oil reserves estimated at 4500 million tonnes. Their value to the British economy may be gauged from the fact that in

An oil-rig being towed to its destination in the North Sea.

1975 Britain imported eighty-six million tonnes of crude oil, mainly from the Middle East, at a cost of £3300 million.

Despite the bonus of North Sea gas and oil Britain's difficulties were far from resolved, for great changes were taking place in government and society. Both unemployment and the rate of inflation remained uncomfortably high. Technological developments such as the micro-processor, or silicon 'chip', each less than a quarter of an inch square and containing 100,000 components, had immense potential for automating industry and communications. Although many people were able to afford the material things of life, the new technology brought great problems; not only because it could create massive unemployment, but also because those countries which failed to modernise their industries were unable to compete in world markets.

At the same time increased government intervention in everyday life led to a feeling that the central government in London was often rather remote from people's needs. Thus the 1970s witnessed the growth of Scottish and Welsh nationalism, whose strength gave rise to fears that the United Kingdom might break up into its different parts. The debate over separate assemblies for Scotland and Wales, however, was not settled by a referendum held in March 1979 (the results of which were inconclusive) and the question of devolution was shelved for the time being. Even more difficult to resolve was the problem of Northern Ireland, whose constitutional links with Britain were violently opposed by Irish nationalists.

Ireland

The outbreak of violence in Northern Ireland in 1968 which spread to mainland England cannot be readily understood without some appreciation of Ireland's recent history and its unhappy relationships with Britain.

Ireland, a country divided by the forces of religion and nationalism, was part of Britain between 1800 and 1921. William Gladstone (1809–1898), the great English Liberal statesman, twice tried to give Home Rule to Ireland, but Parliament refused to pass the necessary legislation. Eventually, in 1912, a Liberal government headed by Herbert Asquith introduced a third Home Rule Bill, which finally became law in September 1914. Under its provisions a united Ireland was to have its own parliament and control over its own affairs, apart from such matters as foreign policy, defence and trade which were reserved for the Imperial Parliament at Westminster.

The outbreak of the First World War caused the operation of the Act to be suspended, in order to avoid civil war in Ireland. The Protestants in Ulster, who were in a majority, were determined not to become part of a united Ireland which was predominantly Roman Catholic. Anxious to keep the constitutional ties with Britain created by the Act of Union in 1800, their motto was 'Ulster will fight, and Ulster will be right'. An Ulster Volunteer Force was formed by Sir Edward Carson, and its threat of armed rebellion if the government tried to impose Home Rule had the sympathy of many people in Britain, including that of Bonar Law, leader of the Conservative party. He stated that he could imagine 'no length of resistance, to which Ulster will go, which I shall not be ready to support, and in which they will not be supported by the overwhelming majority of the British people.'

Meanwhile, the Irish Nationalist party led by John Redmond formed its own private army in reply to the Ulster Volunteers, and both groups illegally purchased guns and ammunition from abroad. In the so-called Curragh Mutiny in 1914, the officers of the British garrison made it clear that they would disobey orders rather than take action against the Ulstermen, and they were allowed to resign their commissions. The government thankfully postponed any solution of the problem to the end of the war.

The Easter Rising 1916

The more extreme Irish nationalists who belonged to the Irish Republican Brotherhood (a secret military society formed in 1858) were not, however, prepared to wait that long. They planned a rebellion, and Sir Roger Casement went to Germany to obtain weapons. British intelligence unearthed details of the plot, and Casement was arrested in April 1916 when a German U-boat landed him in Tralee Bay, in Southern Ireland. (He was later convicted of treason and hanged.) In the meantime, the ship carrying arms to Ireland was intercepted by a British warship.

In spite of this set-back the leaders decided to go ahead with the planned insurrection, in the hope that the rest of Southern Ireland would follow their example and revolt against British rule. On Easter Monday 1916, Irish Volunteers and members of the newly formed Irish Citizen Army seized several important public buildings in Dublin, including the General Post Office, where an Irish Republic was proclaimed. The defeat of the rebellion, however, was a foregone conclusion. Hundreds of Irishmen were arrested, and most of the leaders were court-martialled and shot.

These reprisals completely altered the attitude of the Irish population, most of whom had been indifferent towards the Easter Rising. Those who lost their lives came to be regarded as Irish martyrs, while the survivors became the nucleus of the Irish Republican Army (IRA). Many of Redmond's followers deserted him and joined the *Sinn Féin*★ movement, founded by Arthur Griffith at the beginning of the twentieth century.

★A Gaelic term which, roughly translated, means 'Ourselves, unaided'.

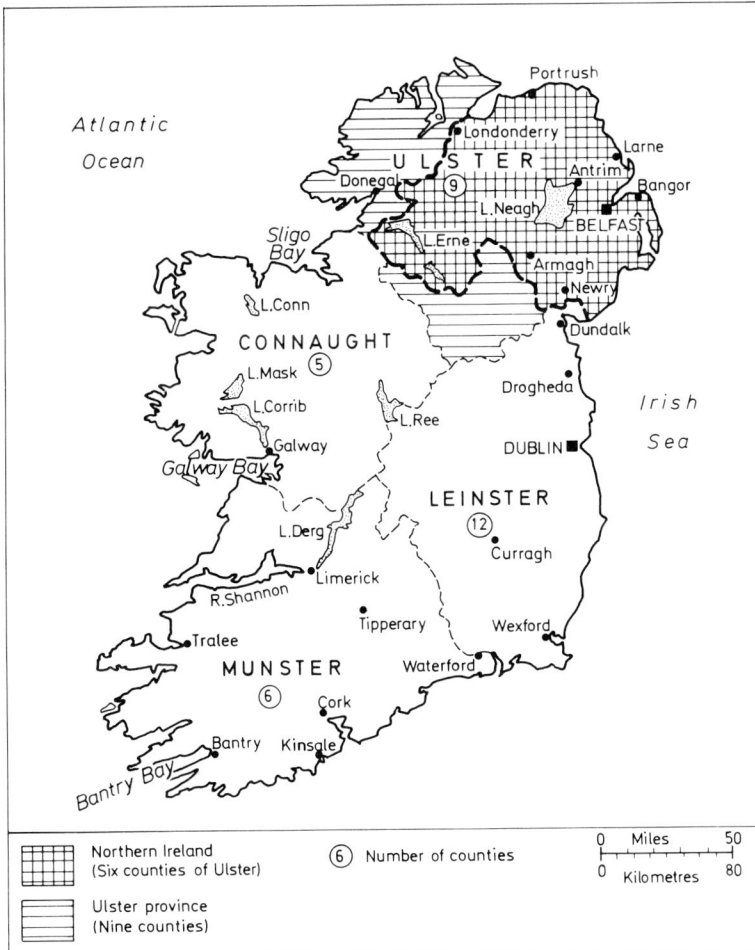

14   *Ireland*

The Irish Free State (Eire)

In the 1918 General Election the Unionists won a clear majority in Northern Ireland, but *Sinn Féin* won every constituency outside the province of Ulster. The *Sinn Féiners* refused to take their seats at Westminster, and set up their own Irish assembly, or *Dáil Éirann*, in Dublin, where they claimed to represent an independent Ireland. Eamonn de Valera (1882–1975), the only surviving leader of the Easter Rising (he was condemned to death, but spared because of his American citizenship), was chosen president of the assembly.

The so-called 'Troubles' began in 1919 when the IRA began a campaign of violence against British rule in Ireland. The government answered terror with terror, employing ex-servicemen to assist the Royal Irish Constabulary in maintaining law and order. These volunteers, known as the 'Black and Tans' (after the colours of their uniform), became a byword for brutality as a result of the methods they employed to combat the IRA.

In 1920 the Westminster Parliament passed the Government of Ireland Act, which separated six of the nine counties of Ulster from the rest of Ireland and set up two parliaments, one at

Stormont in Belfast for Northern Ireland, and another in Dublin for the rest of Ireland. In 1921 an Anglo-Irish Treaty was negotiated, whereby Ireland, with the exclusion of six Ulster provinces, was given Dominion status. At this juncture the *Sinn Féin* movement split into two factions: those who were pro-Treaty, and those who regarded acceptance of the partition of Ireland as a betrayal.

With the establishment of the Irish Free State in 1922, however, and the evacuation of British troops by the end of the year, the 'Troubles' finally ceased.

De Valera, who had resigned in protest against the 1921 Treaty, returned to the *Dail* in 1927 at the head of his party, renamed *Fianna Fail* (Soldiers of Destiny). In 1932 he succeeded William Cosgrave as Prime Minister and, under his rule, Ireland broke its links with the United Kingdom one by one. In 1937 the Irish Free State was renamed Eire, with a president as head of state. Under the new constitution the oath of

allegiance to the British Crown which Irish ministers had been required to swear, was abolished. In 1938 Britain surrendered its right to use three Irish ports as naval bases, and when the Second World War broke out, Eire remained neutral. In 1949 it became a republic and left the Commonwealth.

The British government promised that Northern Ireland would not cease to be part of the United Kingdom without the consent of the people of the province. Since Stormont was dominated by the Unionist party which was closely linked to the Orange Order*, it was unlikely that Northern Ireland would voluntarily join Eire.

*The Orange Order was founded to commemorate the victory of William III (William of Orange) at the battle of the Boyne in 1690, when he defeated the army of James II, thus ensuring the triumph of the Protestant cause over the Catholic cause in Ireland. It was a society dedicated to the preservation of the Protestant ascendancy in the province and to the union with Britain.

British troops charge through the streets of Londonderry, armed with guns, helmets and riot shields.

In the 1960s a Civil Rights campaign developed in Northern Ireland, where the Catholic minority deeply resented the manipulation of electoral boundaries to favour Protestant candidates, and discrimination against it, especially in jobs and housing. In 1968 the province came to the brink of civil war after the Civil Rights movement staged a march through Londonderry in order to draw attention to the Catholics' grievances. This action resulted in a series of communal riots which threatened to bring about a complete breakdown of law and order in the province. The Civil Rights movement was largely taken over by the IRA and left wing extremists, while Protestant neighbourhoods retaliated by forming their own paramilitary forces such as the Ulster Defence Association and the Shankhill Defence Association.

Violence grew as barricades were erected in the Catholic areas of Belfast to protect their communities from Protestant extremists, and in August 1969 British troops were rushed to Northern Ireland. Their role at first was to keep the peace between the Catholic and Protestant sections of the population, but they soon became targets for the IRA, who regarded them as the agents of the hated connection with Britain. In August 1971 the Prime Minister of Northern Ireland, Brian Faulkner, was forced to introduce internment, whereby suspected IRA terrorists could be arrested and interned without trial.

By March 1972, however, organised terrorism had become such a serious problem that the British government assumed full responsibility for Northern Ireland, and William Whitelaw was sent to the province to report on the situation. More troops were sent and in July, during Operation Motorman, the security forces bulldozed the barricades in the Catholic 'no-go' areas of Belfast and Londonderry.

As a result of this action many leading members of the IRA were arrested by the security forces. A temporary lull in the violence followed as the IRA regrouped, but in 1976 it mounted a campaign of bombings in London and other major British cities, in an effort to force the government to concede to its demands. Although the campaign was overcome, a solution to the problem of Northern Ireland seemed as far distant as ever. The government could not be forced into accepting change, while the Protestants, fearing that if Northern Ireland was united with the rest of Ireland they would become a persecuted minority, were equally determined to resist change. A solution to the problem of 'John Bull's other island' remained as elusive as ever.

CHAPTER NINE:
The Soviet Union and Eastern Europe under Communism

In 1945 the Soviet Union emerged from the war as the second greatest power in the world, but its victory over Germany had been achieved at a terrible cost. More than fifteen million Russians had lost their lives and a large area, including hundreds of towns, cities and villages, had been devastated by the savage fighting. Factories, railways, bridges and canals had been deliberately wrecked by the retreating German armies.

Russia displayed impressive powers of recovery, however. By the end of the period covered by Stalin's Fourth Five Year Plan (1946–50) industrial output had been expanded beyond 1940 levels. Russian scientists, aided by captured German scientists, had succeeded in developing the atom bomb, several years ahead of the schedule Western experts had thought possible. Apart from reparations extracted from countries overrun by the Red Army, all this was accomplished without foreign aid.

The driving forces behind Russia's industrial recovery were the obvious need to repair a badly damaged economy, and Stalin's fear of an attack by the Western capitalist countries in an attempt to destroy communism. Thus he refused either to put the huge Red Army on a peacetime footing, or to withdraw Soviet troops from the Eastern European countries they had occupied in the process of defeating Germany. At the same time he sacrificed the desire of the Russian people for a better standard of living in order to build up the country's military strength.

Stalin's obsession with Russia's security was understandable when considered against the background of Soviet relations with Western Europe in the twentieth century. Russia had suf-

fered grievously in two wars with Germany and, since it was the only country to have been expelled by the old League of Nations for aggression, the Soviet government doubted both the impartiality of the new United Nations Organisation, and its effectiveness in dealing with international problems.

The presence of a powerful Red Army in Eastern Europe after 1945 alarmed the Western Allies, who believed that it was only the American monopoly of atomic weapons which deterred the Soviet Union from attacking Western Europe. On the other hand the Soviet Union dared not accept a position of permanent inferiority in atomic weapons. In 1946 therefore, Stalin rejected the Baruch Plan, whereby the United States offered to surrender its stockpile of atomic bombs to an international authority. The offer was made on condition that all other countries promised not to develop atomic weapons, and allowed annual inspections in order to ensure that they could not be manufactured secretly.

The achievement of Soviet scientists in building an atom bomb in 1949 triggered off a nuclear arms race of frightening proportions. President Truman commissioned the development of a hydrogen bomb which was one thousand times more powerful than the atom bomb which had destroyed Hiroshima. The Americans tested an H-bomb on a Pacific island in 1952, while the Soviet Union also acquired this fearsome weapon in the following year. After 1954 both the Soviet Union and the United States had strategic air forces capable of striking each other's cities with nuclear bombs.

Stalin's death and collective leadership

In March 1953 Joseph Stalin, one of the most feared and powerful men in the world, died after a brain haemorrhage and the struggle to succeed him began. The five chief rivals were George Malenkov, who became Chairman of the Council of Ministers, Vyacheslav Molotov, the Foreign Minister, Lavrenti Beria, chief of the secret police, Nikolai Bulganin, the Minister for Defence, and Nikita Khrushchev, who was appointed Secretary of the Communist party.

Beria was soon removed from the political scene, being accused of plotting to seize power, found guilty and executed by a firing squad in December. Malenkov, who wanted greater emphasis on the production of consumer goods in order to improve living standards, was criticised by Khrushchev, who for his part urged the need to concentrate on heavy industry. Khrushchev's 'guns before butter' arguments were more convincing, and in February 1955 Malenkov resigned. He was succeeded by Bulganin, but by this time the idea of collective leadership was already giving way to Khrushchev's ascendancy.

Stalin discredited

Stalin's death was followed by a gradual relaxation of the harsher features of his regime. The powers of the secret police were curbed, some labour camps were closed and many of their inmates rehabilitated. Meanwhile, Stalin's reputation for wise leadership was subtly undermined; his photographs were shown less frequently in newspapers, and his role in the Revolution was given less prominence as the virtues of collective leadership were emphasised.

Nevertheless, Khrushchev's famous speech to the Twentieth Congress of the Communist Party in 1956, denouncing the evils of Stalin's rule and attacking the 'cult of the individual' (or glorification of Stalin), shocked the delegates. Khrushchev accused Stalin of failing to strengthen Russia's defences, despite clear evidence that Germany was planning to invade Russia, and of ignoring accurate information about the precise time and date of the attack. He recounted to astonished delegates how Stalin had employed the apparatus of a police state and mass terror to liquidate thousands of innocent people. As evidence he told them that no fewer than ninety-eight out of 139 members of the Central Committee elected at the Seventeenth Congress had been executed at Stalin's orders, and 1108 out of the 1966 delegates at the Congress had been accused of treasonable offences such as sabotage and espionage. Finally, Khrushchev attributed the success of the Revolution to the self-sacrificing work of the Russian people under the leadership of the Communist party; it was not, he declared, the fruit of Stalin's leadership, as pictured during the period of the cult of the individual.

Khrushchev's revelations had widespread repercussions, not only in the Soviet Union, but also throughout the communist world. Some of his colleagues criticised him for deviating from standard Marxist doctrines, and tried to overthrow him. Khrushchev was outvoted by seven to four in the Praesidium (a standing committee in the Soviet Union) but he out-manoeuvred his opponents by summoning the Central Committee, a body dominated by men he had appointed, which over-ruled the decision of the Praesidium. Malenkov, Molotov and other leading critics were forced to resign their posts, and were later expelled from the Communist party. In March 1958 Bulganin resigned in favour of Khrushchev, who became leader of the Communist party as well as Head of State, thereby occupying the position for which he had denounced Stalin. The important consequences of 'de-Stalinisation' are described later in this chapter.

Khrushchev and peaceful co-existence

One result of Stalin's death was a gradual thaw in the Cold War which had developed after 1947, as the two superpowers realised that they were unable to prevent enormous losses in lives and property in their own country, in the event of a nuclear war against each other. Khrushchev moved away from Lenin's thesis that war between the communist and capitalist countries was inevitable, towards a policy of peaceful co-existence whereby competition between the rival power blocs would stop short of war.

The Stalinist policy of unyielding confrontation with the Western powers was therefore abandoned in favour of a more flexible strategy. Non-communist countries were to be persuaded to align themselves with the communist bloc by means of economic and military aid, and by evidence of the superiority of communism to other forms of government. As part of this process of *détente* (the relaxation of international tension), Bulganin and Khrushchev paid friendship visits to India in 1955 and to Britain and Burma in the following year. The Soviet Union signed the Austrian State Treaty in 1955, whereby the great powers agreed to withdraw their occupation forces from Austria, which promised permanent neutrality in its relations with other countries. Although a Summit Conference of the great powers at Geneva in the same year achieved no positive results, these signs of a thaw in the Cold War produced a feeling of optimism that war could be avoided.

The new direction of Soviet foreign policy was fiercely criticised by China, which interpreted it as showing weakness towards the United States. Disagreement between the two communist powers eventually resulted in the break-up of the Sino-Soviet alliance, signed by Stalin and Mao Tse-tung in 1950. After 1960 the Soviet Union and China became rivals, with Russia's nuclear supremacy and China's territorial claims against its powerful neighbour, additional elements of tension.

Khrushchev's fall from power

Khrushchev's foreign policy was difficult to predict, for peaceful co-existence was endangered by the tough attitude he adopted over Berlin in 1961, and during the Cuban missile crisis in 1962 (see Chapter Nineteen). Soviet prestige was damaged when the Russian leader was forced to back down or risk a nuclear war. Disapproval of his handling of foreign affairs, particularly Russia's relations with China, led to his enforced resignation in 1964.

Khrushchev was succeeded by a triumvirate of Alexei Kosygin, Leonid Brezhnev and Nikolai Podgorny. Their determination to maintain Soviet control of Eastern Europe was shown in 1968, when a rebellion against Soviet influence in Czechoslovakia was crushed, as in Hungary in 1956 (see below), but the policy of *détente* with the West was maintained. During the 1970s Strategic Arms Limitations Talks (SALT) took place in the difficult search for an end to the arms race. At the same time the NATO and Warsaw Pact countries tried to reach agreement on Mutual and Balanced Force Reductions (MBFR). Although progress in both sets of negotiations was very slow, the willingness of both sides to discuss the problem of armaments and security helped to allay fears and lower international tension.

Eastern Europe

For over a century Russia has regarded control of Eastern Europe as vital to its interests. The defeat of first Russia and then Germany in the First World War had enabled the Baltic states and Poland to regain their independence, while Czechoslovakia and Hungary were created out of the ruins of the Austro-Hungarian empire. Their existence as separate nations, however, was short-lived. In 1939 Germany annexed nearly all Czechoslovakia and half of Poland, while Russia seized the Baltic states and the remainder of Poland. Germany's domination of Eastern Europe was the prelude to war with the Soviet Union. After it was over, Stalin was determined to ensure the Soviet Union's safety by subordinating all Eastern Europe to Russian military and political control.

In pursuit of this aim Stalin was greatly assisted by several factors which prevailed at the end of the Second World War. The Soviet Union enjoyed tremendous prestige for its heroic victory over Nazi Germany. Nearly everywhere the Russians were regarded as liberators from German oppression, whereas the Western governments were discredited by their devious policies towards Germany in the 1930s. After the war the United States and Britain were suspected of wishing to revive Germany as a military power,

NORWAY
Oslo

FINLAND
Helsinki

SWEDEN
Stockholm

ESTONIAN SSR
Tallin

USSR

LATVIAN SSR
Riga

Moscow

DENMARK
Copenhagen

LITHUANIAN SSR
Vilna

North Sea

Baltic Sea

BYELO-RUSSIAN SSR

EAST GERMANY
Berlin

POLAND
Warsaw

WEST GERMANY

CZECHOSLOVAKIA
Prague

UKRAINIAN SSR

SWITZERLAND

AUSTRIA
Vienna

HUNGARY
Budapest

MOLDAVIAN SSR

RUMANIA

YUGOSLAVIA
Belgrade

Bucharest

Black Sea

ITALY

CORSICA

Rome

Adriatic Sea

BULGARIA
Sofia

ALBANIA
Tirana

SARDINIA

Ankara

GREECE

TURKEY

Athens

SICILY

CRETE

CYPRUS

Mediterranean Sea

| | USSR after 1945 | | Soviet satellites | | Soviet satellite until 1961 | | Communist but independent of Soviet control | 0 | Miles | 250 |
| | | | | | | | | 0 | Kilometres | 400 |

15   *Eastern Europe after 1945*

an idea which alarmed Germany's eastern neighbours.

Stalin cleverly exploited these fears by encouraging the Poles and the Czechs to expel all German inhabitants from their territories. The Red Army helped the Poles to seize German territory east of the Oder-Neisse rivers, containing the valuable ports of Danzig, Stettin and Gydnia, as compensation for the loss of Polish lands annexed by the Soviet Union in 1939. Thus Poland had an interest in preventing the emergence of a strong Germany, which might seek to recover its lost territory.

The establishment of communist governments in the countries of Eastern Europe was also helped by the fact that, apart from Czechoslovakia, they lacked developed democratic traditions. Political parties in the occupied countries had either been broken up by the Germans, or were unpopular as a result of collaborating with them. The abolition of backward monarchies in Hungary, Bulgaria, Yugoslavia and Rumania between 1945 and 1947 was welcomed by the majority of people.

The support of the peasant populations was won by the seizure of the great landed estates, which were divided among the peasants. Rapid industrialisation, the communist solution to the problem of repairing the ruined economies of Eastern Europe, appealed to the governments of largely agrarian countries. It was only after the Communists had consolidated their power that the harsh nature of their rule became apparent.

The establishment of communist dictatorships in Eastern Europe

With the exception of Yugoslavia, which developed its own brand of communism under Marshal Tito, the wartime resistance leader, Soviet-controlled governments were in office in every Eastern European country by 1949. They were forced to sign military agreements allowing the Soviet Union to station troops on their territories; Stalin being determined that Russia's European neighbours should take their orders from Moscow.

The Communists' techniques of seizing power followed a similar pattern. At first they cooperated with anti-fascist parties. Coalition governments were formed, with Communists occupying key posts, such as those giving control of communications, police and the armed forces. When the Communists had won sufficient power and influence, the non-Communist parties were gradually abandoned or destroyed. The Cominform (Communist Information Bureau), successor to the prewar Communist International, was created in September 1947 to coordinate the tactics of the Communist parties throughout Europe, until its dissolution in 1956.

Poland

Many Poles were suspicious of Soviet intentions, which was not surprising in view of Russia's seizure of 70,000 square miles of Poland. Nevertheless, the Red Army was welcomed as the destroyer of the Nazi tyranny which had claimed the lives of six million Poles. At the Potsdam Conference Stalin promised to hold free elections in Poland, but he refused to recognise the exiled Polish government in London. Instead, the Red Army installed a Communist Government of National Unity at Lublin. Boleslaw Bierut became President, and Edward Morawsky Premier.

Eventually, in 1947, the long delayed elections took place, although they were rigged to enable the Communists and their supporters to win a majority of votes. The Peasant party was mercilessly harassed and when its leader, Mikolajezyk (the former Prime Minister of the exiled Polish administration) fled for his life, the Peasant party collapsed. Poland, however, with its large population, was difficult for the Soviet Union to control effectively; it was discontent in Poland which helped to inspire the revolt against Soviet influence in Hungary (see below).

Czechoslovakia

The Czechs felt that they had been cruelly betrayed by Britain and France in 1938–9, and despite the forced transfer of Ruthenia to the

Soviet Union after the war, they were well-disposed towards the Russians. The exiled President Benes was embittered by the Munich 'sell-out' and cooperated with the Russians. He flew from London to Moscow in 1943, where he signed a Russo-Czechoslovak treaty of friendship, and after the war was restored as President. This raised the prestige of the Communist party, which won nearly forty per cent of the vote in free elections in 1946. Klement Gottwald, a Communist, headed a coalition government of Communists and Social Democrats.

Within two years Czechoslovakia was transformed into a communist 'people's democracy'. The police force was packed with Communists, making it a powerful instrument of the Communist party. When the Social Democrat ministers resigned in protest in February 1948, Gottwald asked Benes to replace them with communist stooges. He threatened communist violence if Benes did not agree and assembled large police forces in Prague. Benes yielded, and in the May 1948 elections, the presence of Soviet troops ensured that the Communists won an unassailable majority.

Hungary

The Communists polled only twenty per cent of the vote in the 1945 elections, but a dictatorship headed by Matyas Rakosi, a ruthless Stalinist, was rapidly developed. The great landed estates were seized and the peasants, despite their opposition, were organised into collective farms. Backed by the secret police, Rakosi instituted a reign of terror. The Roman Catholic Church was persecuted, its property confiscated by the state, and in 1948 Cardinal Mindszenty, the most outspoken critic of the regime, was imprisoned. In 1949 the Communist party itself was purged. Several high-ranking party officials publicly confessed to acting as agents of foreign governments, and were executed.

Bulgaria

Bulgaria had a long tradition of friendship with Russia and proved to be a loyal communist satellite. In October 1944 George Dimitrov, who

had been expelled from his homeland in 1923 as a communist agitator, returned to Bulgaria after its surrender. In September 1946, when the electorate voted to abolish the monarchy, Dimitrov became Premier until his death in 1950. The Communists quickly consolidated their power. Nikolai Petkov, leader of the left wing National Peasant party, was executed for treason, and during a purge of the party almost half the membership of the Bulgarian Central Communist Committee was liquidated after show trials.

Albania

Albania emerged at the end of the war with a communist administration recognised by the Allies. The new Premier was Enver Hoxha, who had organised the Albanian Communist party and led the wartime resistance to the German occupation. Hoxha was a supporter of Stalin. He refused to agree with Khrushchev's criticisms of Stalin's policies, and after 1956 relations between the Soviet Union and Albania deteriorated. Hoxha withdrew Albania from COMECON (the Council for Mutual Economic Assistance), the Soviet counter to Marshall Aid, and in 1961 Albania was excluded from the Warsaw Pact. Relations between the two countries were broken off, and Albania aligned itself with the People's Republic of China in the struggle for the leadership of the communist movement.

Rumania

A Russian sponsored government was established in Rumania by the end of 1945. In February of that year the Kremlin forced King Michael to dismiss General Radescu, the Premier of a coalition government, and to replace him with the Soviet Union's nominee, Petru Groza, leader of the Rumanian Communist party. In April 1948 Rumania became a republic.

Yugoslavia

In October 1944 Tito's partisans liberated Yugoslavia without Russian help. Tito was regarded as his country's saviour and enjoyed massive popular support, but even so, he allowed no opportunity for opposition to his rule to develop. When the non-communist resistance movement collaborated with the Germans rather than see the Communists installed in power, it was exterminated during the final stages of the fighting.

In the November 1945 elections only communist candidates were allowed, and in 1946 Yugoslavia became a communist state. Tito's government was recognised by the Allies, for it clearly had the support of the Yugoslav people, whose heroic resistance to the Germans was much admired. The differences in outlook between Stalin and Tito, however, soon became obvious. After numerous disagreements, Tito and the Yugoslav Communist party were expelled from the Cominform in June 1948.

Three important consequences followed the rift between Yugoslavia and the Soviet Union. The first was the end of the civil war in Greece, when Tito closed the Yugoslav frontier with Greece. The Communists in northern Greece, deprived of their supplies, soon collapsed. Secondly, Tito's defiance made Stalin determined that no other communist countries should be allowed to follow the example of Yugoslavia. The communist hierarchies in Poland, Hungary, Czechoslovakia, Bulgaria, Rumania and Albania were purged to ensure that they would not deviate from Stalin's policies. Thirdly, Tito accepted Marshall Aid in order to reconstruct his country's economy and Yugoslavia forged close trade links with the West.

Nevertheless, Yugoslavia remained a communist state. Agriculture was organised along collective lines, though private plots of land were allowed, and industry and commerce were nationalised. When the country had been thoroughly communised, Tito tried to heal the long-standing divisions between the Croats and Serbs, and the religious differences between Roman Catholics, Muslims and Greek Orthodox. After 1953 the powers of the secret police were reduced, and locally elected councils were given substantial powers of self-government. This process developed with a seriousness unknown in any other communist state in Europe.

The end of the Stalinist era

While Stalin lived the communist satellites were exploited for the benefit of the Soviet Union. Huge quantities of industrial equipment and raw materials were extracted from the Soviet zone of Germany in the shape of reparations, while the other countries supplied agricultural products. People who spoke out against Stalin's rule risked being sent to a labour camp. After Stalin died in March 1953 there was a strong reaction against his grim tyranny. In East Berlin, workers demonstrated in the streets, demanding secret elections and shorter working hours. They set fire to the Communist party headquarters and Russian troops had to be called in to restore order. In Hungary, Rakosi fell from power, while there was unrest in other parts of the Soviet bloc.

The Soviet Union tried to reduce the volume of discontent by allowing the production of more consumer goods, relaxing censorship and curbing the activities of the secret police, and permitting the development of some commercial and tourist links with the West. At the same time attempts were made to strengthen the bonds of the communist world. In 1955 the Russian leaders, Nikolai Bulganin and Nikita Khrushchev, persuaded the satellite countries to sign a military alliance, called the Warsaw Pact, with the Soviet Union. Its members promised each other mutual assistance in the event of an attack by West Germany, which had just joined NATO. The quarrel with Yugoslavia was patched up when Bulganin and Khrushchev visited Belgrade in 1955. Tito himself went to Moscow the following year, when Khrushchev conceded that there could be 'different roads to socialism in different countries'.

The Hungarian revolt 1956

The reversal of Stalin's repressive policies had unexpected consequences in Eastern Europe, where there were demands for greater political freedom. In Hungary mass demonstrations in Budapest for reforms rapidly developed into an anti-Russian revolt. In the more relaxed political atmosphere of the post-Stalin period, Imre Nagy, who was at heart a Titoist, had succeeded Rakosi. In 1955 the latter had recovered power, but his policies were so unpopular that he was removed from office on Moscow's orders, and replaced by Erno Geroe. He refused to consider demands for the evacuation of Russian troops, improved living standards and introduced free parliamentary elections, but had no more success in rallying the support of the Hungarian people than his predecessor. Faced with this dilemma the Soviet Union tried to regain control of the situation by appointing Nagy as Premier. He promptly announced his intention to hold free elections and to withdraw Hungary from the Warsaw Pact in order that the country could follow a neutralist foreign policy.

The Hungarians were overjoyed, believing they had shaken off Russian domination. Nagy, however, had flung down a challenge which the Soviet leaders could not ignore, for acceptance of Hungary's measures meant the collapse of the Soviet satellite system. If Hungary was allowed independence, why not Poland, Czechoslovakia, even East Germany? The Russian leaders therefore decided to crush the revolt by armed force.

On 4 November three thousand tanks and armoured carriers rumbled into Budapest. After a week's bitter fighting during which 30,000 Hungarians and 7000 Russian soldiers died, the rebellion was put down. Military help from the West, which the Hungarian patriots expected as a result of sympathetic radio broadcasts, never came. Without help the Hungarian struggle for freedom was doomed from the start.

The Russians appointed as the new Premier Janos Kadar, who had suffered terribly both under the Nazis and in 1951 at the hands of Rakosi's secret police. He soon broke his promise that the achievements of the revolution would

Hungarians wrench cobblestones from the streets of Budapest, piling them up behind felled lamp posts in an effort to slow down the Soviet tanks.

be kept. The secret police were reorganised, and thousands of suspected rebels were hunted down and imprisoned. Nagy was promised safe conduct from the Yugoslav embassy where he had taken refuge, but he was arrested, handed over to the Russians and secretly shot in Rumania in 1958.

The aftermath of the Hungarian revolt

The failure of the Hungarian revolt showed how difficult it was to overthrow a government which was backed by the secret police and the army of a foreign power, even though it was opposed by the great majority of the population. The events in Hungary also proved that the West, despite its verbal support of a popular anti-Soviet movement, would not risk war to liberate any East European country from Soviet control. This was merely recognition of the simple fact that Russia's conventional military power in Eastern Europe was overwhelming. Even though the Anglo-French invasion of Egypt distracted world attention from Russian aggression, no Western country was prepared to accept the real possibility of nuclear annihilation in order to free a subject people from an alien rule.

The Hungarian revolt also marked an important stage in the development of post-war communist ideology. While it revealed the risks of allowing more open discussions of policy and greater participation in decision-making at all levels (as in Yugoslavia) it confirmed that repression along Stalinist lines could only be maintained by relying upon armed force.

The Czechoslovak crisis in 1968

With the exception of East Germany, Czechoslovakia was the only Soviet satellite which felt itself to be part of Western Europe. Moreover, between the wars a greater degree of democracy existed in Czechoslovakia than in any other East European state. It was the Czech people's desire for a freer society which led to another major crisis within the Soviet bloc.

In early 1968 Alexander Dubcek became Secretary of the Czech Communist party; he replaced Antonin Novotny, a Stalinist, who remained Head of State until March. In March, Ludvik Svoboda, a Czech nationalist, became President and Oldrich Cernik became Prime Minister. Dubcek and Cernik allowed greater freedom of the press, assembly and worship. Czechs were given the right to strike and to travel abroad and arrangements were made for secret elections to be held. Dubcek also argued that member countries of the Warsaw Pact should have a voice in the direction of its affairs.

The Kremlin and the other satellite governments were alarmed by these developments, which were similar to those in Hungary in 1956. The Soviet Union dared not allow Czechoslovakia, with its common frontier with West Germany, to join Yugoslavia as a neutralist country. Troops from several satellite countries consequently invaded Czechoslovakia, where they met passive resistance. Although there was considerable sympathy in the West for Dubcek's aims, there was no open opposition to communist intervention.

Dubcek and Cernik were arrested, and the Czechs were forced to accept an army of occupation. Although Dubcek was soon released from prison he was only allowed to remain in office for a further eight months; after this he was replaced by Dr Husak, who was prepared to follow rigidly the Moscow dictated party line. The liberal measures of Dubcek's government gradually disappeared; Husak purged the communications media and the universities, while many of those who had spoken out against the military occupation were imprisoned. Dubcek himself was formally expelled from the party in 1970, and even years afterwards, he and his supporters were still being harassed by the secret police.

The crisis, however, did not disturb the solidarity of the satellite countries. Dubcek was not a traitor to the communist cause, but rather an idealist who wished 'to give communism a human face'. Nor did the Czechs themselves see the events of 1968 as an attempt to break away from the Soviet bloc. During the 1970s their resentment of the military occupation of their

*Czechs wave clenched fists at a Soviet cameraman, filming from the
safety of an armoured car in the streets of Prague.*

country was largely forgotten, as the Czech
population enjoyed greatly improved standards
of living.

The communist bloc in the 1970s

By this time all the states of Eastern Europe had
advanced far along the road to socialism and the
overwhelming majority of their peoples recognised the futility of opposition, even if they
wanted change. Ties of self-interest, similar
types of government and the presence of Russian
troops bound the satellite countries of Eastern
Europe to their powerful neighbour, the Soviet
Union. Although COMECON, set up by Stalin

in 1949, was but a pale shadow of the Common
Market in Western Europe, it helped to unite the
Soviet Empire. The 'Friendship Oil Pipeline'
pumped oil from Russia to Czechoslovakia,
Hungary, East Germany and Poland. These
countries were not affected by the oil crisis of
1973, as their needs were met in full by the Soviet
Union.

Thus after more than a generation of enforced
partnership with the Soviet Union the frontiers
between the communist satellites and the rest of
Europe corresponded very closely in 1979 to the
military division of Europe at the end of the
Second World War. In this respect, at least, the
events of 1944–5 sealed the fate of Eastern
Europe.

CHAPTER TEN:
The Korean War

For much of the twentieth century Korea has been a victim of great power ambitions and rivalries. Annexed by Japan in 1910, it became the base for Japanese expansion in Manchuria in 1931–32, and on the Chinese mainland after 1937. At the end of the Second World War Korea was occupied by American and Russian troops, as agreed at the Yalta Conference. They accepted the surrender of the Japanese forces in the country, and the thirty-eighth parallel became the dividing line between their two military administrations.

Stalin and Roosevelt had already agreed that Korea should eventually become free and independent. A joint commission was therefore set up by the United States and the Soviet Union, in order to establish a democratic government. The Koreans, however, did not see why they should have to wait so long. They wanted their liberation from Japanese rule to be followed immediately by independence. In the northern zone, controlled by the Russians, communist committees were formed to maintain law and order. They planned to instal in Pyongyang a government for the whole of Korea, headed by Kim Il Sung, a Moscow-trained Communist. In the southern zone, where the Americans were confused by the complexities of Korean politics, little progress was made towards achieving a stable administration.

The Americans refused to accept the Soviet proposal, since they felt it would lead to the formation of a communist government for Korea, and in September 1947 President Truman asked the United Nations to take responsibility for Korea. The UN Assembly resolved that it should become united and independent, and a UN Commission was sent in January 1948 to supervise free elections.

The Communists did not take part in the elections held in South Korea in May 1948, where Dr Syngman Rhee, leader of the South Korean Nationalist Party, was chosen by the Assembly as President of the Republic of Korea, with Seoul its capital. The UN Commission was refused entry into North Korea, where elections to a 'people's assembly' were held in August. The following month this assembly proclaimed the Democratic People's Republic of Korea, with Kim Il Sung its first President. Korea now possessed two governments, each of which insisted that it was the rightful government of the whole country.

On 1 January 1949 the United States recognised the government of South Korea, and arranged to withdraw all its troops from the country within six months, despite the risk that Syngman Rhee's government would be unable to resist North Korean pressures. Truman wished to disentangle the United States from its involvement in Korea, since he was worried by the danger that public opinion would reject American commitments in both Europe and the Far East.

Korea and Taiwan (Formosa) were excluded from the Pacific area the United States would defend against communist aggression. This decision, Truman hoped, would promote the development of a stable peace in the Far East.

In the meantime, however, relations between the North and South Korean governments became increasingly hostile. The division of Korea had disrupted the country's economy, for the south was predominantly agricultural, while the north possessed most of the country's heavy industry and raw materials. When the North Koreans refused to transmit electrical power to the south, on which many light industries and businesses depended, South Korea's economic problems multiplied, and Syngman Rhee lost much of his support. The North Korean government then announced that it would hold elections in the south during August, for the purpose of uniting Korea. On 25 June 1950, without further warning, North Korean forces invaded South Korea, captured Seoul after three days' fighting and drove rapidly south towards Pusan.

The reaction of the United States

At once Truman announced that American troops would be sent to defend South Korea, on the grounds that it was now plain that the Communists were prepared to go to war in order to conquer independent states. At the same time he stated that the United States would protect Taiwan if it was attacked by communist China. This contrasted sharply with Truman's recent statement that the United States did not wish to become involved in China's civil war. What factors lay behind this sudden reversal of foreign policy?

Firstly, American hopes that China would be a friendly power in the Far East collapsed with the communist victory in 1949. One of the first actions of the People's Republic of China was to conclude a thirty year treaty of friendship with the Soviet Union. Secondly, the Cold War between the two superpowers had reached a critical stage. In September 1949 the Soviet Union had exploded its own atomic bomb, so that the United States no longer had the monopoly of atomic weapons. The crisis over Germany (see Chapter Five), where the Berlin blockade had ended in May 1949, seemed to prove that only strong measures, backed by the determination to use force if necessary, could deter communist aggression. Truman also believed that intervention in the Korean War would rally many countries to resist the spread of communism wherever it appeared.

United Nations intervention

The UN Security Council met in emergency session, and condemned the action of North Korea. The Soviet delegate had walked out, as a protest against the UN's refusal to award Nationalist China's seat in the Security Council to the People's Republic of China. In his absence a resolution was passed calling for a ceasefire in Korea, the withdrawal of the North Korean forces behind the thirty-eighth parallel and assistance from all UN members to defend South Korea. The United States also appealed to the Soviet Union to persuade the North Koreans to withdraw, but Stalin replied that the events in Korea were internal matters, over which the UN had no jurisdiction.

Truman therefore ordered American troops into action in Korea, and stationed the US Seventh Fleet between Taiwan and the Chinese mainland to prevent any attempt to seize the island. General MacArthur was placed in command of the UN Force, which was composed largely of American and South Korean troops, although eventually troops from fifteen other nations took part in the war. By the end of July the North Koreans had advanced to within forty miles of Pusan, and it seemed that the UN Force would be driven into the sea. The perimeter was held, however, and throughout August UN reinforcements and supplies poured in, enabling MacArthur to go on to the offensive in September. United States marines landed at Inchon, behind enemy lines, and recaptured Seoul. By the end of the month South Korea had been cleared of invaders.

Chinese intervention

Having gained the initiative, the United States tried to destroy the communist regime in North Korea. Truman ordered MacArthur's army to cross the thirty-eighth parallel, despite China's warning that it would not stand aside if North Korea was invaded. The UN troops advanced rapidly north, but as they approached the Yalu river, they were repulsed by Chinese infantry.

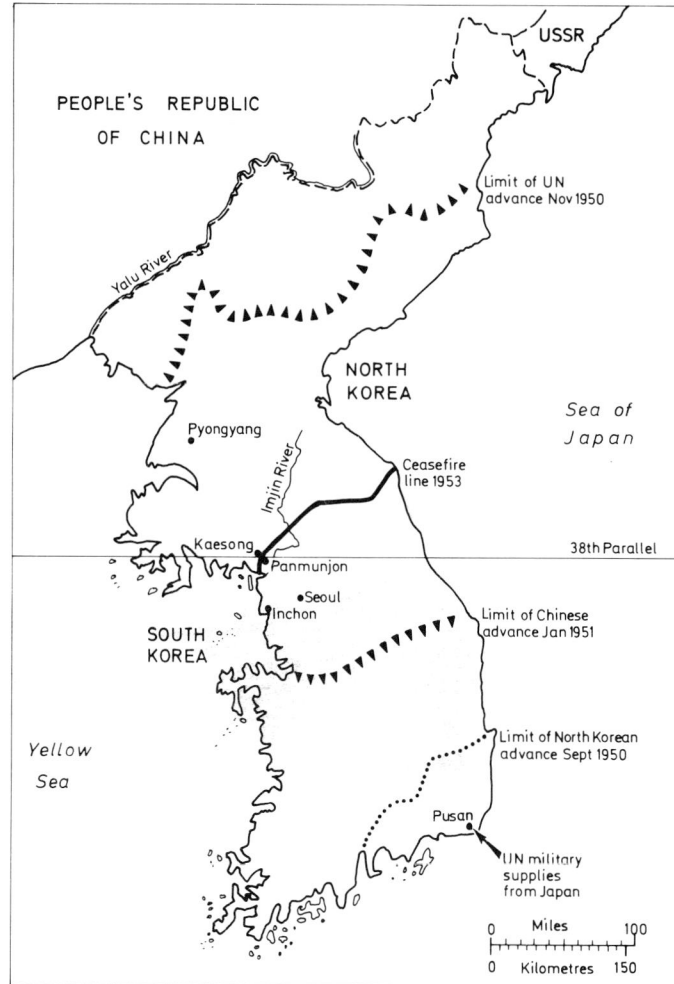

16   *The Korean War, 1950–53*

In the next phase of the war, which lasted until mid-January 1951, the combined communist forces drove the UN Force back over the thirty-eighth parallel, and occupied Seoul.

In February the UN Assembly passed an American resolution which denounced China as the aggressor in Korea. General MacArthur urged Truman to escalate the war by bombing Chinese supply routes and bases in Manchuria, and blockading the Chinese mainland. Truman, however, had no wish to become the architect of a third world war, and in April 1951 Mac-Arthur, who by now had become a liability, was

relieved of his command and replaced by General Ridgeway. Under his direction the communist armies were forced back to the thirty-eighth parallel, where a ceasefire line was eventually fixed in July 1953, two years after negotiations for a truce first began at Kaesong.

The first attempt to end the war soon broke down, but in October 1951 the armistice talks were resumed at Panmunjon, where an agreement was reached after long delays and bitter recriminations. China accused the Americans of using bacteriological warfare in Korea, while the United States complained that the Chinese had

UN anti-aircraft guns fire night and day in the battle against the
North Koreans, close to the capital of Pyongyang.

'brainwashed' their captives. The most difficult problem, however, was China's insistence that all prisoners-of-war should be repatriated when peace was restored, if necessary against their will. A compromise was finally reached whereby a neutral commission was set up to interview prisoners-of-war who did not wish to be repatriated. In the event nearly half of the captured Chinese soldiers chose to go to Taiwan.

The aftermath of the war

Although talks for a peace settlement took place in Geneva in 1954, no agreement was reached over the future status of Korea, so that the war was not officially ended. Subsequent negotiations aimed at bringing about peaceful reunification failed to overcome the mutual hostility of the two rival governments, and for many years afterwards relations between the two countries were embittered by border clashes and propaganda campaigns. Although Chinese troops were withdrawn from North Korea in 1958, the United States maintained military bases in South Korea in order to guarantee its independence. In 1979 President Carter reversed an earlier decision to withdraw American troops by 1982, in view of growing evidence that North Korea had greatly increased its armed forces. Thus the Korean peninsula remained a flashpoint in international affairs.

Democratic rule in South Korea disappeared as Dr Syngman Ree became a virtual dictator in his efforts to suppress all signs of communism. In 1960 he was overthrown and, after a brief interlude, replaced in 1961 by General Park, who maintained himself in power with the help of the army, American support and a booming economy. In 1975 all opposition to his government was made illegal. Meanwhile, the prestige of the Pyongyang government was raised when it was invited to send representatives to the 1975 Conference of Non-Aligned Nations at Lima, Peru, and the number of countries which admitted the legality of the North Korean government rose from thirty in 1970 to over ninety in 1978.

Seen in perspective, the Korean war was a classic example of the concept of a limited war. The United States did not yield to the temptation to use the atomic bomb against China, nor did it bomb Chinese cities by conventional means. China in turn did not attack American ships en route to Korea. Thus a third world war was narrowly avoided. In the Western world public opinion was alerted to the threat from communist aggression, and a programme of rearmament was adopted, led by a massive expansion of the United States' armed forces. For Korea, 'the land of the morning calm', the consequences were less clear and it remained a divided nation. The demilitarised zone separating its two halves symbolised the fragile and uneasy peace which followed the end of the Second World War.

Present day China bears little resemblance to the China of fifty years ago. The Chinese, who inherited one of the oldest civilisations in the world, were very slow to recognise the need for change. Once having done so, however, they transformed Chinese life and society in the space of the quarter century following the communist seizure of power in 1949. By means of propaganda, political indoctrination and violence, the great mass of the population was encouraged to take part in building a new communist society. In this society many traditional Chinese beliefs and customs, as well as the class structure and the old concept of the family, were all denounced and then swept away. The destruction of the ancient system of land ownership and its replacement by huge state farms (communes), was accompanied by rapid urban and industrial growth. Such growth enabled the People's Republic of China to take its place in the 1970s as a world power alongside the Soviet Union and the United States. Within a single generation Mao Tse-tung converted a war-torn country into a strong, revolutionary state, which regarded itself as the champion of the under-developed nations of Asia and Africa against the rich and powerful industrialised Western world.

The resumption of the civil war 1945–49

When the Second World War ended in August 1945, communist control of China seemed a remote possibility. Stalin promised Chiang Kai-shek, the Nationalist (Kuomintang) leader, that he would not assist the Chinese Communists and that Manchuria, occupied temporarily by Soviet troops under Marshal Malinovsky, would be handed back to the Nationalist government. The Americans requested the Japanese commander to order his garrisons to surrender only to Kuomintang forces (a promise he kept), and the American airforce transported Nationalist armies to Peking, Shanghai, Nanking and Tientsin.

Nevertheless, when Chiang Kai-shek and Mao Tse-tung met later that month at Chungking to consider forming a coalition government for the whole of China, it was unlikely that they would agree. The sudden collapse of Japan had enabled the Communists to seize large areas of northern and central China, before they could be re-occupied by the Nationalists. Mao was confident that he could win control of all China north of the Yangtze and Huai rivers. Thus neither leader saw any reason to share power with the other, and a resumption of the civil war was almost inevitable.

The talks between the two leaders were inconclusive. Mao's policy was to seem reasonable in his demands, while yielding nothing of importance. He conceded that Kuomintang forces should outnumber communist forces by a ratio of seven to one but he had no intention of keeping to this agreement. He accepted the proposal from General Marshall (the American Secretary of State who had been sent to China to encourage the formation of a strong, democratic government) for a conference which would draft a new constitution. This resolved that China should be governed by a state council composed of an equal number of Communists and

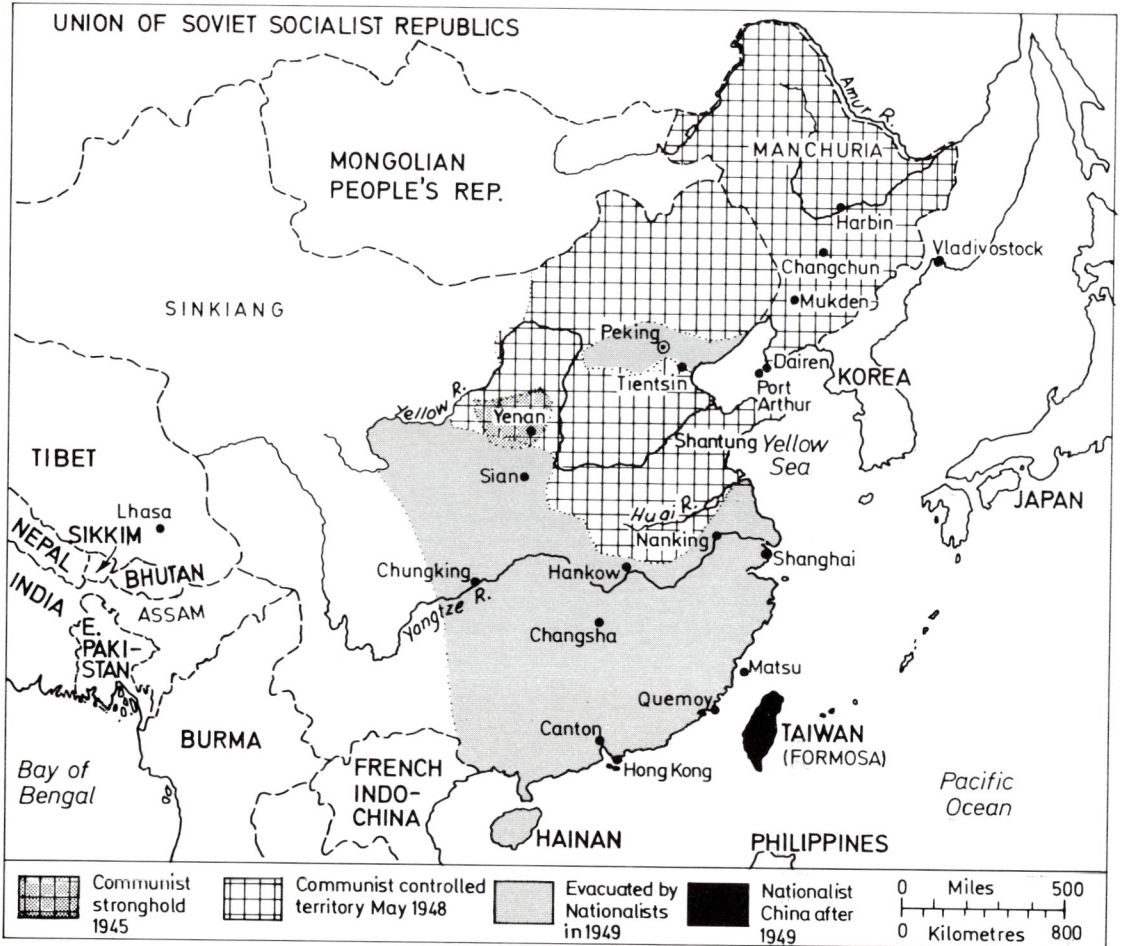

17   *The civil war in China, 1945–49*

Nationalists, together with several representatives from a number of other political parties. Mao, however, did not feel obliged to accept its recommendations.

Soon open warfare developed between the two sides. When Soviet troops evacuated northern Manchuria in 1946 a communist army led by Lin Piao occupied the territory. Although the Nationalists recovered Changchun soon afterwards, they never controlled the countryside, which remained firmly in communist hands.

Even so, Chiang Kai-shek believed that he could easily crush his opponents and that, if he could not, the United States would come to his rescue. Simultaneously he tried to drive the Communists from Shantung province and Manchuria, and to open the railway link between Nanking and Peking. The Communist tactics of avoiding pitched battles and retreating in the face of superior numbers enabled the Nationalists to claim impressive victories; they captured over 150 towns and cities, including Yenan, the wartime communist capital. Their gains, however, were largely illusory, for events were already beginning to slip beyong Chiang Kai-shek's grasp.

Nationalist rule was confined to the towns and cities, which became isolated pockets of influence in a countryside controlled by the Communists. Nationalist air superiority could not prevent the Communists occupying the Liao-tung peninsula and most of Southern Manchuria in 1947. Chiang Kai-shek then bitterly regretted his decision to commit his best troops to its conquest, instead of securing firm control of China between the Great Wall and the Yangtze river.* Desperate efforts to relieve his beleaguered garrisons in Manchuria were to no avail, and by October 1948 Lin Piao's armies had captured Changchun and Mukden, together with 300,000 prisoners. Chiang Kai-shek's best army no longer existed, and Lin Piao's armies were free to advance over the Great Wall and to begin closing in on Peking.

* In reality Chiang Kai-shek probably had little choice. The Manchurian campaign may have been a disaster, but if he had abandoned the province to the Communists without a fight, it is unlikely that he would ever have been able to dislodge them from it.

Communist troops advancing over a hilltop in the South Yangtse area.

Meanwhile, the decisive battle of the civil war was being fought at Huai Hai (a shortening of the names of the Huai river and the Hai railway), an area vital for the Nationalist defence of southern China. The two-month battle ended in December, when over 300,000 demoralised Nationalist troops surrendered, and the Communists advanced to the banks of the Yangtze river. After a four months' lull in the fighting, during which the remnants of the Nationalist armies escaped to the safety of Taiwan (Formosa), and the offshore islands of Quemoy and Matsu, the Communists resumed their advance. Nanking and Shanghai soon fell, and in October 1949 the People's Republic of China was proclaimed in Peking.

Reasons for the Nationalist defeat

The Nationalists lost chiefly because they had been fighting too many enemies for too long. During the course of two decades the Kuomintang had resisted warlords, Communists and the Japanese. The victory over the latter after eight years of fighting was accompanied by a sense of relief that peace was near at hand. As this hope proved to be an illusion, so Nationalist morale faltered with the resumption of the civil war. It then collapsed once the Communists became strong enough to make the transition from guerrilla warfare to a full-scale assault upon the Kuomintang armies.

In its desperation to achieve victory the Kuomintang alienated the bulk of the population. Since most of its income was derived from taxes on city dwellers and customs duties levied at the ports, the Kuomintang had little interest in rural affairs. Its close links with the landowning class meanwhile virtually ruled out any possibility of much-needed land reforms. In those areas liberated from the Japanese the inhabitants were treated more as collaborators with the enemy who deserved to be punished, than as the victims of foreign conquest. The local Japanese currency was replaced at a conversion rate which caused great hardship, while corruption among Kuomintang officials was so rife that in many instances, Kuomintang rule seemed no better than Japanese rule.

If the Nationalist troops, badly paid and inefficiently led, behaved with scant respect for the people they were supposed to be defending, the Communists won increasing support by their consideration for peasant and town dweller alike. Moreover, by distributing lands to the peasants they gave them a good reason to hope for a communist victory. Thus by 1948, when inflation had soared to dizzy levels, the Nationalist cause was so discredited that only massive American intervention in the war could have saved it.

The revolution in the countryside

Mao Tse-tung remained a revolutionary until his death in 1976, devoting all his energy to the twin tasks of strengthening China and establishing communism. In 1950 the existing system of land ownership was abolished. The peasants were encouraged by Communist party officials, or 'cadres', to accuse landlords in 'speak bitter' meetings of cheating the villagers by charging excessive rents, or of seizing land not rightfully theirs. In more serious cases landlords were brought before open air 'people's courts', where they might be severely punished if found guilty. Many thousands were, in fact, executed during the land reform campaign, and many more were sent to forced labour camps.

When the landlord's property and farm equipment had been confiscated, the cadres arranged for its redistribution. The inhabitants in the countryside were classified into four groups: poor peasants, middle peasants, rich peasants and landlords. The landlords were eliminated as a class, and were allowed to keep only as much land as they could cultivate personally. The rich peasants were allowed to keep their land, while the lands formerly belonging to the landlords were shared out among the poor and middle peasants. The villagers were encouraged to join 'mutual aid teams', whereby several families cooperated in working the land, particularly at busy times of the farming year, such as seed-time and harvest. The peasants still owned their land privately, but they shared their farm equipment, and worked on each other's land in turn.

Members of a commune near the Yellow River level the ground in a newly-formed terrace farm.

The second stage of the revolution in the countryside began in 1953, when the government exerted pressure on the 'mutual aid teams' to combine and form small collective farms of between twenty and thirty households. The 'pooling' of land into larger, more efficient units was encouraged by tax reliefs and guaranteed prices for their produce. The land belonging to the collective farm was worked in common, with wages based upon the amount of land contributed by the peasant and the value of his labour. In theory the peasants still owned their land, since they were able to withdraw from the collective if they wished, although this must have been very difficult in practice.

The drive towards large scale collectives, where the land was owned by the community, began in 1955. It meant that those peasants who had acquired land following the communist seizure of power, now lost it, as did the rich peasants. The collective farms were controlled by the government, which fixed production targets and compulsorily purchased the crops. It did so in order to feed the rapidly growing populations of the cities and to achieve surpluses for sale abroad, thus earning foreign currency needed for buying capital equipment. Despite criticisms that the speed of change was too fast, and that peasant support might be alienated, Mao pressed ahead. By 1956, ninety per cent of the peasants were organised into advanced cooperatives, where they owned only their house, a garden plot, personal savings and some domestic animals.

Industrial recovery

The task of increasing food production was only one problem facing the Communist leaders in 1949. During twelve years of warfare, road and rail communications had been neglected and industrial output had fallen well below pre-war levels. The value of money had declined sharply, and goods of all kinds were in short supply. Moreover, apart from the Soviet Union, China could expect little help from other countries.

Within a few years, nevertheless, China's industrial growth was impressive. The government closed all private banks and replaced them by a State Bank, which gave credit facilities only to officially approved projects. The most important industries were nationalised, and the rise in prices was slowed down. At the same time, wages were based upon the cost of necessities, such as food, shelter and clothing. Industry was revitalised during the Korean War (1950–53), when a 'Resist America, Aid Korea' campaign created an intense spirit of self-sacrifice and patriotism among the Chinese people.

In 1951 Mao Tse-tung inaugurated the Three Anti Movement, designed to eliminate corruption, waste and unnecessary bureaucracy. This was succeeded one year later by the Five Anti campaign, which attacked the evils of bribery, tax evasion, fraud, theft of public property and the sale of important economic information. In 1953 the long-delayed First Five Year Plan, based upon the Soviet model, set production targets for all the major industries. When it ended in 1957 the productivity of farming, and of the coal, oil, cement, steel and machine tool industries showed significant increases, while the network of roads and railways had also greatly expanded.

The Great Leap Forward

The Second Five Year Plan, announced in May 1958, set even higher targets than the First. Mao Tse-tung boldly declared that a 'Great Leap Forward' in technology and industrial output could be achieved as a result of the united efforts of the Chinese people. By mobilising the peasant population into labour battalions that would serve as farmers or workers as conditions demanded, the countryside would become a hive of manufacturing industry. Class distinctions based upon different occupations would slowly disappear, so that China would be transformed simultaneously into a communist society and a great industrial nation, in accordance with the revolutionary doctrines of the Chinese Communist party.

By the end of the year 26,000 communes had been established, each consisting of about 5000 households, mainly in rural areas. Each commune was responsible for organising all means of production and distribution, and for providing necessary public services such as hospitals, schools, nurseries and recreation centres. The population of each commune was divided into production brigades and production teams, whose work priorities were fixed by elected managers. Throughout China a tremendous effort was made to increase industrial output by such means as 'back-yard' steelworks and brick kilns, and small factories and workshops.

The failure of the Great Leap Forward

The targets set by the Second Five Year Plan were unrealistically high, however, and the results were disappointing. Food production actually fell, making necessary not only the return to the land of twenty million people who had been employed in manufacturing industries, but also purchases of large quantities of grain from abroad in order to prevent famine. Much of the 'back-yard' steel produced had to be scrapped, while hundreds of primitive coal mines fell into disuse, and many other ambitious projects had to be shelved.

The Great Leap Forward failed for a variety of reasons. The hastily established communes upset the traditional social and economic patterns of life, with most covering such a large area that they were unable to foster a spirit of local pride. Family morale was lowered by experiments in communal living; the more prosperous villages resented their enforced association with poorer villages; many cadres lacked the necessary managerial skills for operating factories, mines and transport systems. Finally, the withdrawal of Soviet technicians and financial aid as a result of the growing Sino-Soviet quarrel (see Chapter Twelve) was a serious blow to China's hopes of becoming an industrial power almost overnight.

The partial failure of the Great Leap Forward led to criticisms of Mao's leadership and he resigned as Chairman of the People's Republic, being succeeded by Liu Shao-chi. Mao remained Chairman of the Chinese Communist party, however, and he shortly dismissed Peng Teh-

huai, the Minister of Defence, who had presented the most serious challenge to his authority. He was replaced by Lin Piao, one of the heroes of the Long March. Mao also took a sharp line against the Soviet Union's policy of reducing international tension by improving its relations with the United States.

The Great Proletarian Cultural Revolution

The struggle for power which followed the Great Leap Forward was also a struggle of ideas between the Maoists, who wished to preserve the revolutionary spirit by involving the masses in a continuous revolution, and the moderates, who wanted to consolidate China's achievements since 1949 by more gradual change. Mao believed that the Chinese Revolution was in

Red Guards carrying portraits of Mao Tse-tung parade along a street in Peking.

danger of being undermined by a whole new generation growing up which had no experience of the revolutionary struggle against imperialism and capitalism. The decline in revolutionary enthusiasm was evident in the desire for self-advancement and material incentives (particularly among the well-educated, who therefore often seemed the least reliable ideologically). The only way to understand revolution, Mao argued, was not through history books or listening to accounts of it, but by actually making revolution.

The origin of the Great Proletarian Cultural Revolution was a play called *The Dismissal of Hai Jui*, whose subject, the sacking of an important party official, was a thinly veiled reference to Mao's dismissal of Peng Teh-huai in 1959. Chiang Ching, Mao's wife, organised a revolutionary opera in Peking in 1964, and a propaganda war began between the Maoists and their opponents, who were branded as 'revisionists' and 'capitalist roadsters'.

In 1966 Mao demanded that the masses should be actively involved in creating a 'pure' communist society. In such a society, distinctions between mental and manual labour, town and countryside, peasant and worker, would be eliminated. (Mao had provided evidence of his own good health by swimming nine miles down the Yangtze river.) All over China young people were encouraged to criticise and purge party officials and anyone else who lacked revolutionary enthusiasm. Schools and colleges were closed down as millions of students enrolled as Red Guards. They attended mass meetings where they studied *The Thoughts of Chairman Mao* (*The Little Red Book*), and debated political ideas. Many went on symbolic 'long marches' in an attempt to recapture the spirit of the early days of the revolution. Others went into the countryside, where they worked on the land and shared the life of the ordinary peasant, spreading the Cultural Revolution as they did so. In many towns and cities Red Guards took over factories and business premises, and intimidated or attacked people accused of being 'reactionaries' or 'class enemies'.

The Red Guards' excesses created chaotic conditions in China and led to clashes with the People's Liberation Army. Order was gradually restored, and the Red Guards returned to their colleges and schools. Under the moderating influence of the Premier, Chou En-lai, the party organisation was repaired; the great majority of the party members were reinstated, though not necessarily in the same posts they had occupied before the start of the Cultural Revolution. Meanwhile, the army had emerged from the struggle stronger than ever, once again demonstrating the truth of Mao's maxim, 'Political power grows out of the barrel of a gun'.

The death of Mao Tse-tung

Mao's death in September 1976, at the age of eighty-three, was preceded by several years of intense speculation over who would succeed him. Upon this would largely depend the future course of China's domestic and foreign policies. Several candidates for the position of head of the world's most populous state had already disappeared from the political scene. During the Cultural Revolution Liu Shao-chi was removed from office and replaced by Lin Piao. In 1973, however, it was officially announced that Lin Piao had been killed in September 1971 in a plane crash, while he was attempting to escape to the Soviet Union after his plot to overthrow Mao had been discovered.

When Teng Hsiao-peng was ousted from the Premiership in 1976, suspicions mounted that Madame Chiang Ching and her three closest political associates (the so-called 'Gang of Four') were quietly removing their rivals from positions of authority. Whether or not the succession of Hua Kuo-feng, who became Premier when Chou En-lai died in January 1976 and received Mao's approval as his heir, marked the beginning of a period of stability, only subsequent events will prove. Beyond all doubt, however, is the fact that Mao's rule was only one stage in the course of the Chinese Revolution.

When eight years of war against Japan ended in 1945 the Chinese people seemed at last to have cast aside the shackles of foreign imperialism. All Japanese conquests of Chinese territory since 1895 were restored, while the Western powers renounced their rights and privileges in China. At the same time China became a founder member of the United Nations, with a permanent seat in the Security Council.

The Chinese wanted peace, but the fierce struggle for power between the Kuomintang and the Chinese Communist party made the resumption of civil war inevitable. It was this threat, together with the lack of support from his allies the United States and Britain, which forced Chiang Kai-shek to grant Stalin's demands for the restoration of Russia's rights in Manchuria and Outer Mongolia.

Soviet and American attitudes towards Nationalist China

The Soviet Union and Nationalist China signed a thirty year military alliance against Japan in August 1945, when each country promised to respect the other's territorial integrity. Stalin also agreed that he would not assist the Chinese Communists, but would, instead, give friendly support to the Kuomintang government. The Soviet Union recognised China's claims to Sinkiang and Manchuria, and Stalin agreed to evacuate within three months the Russian troops who had occupied Manchuria during the final stages of the war against Japan. The Chinese recognised reluctantly the independence of Outer Mongolia, where the Russians had encouraged a breakaway movement to set up the Mongolian People's Republic in 1944. China gave the USSR permission to use Port Arthur and Dairen as naval bases, and agreed to the joint ownership of the Manchurian railway system.

At the end of the Second World War, both the Soviet Union and the United States miscalculated by greatly over-estimating the strength of the Nationalists and under-estimating that of the Communists. The Soviet Union preferred a weak China, but the United States wanted a strong China as an ally against Japan and if need be, against Russia. Thus Stalin, who wanted to secure Russia's objectives along its borders with China before the Kuomintang established itself in power, broke his agreement with Chiang Kai-shek. Indirectly, he helped the Communists by allowing them to overrun much of Manchuria before the Nationalists could take control. The Americans, who had no desire to intervene in China's internal affairs, advised Chiang Kai-shek to negotiate with Mao Tse-tung. They themselves did not give the Kuomintang substantial financial aid until 1948, when Congress passed the China Aid Act. By this time it was much too late to prevent a communist victory.

The establishment of the People's Republic of China was not welcomed by the United States. It killed any lingering hopes that post-war China would be an ally, and it widened the Cold War to include the Far East. Having only recently constructed the North Atlantic Treaty Organisation to act as Western Europe's shield against communist aggression, the United States now began to consider making Japan its ally, as a counter-balance to communist China's influence. This change of policy, combined with considerations of Communist party unity, dictated that China should, in Mao Tse-tung's words, 'lean to one side', and seek the support of the Soviet Union.

The Sino-Soviet alliance 1950

Mao Tse-tung's relations with Stalin were never very cordial. They did not trust each other, and Stalin had long doubted the wisdom of Mao Tse-tung's strategy of winning control of the countryside. According to orthodox Marxist teachings, communist revolution would be the achievement of the urban proletariat, or working class, not the peasants. Even in 1945, Stalin was convinced that the Chinese Communists were doomed to failure unless they disbanded their forces and accepted a subordinate role in the Kuomintang government, with the aim of undermining it from within. It was not until the eve of the communist victory in China that Stalin admitted he had been wrong.

In December 1949 Mao Tse-tung went to Moscow, where he eventually signed a thirty year Treaty of Friendship, Alliance and Mutual Assistance in February 1950. This cancelled the 1945 treaty, and agreed to the restoration of Chinese control over Port Arthur and Dairen and the Chinese Eastern and South Manchurian Railways (now renamed the Changchun Railway). China agreed that Outer Mongolia should remain independent, and the USSR made available a loan to aid China's economic recovery.

Chinese encouragement of communist movements in Asia

The 1950 Sino-Soviet treaty acknowledged the fact that the two countries had many common interests, such as their opposition to Western imperialism and their fear of American military power. Mao Tse-tung, however, was not willing to shape China's foreign policy in accordance with the Kremlin's wishes. He was in fact determined that communist China should play the leading part in helping anti-colonial movements in Asia. Thus China recognised Ho Chi Minh's regime in North Vietnam in January 1950 even before the Soviet Union did so. China also assisted the communist movements in Indonesia, Malaya, Burma, and the 'people's wars' in Vietnam and Korea.

Chinese students show their determination to fight in Korea.

China's involvement in Korea

The Korean problem was almost certainly discussed in Moscow by Mao Tse-tung and Stalin. Both communist leaders wished to lessen American military power in the Far East, particularly when the United States was planning to rearm Japan after the projected peace treaty had been signed. The extension of communist influence to the whole of Korea would strengthen China, and Mao Tse-tung encouraged the North Koreans to invade South Korea. The United States had no commitment to defend South Korea, and the Chinese were surprised by its decision to resist the communist attack. Nevertheless, they were determined that the Korean peninsula should not be reunited under an American sponsored government, since it might again become a springboard for an attack upon China. Just when the United Nations Force seemed on the verge of victory, thousands of Chinese volunteers poured across the frontier to help the North Koreans. Eventually, a ceasefire was arranged and the thirty-eighth parallel became the frontier between North and South Korea.

Tibet

In the meantime, China had secured control of neighbouring Tibet. Ever since the early eighteenth century China had claimed the right to supervise the Tibetan government, headed by a Dalai Lama, whom the Tibetans regarded as the reincarnation of a god. During the latter part of the nineteenth century Tibet became more independent of Manchu rule, only to find itself in danger of coming under Russian control. This threat was averted by the British, who invaded Tibet in 1904 and forced the Dalai Lama to renounce Russia's influence. In 1906 the British government secretly informed the Chinese government that it regarded Tibet as China's responsibility. China attempted to reassert its authority over the protectorate of Tibet, but the 1911 Revolution forced the withdrawal of Chinese troops, and Tibet proclaimed its independence in 1912. Thereafter, until the communist victory in 1949, the Chinese were too preoccupied with internal difficulties to interfere in Tibetan affairs.

In 1950, while the Korean War was in progress, Chinese forces invaded Tibet. Mao Tse-tung

Chinese troops construct a bridge across a river in Tibet, and in the foreground, use rubber dinghies to float trucks across.

was anxious to prevent Tibet becoming a refuge for the defeated remnants of the Kuomintang army, while its incorporation into China would strengthen the borders with India and Russia, particularly in the outlying region of Sinkiang. In May 1951 the Chinese recognised the Dalai Lama as the religious head of state, and promised the Tibetans a measure of self-government. Nevertheless, the Dalai Lama was expected to follow the advice of Chinese officials, and Chinese troops were stationed on Tibetan territory.

Tibet was in many respects a backward country, ruled by priests and feudal landlords. Communications were poor, and much of the country, lying above 1500 metres, was barren. The Chinese built roads, levied taxes on the monasteries, abolished feudal labour in 1953 and confiscated land from the Tibetan landlords. The Chinese regarded themselves as liberators, but the priests, who feared that their influence would decline, encouraged armed resistance to Chinese rule. By 1959 sporadic acts of sabotage had developed into a full-scale revolt by the Khamba tribe in eastern Tibet. The Chinese government accused the Dalai Lama of encouraging the revolt by refusing to use the Tibetan army against the Khamba tribesmen. He isolated himself in his palace in the capital, Lhasa, but when the Chinese threatened to bombard the town he fled to India. Chinese troops quickly crushed the rebellion, and Tibet was annexed by China.

The People's Republic of China, and India

Although India was one of the first countries to recognise the People's Republic of China, Sino-Indian relations soon deteriorated. India was a rival for the leadership of the emerging nations of southern Asia, while its desire to steer a middle course between the two great power blocs was suspect to China. According to Maoist philosophy, in a world dominated by the struggle between the socialist and capitalist systems there could be no place for neutralism. Each state had to 'lean to one side', i.e. align itself either with the forces of 'imperialism' or 'socialism'. Finally, although the Indian government accepted Chinese intervention in Tibet, it would have preferred that territory to have remained a buffer zone between India and China. Its occupation by the Chinese brought to the forefront the border problems which existed between the two countries.

Much of the Indo-Chinese frontier had never been properly defined, but there were two main areas of dispute. The first was the region of Ladakh, where the Aksai Chin, which bordered Tibet and Sinkiang Province, was regarded by India as part of Kashmir. The second was a territory north of the Assam Plain known as the North East Frontier Agency, established in 1914 by an agreement between the British government-in-India and the Tibetan government. The frontier between India and Tibet was the McMahon Line, named after the British civil servant who conducted the negotiations. The agreement, however, was of doubtful legality, since neither Britain nor China recognised Tibet's sovereignty.

The Sino–Indian War 1962

In the late 1950s India moved troops into both disputed areas. Chou En-lai (1897–1976), the Chinese Premier, hinted that China was willing to accept Indian control of the NEFA if India accepted Chinese control of the Aksai Chin. India, however, had no intention of relinquishing its claims to either region, and Chou En-lai's proposals fell upon deaf ears. Fighting broke out in October 1962, and the Indian troops were forced to retreat rapidly to the Assam Plain. Just when it seemed that India was on the verge of defeat, however, China announced that it was withdrawing its forces to the line they had previously occupied.

Mao Tse-tung declared that China had only acted to prevent India from seizing Chinese territory by armed force. The Soviet Union, however, was sympathetic towards India, and Mao Tse-tung feared that the end of the Cuban missile crisis (see Chapter Nineteen) might result in open support of India by both the United States and the Soviet Union. Mao Tse-tung did not want China to become involved in a long war with India, which would damage China's economy and antagonise neutral countries.

Despite the end of the fighting, Sino-Indian relations did not improve. China again pressed its claims to territory in 1965, when war broke out between India and Pakistan, and it supported the newly created state of Bangladesh in 1971. In the meantime, China's frontier with India remained unsettled. Isolated border incidents still occurred, but the Chinese government had become more concerned over the developing quarrel with the Soviet Union.

Sino-Soviet relations

Mao Tse-tung had welcomed Soviet predominance in Eastern Europe after 1945 because it forced the United States to concentrate upon the problem of defending Western Europe. Thus he agreed to the expulsion of President Tito of Yugoslavia from the Cominform in 1948, for his refusal to obey the Communist party line; neither did he object to the Soviet invasion of Hungary in 1956. Thereafter, however, disagreements between Peking and Moscow became more frequent and bitter.

After 1955 both China and the Soviet Union competed with each other for the leadership of the under-developed countries, the so-called Third World. Both Khrushchev, who eventually succeeded Stalin, and Mao Tse-tung were moving away from the conviction that neutralist countries such as India were camp followers of the capitalist nations. Khrushchev wanted to reduce the risk of a nuclear confrontation between the two superpowers through a general acceptance of the idea that they could 'co-exist peacefully'. Meanwhile, Mao Tse-tung realised that the opportunities for communist expansion, which the anti-colonial movements after 1945 appeared to offer, had been exaggerated.

Communist China therefore set out to reassure the Afro-Asian countries of its peaceful intentions and to win their confidence. By doing

Mao Tse-tung in 1937.

so, it hoped to counter-balance the influence of the United States, which had concluded defensive alliances with Japan (1951), South Korea (1953) and Nationalist China (1954). Moreover, the United States was a prominent member of the South East Asia Treaty Organisation, formed in September 1954 in order to check communist expansion in Asia.

In 1954 China and India agreed to abide by the principles of peaceful co-existence. At the Bandung Conference held in Java in 1955, China was quick to declare support for the policy of 'neutralism' agreed by the twenty-nine Afro-Asian nations attending the conference. This meant that the nations were equally opposed to old and new style imperialism, by which they meant interference by other powers in their internal affairs. Chou En-lai promised the Afro-Asian states that China would respect their wishes, and would not support communist movements aimed at over-throwing their governments – provided that they did not side with the United States.

The Sino-Soviet split

Mao Tse-tung disapproved strongly of Khrushchev's denunciation of Stalin's rule in 1956, because it weakened communist solidarity throughout the world. As time went on the quarrel between the Chinese and Russian leaders over communist ideology and strategy grew more and more bitter. When the Soviet Union launched the first *sputnik*, or earth orbiting space satellite, in 1957, Mao Tse-tung urged the Kremlin to exploit Russia's lead in space rocketry and nuclear missiles to force American imperialism on to the defensive.

Mao Tse-tung thought that world-wide communism could be achieved by war, whereas Khrushchev believed that a nuclear war would be so devastating that it would render meaningless any communist victory. He wanted to take advantage of Russia's military superiority by proposing general world disarmament. The socialist countries with their superior economic systems, Khrushchev argued, would out-produce the capitalist states and thereby ensure the triumph of communism. In the meantime, the communist and capitalist countries should co-exist peacefully, a policy which Mao Tse-tung regarded as cowardly.

Thus when Khrushchev was asked to supply China with nuclear weapons and technical assistance, to offset the American decision to base tactical nuclear weapons in South Korea, the Russian leader would only agree provided China placed its armed forces under joint Soviet-Chinese control, which would mean, in effect, Soviet control. The Chinese refused, and decided to press on with the development of their own nuclear weapons. Soon afterwards, in 1959, the Russian technicians in China were summoned home. (Despite this set-back China succeeded in joining the 'nuclear club' within a few years, testing an atomic bomb in October 1964, and developing the hydrogen bomb by

1967. In 1970 China launched its own space satellite, and by the latter part of the decade the necessary technical skills had been acquired for the manufacture of inter-continental missiles.)

The gulf between Peking and Moscow widened during the 1960s. China received no support from the Soviet Union over its quarrel with India; on the contrary, Russia agreed to supply arms to India. Mao Tse-tung retaliated by supporting the Albanian government when it rejected the official Soviet line on 'de-Stalinisation'. In 1963 China claimed the Maritime Province of Russia and part of Siberia and Russian Central Asia, which according to the Chinese view had been illegally acquired by Russia as a result of unequal treaties. During the seventeenth and eighteenth centuries the Manchu dynasty had been forced to cede over 130,000 square miles of territory to Tsarist Russia. Further concessions by China were made in the nineteenth century; by the Treaty of Aigun (1858) China lost 185,000 square miles in Amur Province, and another 130,000 square miles of land east of the Ussuri River (which became the Maritime Province) by the Treaty of Peking in 1860.

Sino-Soviet relations did not improve when Khrushchev fell from power in October 1964, for his successors, Brezhnev and Kosygin, followed similar policies. On several occasions the Soviet Union tried unsuccessfully to secure China's expulsion from the socialist camp. Between 1964 and 1969 there were over 4000 border incidents, which culminated in large scale fighting involving hundreds of casualties along the banks of the Ussuri river, as both nations indulged in a 'war of nerves' in these sensitive regions.

The Sino-American *détente*

The worsening relations between China and the USSR prompted the Chinese leadership to seek reconciliation with the United States of America. Soviet intervention in Czechoslovakia in 1968 aggravated the situation, with Russia claiming the right to intervene in the internal affairs of neighbouring communist states

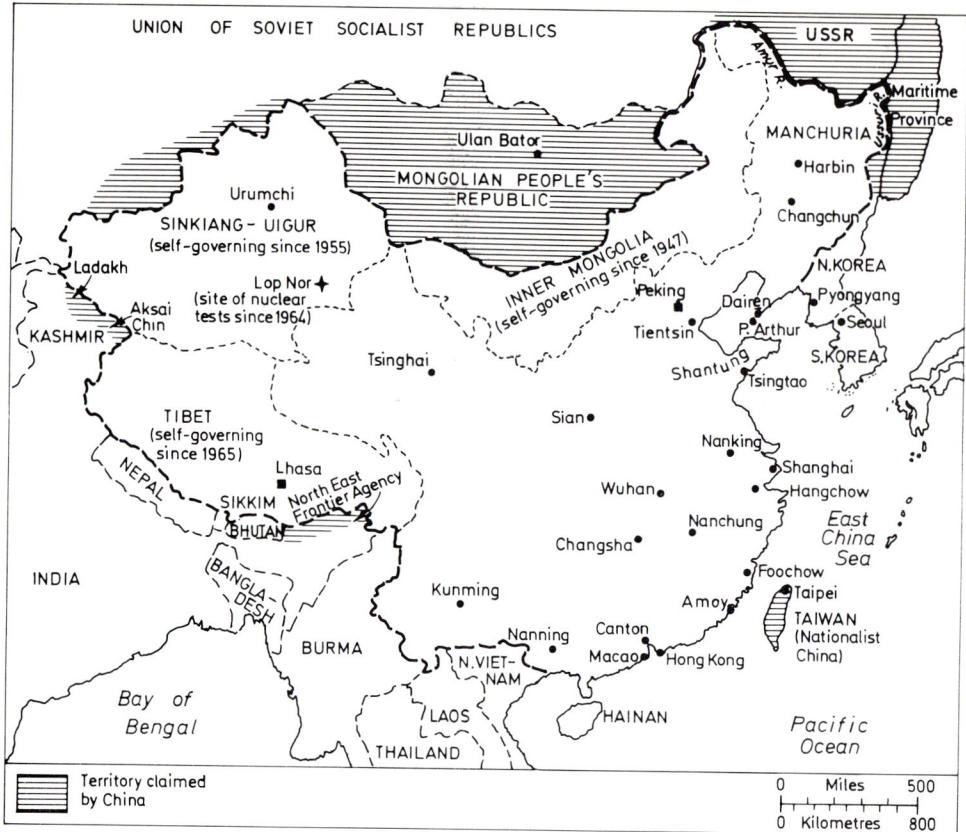

UNION OF SOVIET SOCIALIST REPUBLICS

USSR

Ulan Bator

MONGOLIAN PEOPLE'S REPUBLIC

Maritime Province

MANCHURIA

Harbin

Changchun

Urumchi

SINKIANG – UIGUR
(self-governing since 1955)

INNER MONGOLIA
(self-governing since 1947)

N.KOREA

Ladakh

Lop Nor
(site of nuclear
tests since 1964)

Peking

Dairen

Pyongyang

Aksai
Chin

Tientsin

P. Arthur

Seoul

KASHMIR

Tsinghai

Shantung

Tsingtao

S.KOREA

Sian

Nanking

TIBET
(self-governing
since 1965)

NEPAL

Lhasa

SIKKIM

North East
Frontier Agency

BHUTAN

Shanghai

Hangchow

Wuhan

Nanchung

East
China
Sea

INDIA

BANGLA-
DESH

Changsha

Foochow

Kunming

Amoy

Taipei

Nanning

Canton

TAIWAN
(Nationalist
China)

BURMA

Macao

Hong Kong

N.VIET-
NAM

Bay of
Bengal

LAOS

HAINAN

Pacific
Ocean

THAILAND

Territory claimed
by China

0   Miles   500
0 Kilometres 800

18   *The People's Republic of China, 1972*

in order to safeguard the interests of the communist bloc (the so-called Brezhnev doctrine). Khrushchev's policy of *détente* (i.e. relaxing the tension between the Soviet Union and the USA) had succeeded to such an extent that the Soviet Union was free to exert pressure upon China by building up its forces along its frontiers. In these circumstances, Mao Tse-tung feared a pre-emptive strike to destroy China's developing nuclear capability; an understanding with the United States would reduce this risk.

The United States also welcomed the chance of improving its relations with China. Trade restrictions between China and America were eased and in 1971 an American table tennis team visited Peking. The United States of America also dropped its opposition to China's membership of the United Nations (although it still opposed the expulsion of Nationalist China [Taiwan]

from the Assembly), and the representative of the People's Republic of China took his place in the UN Security Council.

Following on from what was popularly called 'ping pong diplomacy', President Nixon accepted an invitation to visit China in February 1972. The result was a diplomatic success for both countries. Addressing the Chinese people in Peking, Nixon declared that neither the People's Republic of China, nor the United States sought to dominate each other. Instead, he urged, 'Let us start a long march together, not in lock step, but on different paths leading to the same goal, of building a world structure of peace and justice, in which all may stand together with equal dignity'.

The Shanghai Agreement, which was announced at the end of Nixon's visit, marked the end of China's isolation in world affairs. The

United States recognised that there was only 'One China', and that Taiwan was part of it. Although no reference was made to the People's Republic of China it was clearly implied that the real China was mainland China. Both countries affirmed their desire for a peaceful solution to the Taiwan problem. Mao Tse-tung secured a promise that the American forces would eventually evacuate Taiwan, though no date was specified.

The problem of the 'two Chinas'

Taiwan, or Formosa, as it was called by the Portuguese, lies 100 miles east of the Chinese mainland, and 700 miles south of Japan. Annexed by Japan in 1895, it was restored to China fifty years later. Together with the offshore islands of Quemoy and Matsu, Taiwan became the refuge for Chiang Kai-shek's Nationalist army when the Kuomintang collapsed in 1949. Chiang Kai-shek ruled a mere 14,000 square miles of territory populated by fifteen million Chinese (until his death in 1975, when he was succeeded by his son, Chiang Ching-kuo). Despite this, however, he was regarded by many countries as the legitimate ruler of Nationalist China. As a founder member of the United Nations, this country had a seat in the Security Council until 1971.

Taiwan therefore assumed a position of great importance in international affairs, especially when it came under American protection during the Korean War. General MacArthur once described the island as an 'unsinkable aircraft carrier', from which the Nationalists might one day launch an attack upon mainland China. The People's Republic of China, on the other hand, claimed that Taiwan was part of its territory, and it refused diplomatic relations with any country which did not accept this view.

In 1954 the Chinese bombarded Quemoy and Matsu in an effort to compel the Nationalists to surrender, and threatened to invade Taiwan. China resumed its efforts in 1958, when the United States persuaded Chiang Kai-shek to withdraw his troops from Quemoy and Matsu, and made it clear that it would not support any

attempt to reconquer the mainland. With the passage of time, China's admission to the United Nations, the Sino-American *détente* and China's achievement of superpower status, it is likely that Taiwan will one day be incorporated into the People's Republic of China.

Hong Kong

The island of Hong Kong was acquired by Britain by the Treaty of Nanking (1842), which ended the Opium War between Britain and China, and has remained a British possession ever since. Despite Chinese protests in 1967 against the continued occupation of Chinese territory by foreigners, the status of Hong Kong remains unchanged. China tolerates the colonial status of Hong Kong because it is able to earn valuable foreign currency by its exports to the island. Nor has British possession prevented the establishment of friendly relations between Britain and China, marked by the visits to China of ex-Prime Minister Edward Heath in 1974, and Margaret Thatcher, leader of the British Conservative Party, in 1977. In July 1978 Mrs Shirley Williams, the Education Secretary, went to Peking, where agreement was reached on a scientific and technological programme involving student exchanges.

China's influence in the 1970s

China has often professed its desire for peace, and it has said that it will never be the first to use nuclear weapons in any war. It suspects the other two superpowers of having ambitions for world domination. At the same time China's readiness to help revolutionary movements in Black Africa, Latin America and Asia, together with its vast size and huge population, have created apprehension and suspicion of its motives in international affairs; not only among its immediate neighbours in southern Asia, but also in the West and in the Soviet Union. Thus the People's Republic of China remains a puzzle to statesmen, and it may take the rest of the century before the mystery is finally unravelled.

When the Second World War began, most of South East Asia formed part of the Dutch, French and British empires. The only exceptions were the Philippines, which were annexed by the United States in 1898, and Thailand (Siam), which had managed to safeguard its independence. The Japanese conquests in this area pronounced the death sentence on colonialism, and after the war the countries of South East Asia opposed the restoration of European rule.

Between 1945 and 1957 foreign rule virtually ceased. The Philippines were granted independence after their liberation by the Americans. India and Pakistan achieved their freedom in 1947, Burma and Ceylon (now Sri Lanka) in 1948 and Indonesia in 1949. French rule in Indochina ended in 1954 and Malaya obtained its independence from the British in 1957. In 1975 the only survivals of colonial rule were Brunei, part of New Guinea, and Portuguese Timor. Unfortunately, Japan's defeat did not bring peace to South East Asia, and for the next thirty years there was warfare in one part or other of the region. The birth of the new nations was often accompanied by war and revolution, and South East Asia had the misfortune to become involved in the Cold War rivalries of the great powers.

The end of French rule in Indochina

After the Fall of France in 1940, French Indochina (Cochin-China, Cambodia, Annam, Tongking and Luang Prabang [Laos]) was at Japan's mercy. General Pétain, the Vichy French leader, collaborated with the Japanese in the hope that France would be allowed to keep possession of Indochina. Japanese forces, however, soon occupied Tongking in order to close one of the supply routes to the Chinese Nationalists, and in July 1941 the rest of Indochina was occupied as a base for Japanese expansion to the south. French officials in the occupied areas were tolerated for the sake of a stable administration.

When Japan's defeat became certain the French made plans to reassert their authority when the war ended, but the Japanese seized the initiative by interning the French and announcing the end of French rule. The nominal Emperor of Annam, Bao Dai, was installed as ruler of the three coastal territories which were renamed Vietnam, or 'the land south of China'. The kings of Cambodia and Luang Prabang (Laos) were encouraged to declare their countries independent.

Neither the Vietnamese nor the French accepted this solution. A Vietnam Independence League, opposed to both French and Japanese imperialism, had been formed in 1941 by Ho Chi Minh for the purpose of waging guerrilla warfare against the Japanese, and by 1945 it controlled most of Tongking. When the Japanese surrendered, the Vietminh persuaded Bao Dai to abdicate and proclaimed the Democratic Republic of Vietnam. Ho Chi Minh became President of the new state until his death in 1969.

Bao Dai advised General de Gaulle to recognise Vietnamese independence as the only way to protect French interests in Indochina. In a personal letter to the French President, Bao Dai wrote:

You have suffered too much during four years not to understand that the Vietnamese people no longer wish, can no longer support, any foreign domination or foreign administration. You could understand even better if you were able to sense this desire for independence which has been smouldering in the bottom of all hearts, and which no human force can any longer hold back. Even if you were to re-establish a French administration here, it would no longer be obeyed; each village would be a nest of resistance, every former friend an enemy, and your officials and colonists themselves would ask to depart from this unbreathable atmosphere.

The French, however, were determined to reclaim Indochina, which they proposed should form part of the French Union. In February 1946 they reassumed military control in the south, and in April they re-occupied the northern part of the country, following the departure of the Nationalist Chinese forces who had supervised the surrender of the Japanese at the end of the war.

The First Indochinese War 1946–54

As it was clear that the French government had no intention of granting the Vietnamese people real independence, the Vietminh stepped up their campaign of terrorism and sabotage. In November 1946 French troops bombarded the port of Haiphong in order to drive Vietminh forces out of the city. The following month Vietminh guerrillas attacked the French garrison in Hanoi. These events marked the start of a long war in which the Vietminh used the same tactics they had successfully developed against the Japanese. Ho Chi Minh's strategy was to win the support of the peasants first, then attack the enemy supply lines, and finally assault their strongholds. Soon French authority in North Vietnam was restricted to the towns, while the Vietminh controlled the countryside. Meanwhile, the French tried to gain the support of the Vietnamese people. Bao Dai was persuaded to head a government of the whole of Vietnam, in opposition to that of Ho Chi Minh. In July 1949 he became Prime Minister, and Cambodia, Laos

and Vietnam officially became Associated States within the French Union.

The communist conquest of mainland China, completed in October 1949, revolutionised the situation in South East Asia, since the Vietminh received increased aid from the Chinese Communists, as well as from the Soviet Union. The United States and Britain responded by recognising the French-sponsored governments of Vietnam, Laos and Cambodia. The outbreak of the Korean war in February 1950 finally convinced President Truman that the Communists were determined to bring all South East Asia under their sway, either by helping guerrilla movements to undermine the legal governments of countries by subversive tactics, or by actual invasion. Indochina and Korea thus became drawn into the Cold War between the rival superpowers.

Despite American aid the war in Indochina went badly for the French, and by 1953 the three states were seeking to sever their connection with France altogether. The war had spilled over into neighbouring Laos, where the Laotian Communists, known as *Pathet Lao* (which means Lao State), were openly helping the Vietminh guerrillas and beginning to challenge the authority of the Laotian government.

The French economy could no longer stand the strain of the war in Vietnam, and at France's prompting a conference of the great powers at Geneva was arranged in order to bring about a ceasefire. In March 1954 the Vietminh forces, led by General Giap, launched a major offensive against the French stronghold at Dien Bien Phu, close to the Laos-Vietnam frontier. Surrounded by Vietminh forces on all sides, the beleaguered garrison surrendered in May. This disaster killed any lingering French hopes of retaining some colonial influence in Indochina.

The Geneva Agreement 1954

The ceasefire negotiations dragged on until July, when a settlement was finally reached. French and Vietminh forces were to withdraw from Cambodia and Laos, whose independence was recognised. A demilitarised zone along the seventeenth parallel was created in Vietnam. French

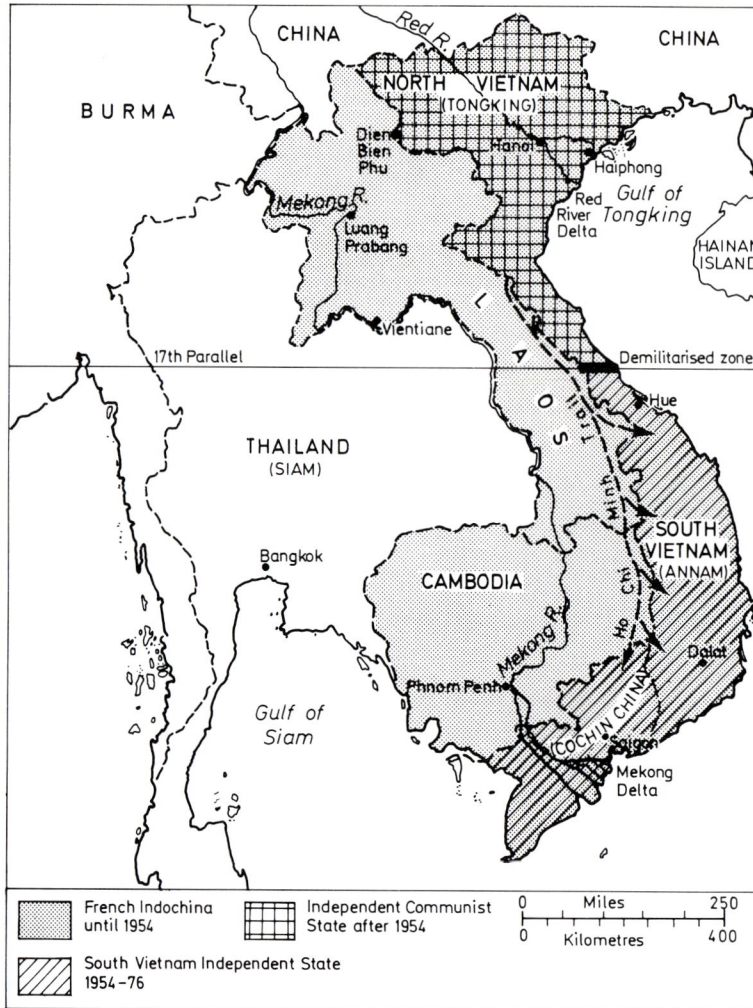

19   *Indochina*

troops were to withdraw to the south of this line within 300 days, while Vietminh forces were to withdraw to the north of it. Neither zone would join any military alliance. Lastly, elections were to be held within two years in order to bring about the unification of Vietnam.

The 'domino theory' of communist advance

The United States viewed the collapse of French power in Indochina with alarm, for communist China had entered the ranks of the great powers and communist aggression in Korea had only been checked by full-scale war. Now a communist regime had consolidated its hold on North Vietnam. To many Americans it seemed that the whole of South East Asia was in danger of falling under communist control. As the Communists seized power in one state, the neighbouring state came under communist pressure. If it was allowed to collapse, the others might be knocked down one by one. This was the so-called 'domino theory' developed by President Eisenhower. His solution was to strengthen South Vietnam and form SEATO, the South East Asia Treaty Organization, which was signed at Manila in September 1954.

SEATO

SEATO was limited in its application; it covered South East Asia, but the position of India was left uncertain. The member governments – the United States, Australia, New Zealand, Philippines, Thailand, Pakistan, France and Britain – promised to consult each other in the event of an armed attack, or if the peace of the area was endangered, but they were not bound by the treaty to come to each other's assistance. SEATO did not actually prove very effective in providing collective armed support.

Thus Cambodia insisted on its neutrality in 1956 and Laos was neutralised in 1962. Britain refused to associate with the United States' military intervention in South Vietnam after 1961, and France withdrew from SEATO for similar reasons in 1966. SEATO was also weakened by the conflicts between Pakistan and India in 1962, 1965 and 1971.

South Vietnam under the rule of Ngo Dinh Diem 1954–63

Ngo Dinh Diem, who became head of the South Vietnam government in June 1954, faced a difficult situation. The economy was in disarray, transport and communications were disorganised and the army was demoralised. In Saigon itself the administration was controlled by gangsters known as *Binh Xoyen*. The government also faced opposition from various religious groups, which were attempting to seize control of parts of the south.

Diem regained control by breaking the power of the *Binh Xoyen* and the religious sects. Eventually, in October 1955, his position was sufficiently strong for elections to be held to determine the future form of government of South Vietnam. The South Vietnamese were asked to decide whether Diem or the Emperor Bao Dai should rule. Diem claimed ninety-eight per cent of the votes cast and he proclaimed the Republic of Vietnam, with himself as President.

With United States' support Diem refused to hold further elections on the reunification of Vietnam, claiming that a vote free from illegal communist pressures could not be guaranteed. Ho Chi Minh accused Diem of being a puppet of American imperialism and the Communists exploited the discontents of the peasants, who had not been affected by the economic prosperity which the towns enjoyed. Sympathy with the peasants' grievances was combined with a ruthless policy of terrorism. Village leaders, government officials and teachers who openly opposed the Communists were assassinated. Diem's repressive rule, his alienation of the peasants and Buddhists, inflation and the outbreak of civil war, gradually lost him the army's loyalty. In 1963, after several abortive attempts, Diem was deposed by a military coup and murdered.

The Second Indochinese War 1961–73

Meanwhile, civil war had broken out in South Vietnam, where the Communists virtually controlled the Mekong Delta and the provinces north-east of Saigon. The South Vietnamese Communists called themselves the National Liberation Front, although they were more popularly known as the Vietcong. They were farmers by day and guerrilla fighters by night.

The United States was determined that communism should not spread below the seventeenth parallel, and thousands of American troops were sent as combat advisers to train and strengthen the South Vietnamese army. Diem's government adopted a 'strategic hamlet' policy similar to that which the British had successfully employed during the Emergency in Malaya. The peasants were gathered into fortified villages where they could be protected by government troops. In this way it was hoped to deprive the Vietcong of recruits, supplies and provisions. Despite these measures, however, the South Vietnamese forces were unable to pacify the countryside, and the build-up of American troops, which broke the Geneva Agreement, continued.

The war escalated in 1964 when the United States encouraged the South Vietnamese forces to mount commando raids on Vietminh positions in North Vietnam. When two American destroyers were fired upon by North Vietnamese gunboats in the Gulf of Tongking the United States took action. Congress voted President Lyndon Johnson powers to take all necessary measures, including the use of armed force, to protect South Vietnam, or any South East Asian country whose security was threatened by communist aggression.

From October 1964 onwards American B52 aircraft bombed the Ho Chi Minh Trail, along which supplies of arms and equipment were carried to the Vietcong. In March 1965 Johnson authorised the bombing of strategic targets and supply depots in North Vietnam itself. By these strong measures Johnson hoped to convince the

Communists that they could not achieve their aims by force. The North Vietnamese responded by increasing their aid to the Vietcong. Thus despite the fact that the number of American combat troops and advisers in South Vietnam rose to half a million men by 1968, victory for either side seemed as far away as ever.

The United States' resolve to win the war, however, was weakening. At home there was mounting criticism of the conduct of the war, as realisation of the full horrors of the Vietnam conflict grew. In the chaotic situation of a civil war in which each of the opposing sides was supported by an external power, it was often difficult to distinguish Vietcong guerrillas from ordinary peasants. Friendly villages were sometimes bombed by mistake, while the tactic of pattern bombing, in which a whole area was systematically devastated by high explosive bombs, could not differentiate between friend and foe on the ground. Thousands of peasants, trapped in the crossfire of a war from which they could not escape, were made homeless refugees. The most controversial issues, however were the use of napalm or jellied petrol which exploded on contact, and defoliants, which were widely employed to destroy the forest cover of communist supply trails. Furthermore, only Australia, New Zealand, Thailand, South Korea and the Philippines supported America's Vietnam policy abroad.

Peace talks between representatives of the American and North Vietnamese governments were begun in Paris in May 1968; they were deadlocked until October, however, when President Johnson agreed to call a halt to the bombing of North Vietnam and to admit Vietcong delegates to the negotiations. The Communists' Tet (Lunar New Year) offensive against the towns, arranged to coincide with the Paris talks, was intended to convince the United States that they were determined to win the war. Saigon, the capital of South Vietnam, nearly fell to the communists, but the South Vietnamese army inflicted heavy casualties upon the Vietcong, and even recovered control of some areas formerly administered by the National Liberation Front.

In May 1969 the newly elected President of the United States, Richard Nixon, announced his

South Vietnamese troops discover a child in hiding during an operation in the Mekong River Delta.

intention of ending the war in Indochina. Nixon's strategy was 'Vietnamisation' – to extricate American forces from the conflict, and leave Vietnamese to fight Vietnamese. Nixon, nevertheless, was not prepared to accept peace at any price, and the withdrawal of American troops was made subject to three conditions. The first was progress in the Paris peace talks, the second was a decline in the level of North Vietnamese military activity, and the third was the ability of the South Vietnamese army to accept responsibility for the conduct of the war.

North Vietnamese forces, however, had by now begun to operate against South Vietnam from bases in Laos and Cambodia with increasing success. The National Liberation Front (Vietcong) set up a Provisional Revolutionary Government in 1969 to administer 'liberated areas' of South Vietnam. Nixon was therefore compelled to offer the Hanoi government further concessions in his desire to end the Vietnam war. In January 1972 he proposed a ceasefire to cover the whole of Indochina, and the exchange of prisoners-of-war. He also agreed to the reunification of the whole of Vietnam after country-wide elections, and offered to withdraw all American troops from South Vietnam within six months. A ceasefire agreement was eventually signed in January 1973.

Peace was now in sight, though fighting continued until December 1974 when the Vietcong launched a major offensive and routed the South Vietnamese forces. Nguyen Van Thieu (who had been President of South Vietnam since 1967) resigned, and a Provisional Revolutionary Government of South Vietnam was formed. After rapid progress towards reunification, elections to a single National Assembly for a united Vietnam were held in April 1976. The Socialist Republic of Vietnam then came into existence and the thirty year struggle for independence, which had brought misery to millions of Vietnamese and turned large tracts of the countryside into wasteland, was finally over.

Just a part of the scenery—the havoc caused by bombs and napalm. This soldier doesn't notice it any more.

Thailand, Laos and Cambodia

The kingdom of Thailand abandoned its traditional neutrality during the Second World War when it made an alliance with Japan. Despite its mistake of joining the losing side, Thailand was treated very leniently after the war. Apart from having to expel the Japanese from the country, and make the surplus rice crop available for distribution in South East Asia, the Thai government was only required to return former Burmese and Malayan territories which had been annexed with Japanese help. The generous peace terms encouraged a pro-American attitude on the part of post-war Thai governments.

Between 1945 and 1947 there were no fewer than nine ministries before Field Marshal Phibun Songgram seized power, supported by the army, and formed an administration which ruled Thailand for ten years. In 1957, however, Songgram was accused of following weak and inefficient policies, and of failing to check inflation and corruption. He was overthrown by a bloodless *coup d'état*, and his place was taken by another field marshal, Sarit Thanarat.

Thanarat banned all political parties except his own, the Revolutionary party. Stern measures, such as strict censorship and the arrest of suspected Communists, made clear his hatred of communism, and a new constitution conferring substantial powers upon the Premier was drawn up. Key posts in the government, state industries and the armed services, were filled with his friends, and until his death in 1963 Thanarat ruled as a virtual military dictator.

In 1968, after ten years of military rule, Thanom Kittikachorn, Thanarat's successor, introduced a civil constitution. It was short-lived, as political unrest and the growth of communist terrorist activities forced the government to bring in martial law in 1971. Two years later, anti-American feeling and resentment against high prices brought about Kittikachorn's downfall in October 1973. Dr Sanya Dharmasaki, who became Premier, permitted the existence of political parties, except the Communists, in an effort to encourage the growth of democracy. In the 1975 elections forty-two separate parties fielded candidates.

Meanwhile, events had forced the Thai government to reappraise its foreign policy. Hitherto, Thailand had supported the United States' objectives in South East Asia, in the process becoming dependent upon American military aid. The Thai government sent troops to fight alongside UN forces in the Korean War (1950–53) and welcomed American military aid when the Communists stepped up their activities in Laos after 1959. The Thais also sympathised with the South Vietnamese regime, and American B52s were allowed to operate from bases in Thailand in order to bomb the Ho Chi Minh Trail.

At the same time Thanarat had been careful not to alienate communist China, whose power and geographical proximity could have made it a dangerous neighbour. After 1972, when the United States began to gradually withdraw its forces from South East Asia, Thailand reverted to its traditional role of neutrality. The collapse of American policies in Indochina in 1975 speeded up this process, and the last American troops left Thailand in March 1976. Meanwhile, when the Communists seized control of neighbouring Laos in 1975, Thailand closed its frontiers with Laos in an effort to isolate itself from events taking place in the rest of Indochina.

Laos

Laos, sandwiched between Vietnam, Cambodia and Thailand, occupied a strategic position in South East Asia, with the result that even before its independence was granted by the 1954 Geneva Agreement, Laos was being drawn into the Indochinese war. A communist organisation, the *Pathet Lao*, was set up in 1950 with the aim of securing national independence of French rule. Its leader was Prince Souphanou Vong, a friend and supporter of Ho Chi Minh. *Pathet Lao* forces readily cooperated with Vietminh guerrillas, who entered Laos in 1953 in order to gain easy access into South Vietnam by means of the Ho Chi Minh Trail.

In 1957, after negotiations which dragged on for three years, a coalition government was established in Vientiane, the capital of Laos. The

20   *South East Asia, 1978*

Royal Laotian Government, so called because the leaders of the two main factions, Prince Souphanou Vong and Prince Souvanna Phoumi, were of royal blood, brought neither peace nor progress to Laos. A confused struggle developed between the two factions, with the Americans backing Prince Souvanna Phoumi, and the Russians, Chinese and North Vietnamese supporting the *Pathet Lao* led by Prince Souphanou

Vong. The involvement of the United States and the Soviet Union threatened to bring about war between the two superpowers. Fortunately, both governments were anxious to avoid coming to blows over Laos. In 1962 President Kennedy and the Russian Premier, Khrushchev, agreed to recognise the neutrality of Laos, and to limit their aid to the two sides. The Chinese and the North Vietnamese, however, continued to assist and encourage the *Pathet Lao* forces, since a communist victory in Laos would greatly help the Vietminh in their struggle to win control of South Vietnam.

By 1970 the *Pathet Lao*, which had formed a rival administration at Khang Khay, controlled one third of the country and in 1975 the flimsy coalition government fell to pieces. Anti-American riots in Vientiane led to the withdrawal of United States troops and *Pathet Lao* forces occupied the whole of Laos. The royal family and many right wing supporters fled into Thailand. The monarchy was abolished, and Prince Souphanou Vong was made Premier of the People's Democratic Republic of Laos.

Cambodia

Prince Sihanouk, who ruled Cambodia first as king (1954–58), then as an elected Head of State from 1960–70, desperately tried to prevent Cambodia becoming entangled in the Indochina War. After 1964, however, his government was challenged by Cambodian Communists, called *Khmers Rouges*, and by North Vietnamese irregulars who operated from Cambodia against South Vietnam. Cambodia's neutrality was also violated by American and South Vietnamese troops in their 'search and kill' operations.

In March 1970 Prince Sihanouk was removed from office by a military coup, and the Khmer Republic was proclaimed in October. Lon Nol, its new leader, appealed for American help in driving the Communists from Cambodia. In June 1972 Lon Nol became President of the Khmer Republic, but his rule was opposed by the royalist supporters of Prince Sihanouk, who made an alliance with the *Khmers Rouges*. After the American withdrawal from Indochina their combined forces captured Phnom Penh early in 1975 when, under communist rule, the Khmer Republic was renamed Cambodia.

Indochina in 1979

The history of Indochina from 1942 was one of almost continuous warfare. In successive wars its peoples fought firstly the Japanese and then the French. In the third war they fought the Americans who, ironically, in trying to check the spread of communism in South East Asia, forced the nationalist parties in each state to choose between communism and support for American involvement in its affairs. In each case, with the exception of Thailand, they eventually decided against foreign intervention. Finally, they fought each other, as the Hanoi government tried to achieve Ho Chi Minh's goal of an Indochinese federation dominated by Vietnam. In December 1978 the Vietnamese army invaded Cambodia, following border clashes between the two countries which had occurred at intervals since 1975. Consequently in February 1979 China invaded Vietnam, its former ally, in order to support Cambodia and teach Vietnam a short, sharp lesson.

These events led directly to a mass exodus of refugees, not only from Cambodia but also from Vietnam, where the government decided to drive out of the country one million Chinese whose loyalty was suspect. As hundreds of thousands of people fled by land and sea in the hope of settling in neighbouring countries, they created a major problem for the world community. The governments of Thailand, Malaysia, Indonesia and Hong Kong feared that they would be swamped by the thousands of 'boat people' who were landing on their shores, and they demanded that other, more fortunate countries, accept their share of the refugees. Meanwhile, as tensions rose in the region, the United States promised to support the ASEAN countries if they were attacked by their powerful neighbour, Vietnam.

An awareness that India was part of a continent emerging from Western controls to take its proper place in world affairs was a major theme in Indian nationalism in the early twentieth century. This belief that European imperialism in Asia was an interlude was supported by Japan's victory over Russia in 1905, by the Young Turk Revolution of 1908 and by the Chinese Revolution in 1911.

When the First World War broke out in 1914, however, British rule in India seemed secure. Although two Indian nationalist movements existed – the Indian National Congress, founded in 1885, and the Muslim League, formed in 1906 – they were composed mainly of rich and educated Indians, and neither organisation enjoyed mass popular support. At the great imperial *durbar* held in Delhi in 1911 to celebrate his coronation, King George V received the homage of hundreds of Indian princes and potentates. They loyally supported Britain when war was declared; Indian troops fought bravely in East Africa, in the Middle East and even in the trenches of northern France in defence of the British Empire. Nevertheless, the celebrations and protestations of loyalty merely glossed over the growing unrest among Indians, and within a generation after the end of the First World War, British rule in India was no more.

The growth of Indian nationalism

At the turn of the century the Congress movement campaigned for active participation in the government of India, not complete independence. Most of its leaders, believing that British rule had brought many benefits to the country, were not anti-British and they promised unswerving loyalty to the Crown. An important exception, however, was Bal Gangadhar Tilak, who was convinced that the British would never voluntarily give India its freedom. His goal was a revival of Hindu India, to be achieved by revolution not reform, and he quickly gained a large following in Bombay province. Tilak was imprisoned twice by the British for his inflammatory nationalism, but his ideas spread and secret revolutionary societies sprang up in various parts of India. Their chief weapons of protest were economic boycotts of British goods and political assassinations.

The British government responded with a mixture of repression and reform. Public meetings were severely restricted, newspapers were censored and agitators were deported without trial. At the same time, in order to encourage Indians who were loyal to Britain, small concessions were granted. After 1909 some members of the provincial assemblies were elected by Indians. A proposal to partition Bengal into two separate provinces – West Bengal with its Hindu majority, and East Bengal and Assam with its Muslim majority – which had infuriated Hindus throughout India, was revoked in 1911. The nationalists were also promised in 1914 that India's partnership in the Empire and in the Allied war effort would not be overlooked.

As the First World War dragged on, with little sign of progress towards responsible government in India, many Indians became disillusioned, feeling that their country's contribution was very largely unrecognised and unrewarded. They were also influenced by the slogans for national self-determination, which seemed to provide the basis for the post-war settlement of international problems. Muslims' loyalty to Britain was further strained by the failure to partition Bengal and by the fact that the Caliph of Turkey, their spiritual overlord as the leader of Islam, was at war with Britain. Mohammed Ali Jinnah, the future creator of Pakistan, urged the Muslim League to rejoin the Congress in 1916, so that Britain was faced with a united Indian opposition. Jinnah declared:

India is for the Indians. Be the time near or distant, the Indian people are bound to attain their full stature as a self-governing nation. No force in the world can rob them of their destiny.

In 1917 the British, worried by the collapse of their ally Tsarist Russia, promised that they would involve more Indians in the government of their country. In the Montagu-Chelmsford Report, they accepted the principle of self-government for India, and began to prepare for it by handing over certain government departments (such as those responsible for public health and education) to elected Indian ministers. A review of the reforms was promised after they had been in operation for ten years, when the next stage towards responsible government would be decided.

The prospects of keeping any remaining Indian goodwill, however, were clouded over by three events in 1919. The first was the passage of the Rowlatt Acts, as a result of which agitators and anyone suspected of conspiring against British rule could be arrested and tried without benefit of legal counsel, jury, or appeal against sentence. The other two events were the emergence of a new leader, Mohandas Karamchand Gandhi, who became the symbol of Indian independence until his death in 1948, and the Amritsar Massacre.

Gandhi and the Indian independence movement

Gandhi returned to India in 1915 from South Africa, where he had led the Indian community in their fight against racial discrimination by the South African government. There he had devel-oped the strategy of civil disobedience and non-cooperation, which he called *satyagraha*, or 'soul force', as a method of protest.

Gandhi, more than anyone else, realised that the millions of Indian peasants constituted an immense political force if only they could be involved in the struggle for freedom. Furthermore, he was convinced that British rule, based as it was on the support of 4000 administrators and 70,000 troops, could only survive so long as it had the goodwill of Indians. Faced with the passive resistance of the whole population, he believed that Britain's authority in India would rapidly crumble away.

Gandhi's impact was astounding. By using religion as the basis of political action, he transformed the independence movement. Jawaharlal Nehru, who became India's first Prime Minister, was captivated by the teachings of the *Mahatma*, or 'great soul', as Gandhi was called, and described his effect upon the Indian political scene in these words:

Then Gandhi came. He was like a beam of light that pierced the darkness and removed the scales from our eyes; like a whirlwind that upset many things, but most of all the working of people's minds. He did not descend from the top; he seemed to emerge from the millions of India, speaking their language and incessantly drawing attention to them and their appalling condition. The essence of his teaching was fearlessness and truth, and action allied to these.

Gandhi condemned the new security measures introduced by the Rowlatt Acts, and called for a *hartal*, a Hindu method of protest, when all shops and businesses were closed as a sign of mourning. Everywhere Hindus responded to Gandhi's call, but what was intended to be a peaceful demonstration of Indian unity and opposition to foreign rule led to riots and killings all over India. This was especially so in Amritsar, a holy city in the Punjab, where tensions were high as a result of economic distress and bitter religious rivalries between Sikhs, Muslims and Hindus.

British officials in the Punjab believed that communist agitators were responsible for organising the *hartal*, and they feared a general uprising of the population, with the lives and property of Europeans at the mercy of the mob. On 10 April 1919 a large crowd tried to enter the European residential quarter of Amritsar. Turned back by armed police the crowd burned public buildings in the city centre and killed a number of Europeans. Thereupon General Dyer banned all public meetings. When this order was disobeyed on 13 April he took a detachment of ninety soldiers to break up the meeting. He arrived at the meeting place to find a large crowd, which he believed was being roused to violence. Fearing for the lives of his troops, he ordered them to open fire without warning. Within minutes, 379 people had been killed, and over 1000 had been wounded. Dyer was convinced he had prevented the outbreak of a revolt, but his action inflamed Indian public opinion.

In the aftermath of the Amritsar Massacre, Gandhi pleaded with Muslims and Hindus to unite in a campaign of civil disobedience which, he declared, would achieve *swaraj* (self-government) within one year. His call for non-violence, however, went unheeded; as religious riots and killings spread, Gandhi brought about an end to passive resistance, horrified by the hatreds he had released. Arrested and sentenced to six years' imprisonment, he was freed after two years on the grounds of his ill-health, since the authorities dreaded the consequences if Gandhi died in prison.

For several years Gandhi dissociated himself from the struggle for independence, preferring to work for the admission of the large class of 'untouchables' into Hindu society, and encouraging cottage spinning and weaving of cloth in order to make Indians feel self-reliant. This aspect of Gandhi's work is commemorated by the inclusion of the spinning wheel as the symbol of freedom on India's national flag.

Gandhi's seclusion from political life mystified many of his followers, but in 1930 he returned to the forefront of the independence movement. In 1928 Nehru, by now President of the All India Congress, demanded complete independence for India. In January 1930, at meetings all over India, the Congress flag was raised and proclamations of independence were read out. Neither the British authorities, however, nor the Indian population as a whole, took

any notice. What was needed was a dramatic event in order to focus public attention on the issue. Gandhi, with his gift for publicity, supplied the answer.

He decided to break the laws regarding the salt tax. The manufacture and sale of salt was a government monopoly from which it derived a large income, since salt was a vital commodity in everyone's lives. Gandhi stated he would walk 240 miles from his home in Ahmedabad to the coast at Dandi, where he would gather his own salt free of charge. Setting out on his journey with seventy-nine followers he was soon joined by thousands of others. At first the government ignored this defiance of its authority, but as violence erupted in one city after another it decided to act. In May 1930 Gandhi was arrested, and in the next few months 60,000 people were imprisoned for civil disobedience. They included Nehru, who was sentenced to six months' gaol for breaking the salt laws.

With the Congress Party and Britain locked in a bitter confrontation, a Round Table Conference was convened in London to discuss the problem of India. The Congress leaders refused to attend, but Gandhi, who was anxious for a peaceful solution, shocked the die-hards by agreeing to a truce. By this agreement, the government released all political prisoners in return for Congress abandoning the civil disobedience campaign. Gandhi and the Congress leaders went to London in 1931 and attended the talks.

The Round Table Conference achieved very little, for neither Congress nor Gandhi would be satisfied with anything less than complete independence, which the British were not prepared to consider at that stage. A stalemate followed: Britain realised that the Congress was a major political force in India, without whose participation no permanent solution to the Indian problem was possible, while Congress leaders admitted that British rule could not be overthrown by force.

In 1935 the London government passed a new Government of India Act. This established a federal system for India by giving the provinces self-government, with elected assemblies and Indian ministers responsible to them, and making provision for the admission of the princely states into a future Indian Union. Congress took part in the elections held in 1937, winning clear majorities in five out of eleven provinces, and emerging as the largest party in three others. Flushed with victory, Nehru rejected cooperation with the Muslim League, declaring that the only two forces in India were British imperialism and Indian nationalism, as represented by Congress.

Nehru strove to maintain Indian unity, but the Muslim and Hindu communities' fear and mistrust of each other grew. Congress was infuriated when Britain involved India without consultation in the war against Germany, and demanded a promise of independence after the war, with virtual self-government in the meantime. When this was refused, the provincial Congress governments resigned, and Congress waged a 'Quit India' campaign against the British. Although Sir Stafford Cripps was sent to India in 1942 to offer the Indians Dominion

status after the war, this did not satisfy the Congress leaders (who had been imprisoned by the British), since they still wanted independence without delay. The Muslim League was overjoyed by the tactics of Congress, and the chance of a compromise between the two nationalist movements vanished. India was now set firmly upon the road to partition.

Indian independence and partition 1947

Gandhi once declared:

I shall work for an India in which the poorest shall feel that it is their country, in whose making they have an effective voice, an India in which there shall be no high class and low class of people, an India in which all communities shall live in perfect harmony. This is the India of my dreams.

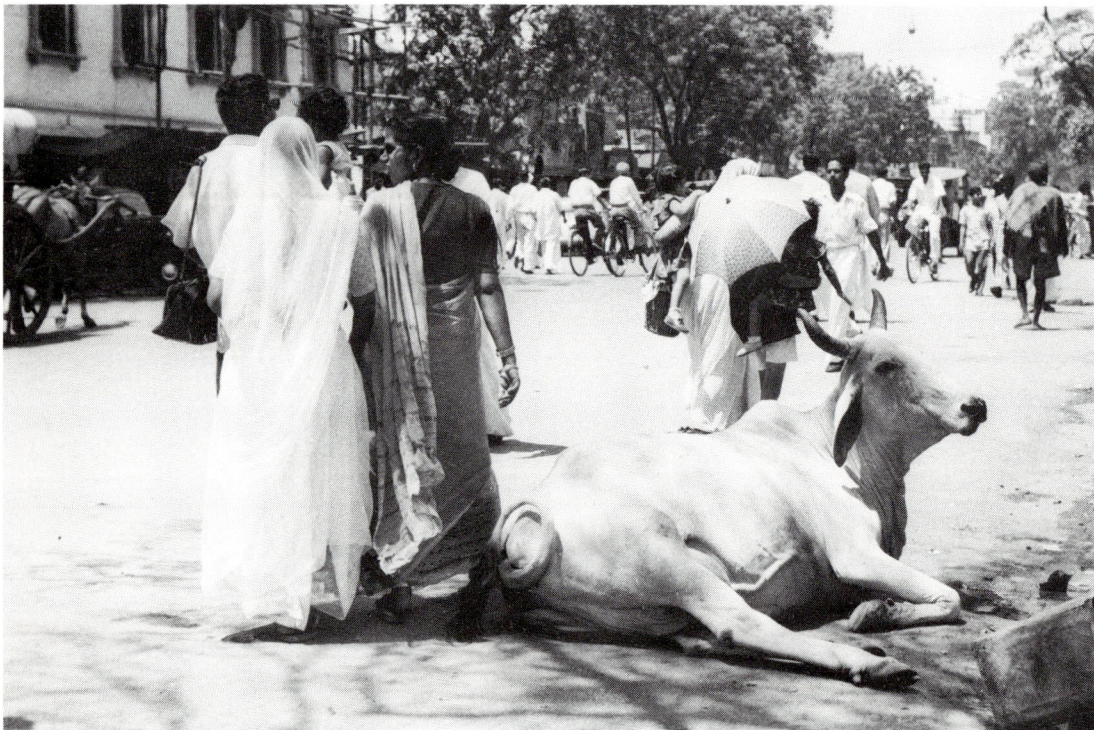

A sacred cow lies undisturbed in the old city of Delhi.

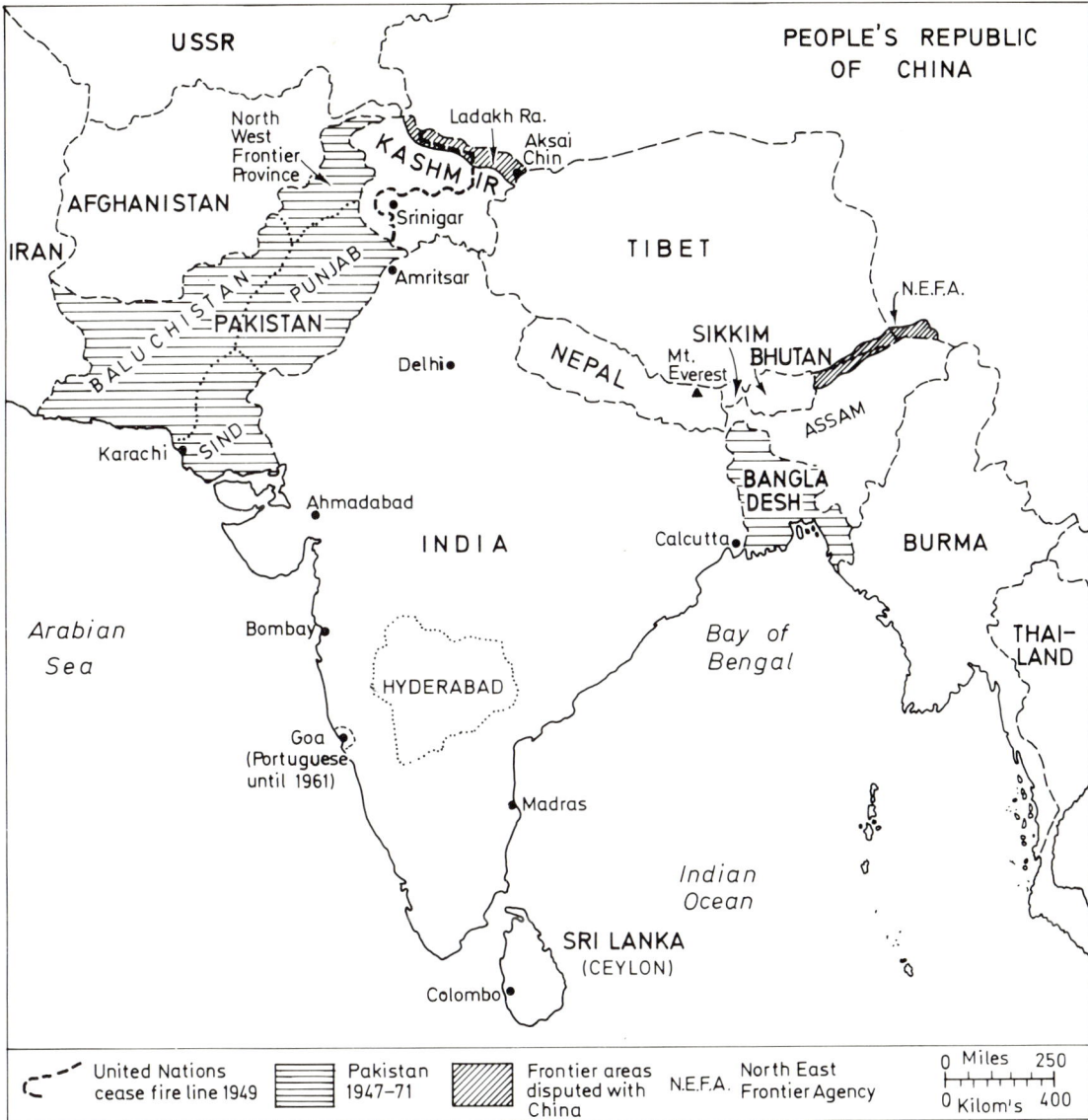

21   *The Indian sub-continent since independence*

Sadly, Gandhi's dreams of Indian unity proved impossible. To understand why this was so it is necessary to appreciate the intensity of religious beliefs among Hindus and Muslims.

In the Hindu faith the cow is sacred, venerated as the symbol of a life-giving force. Cows are allowed to wander freely unharmed, and to eat whatever they wish; the sin of killing a cow is, in Hindu eyes, no different in degree from the sin of killing a human being. Muslims, on the other hand, have no such regard for the cow, and they infuriated their Hindu neighbours by openly displaying the slaughtered carcasses of cows in their butchers' shops. Hindus, knowing

Muslims require silence during their prayers, arranged for noisy processions to file past mosques while devout Muslims were attending their compulsory prayers. Killings for religious motives were commonplace, and where Hindus or Muslims were in a minority they lived in fear for their lives. Leaders of both communities urged their members to avenge the wrongs done to them in the past.

The great majority of Indians were Hindus, but there were over ninety million Muslims. After the Second World War the Muslim minority, led by Jinnah, demanded that those parts of India where the Muslim population was most heavily concentrated should become the separate state of Pakistan. The name was derived by taking the first letters of Punjab, Afghanistan, and Kashmir and the last five letters of Baluchistan.

Bodies litter the streets of Calcutta after riots on the eve of a Muslim religious festival. Over 3000 people were believed to have been killed.

The Muslim demands, and the Congress opposition to them, caused communal riots in many parts of the country. Lord Wavell, the Viceroy of India, consequently advised the British government to postpone independence for fear of even greater bloodshed. The Labour government, however, led by Clement Attlee, was determined to achieve a rapid solution to the Indian problem. Wavell was thus replaced in 1947 by Lord Mountbatten, who had instructions to arrange for the transfer of power to India no later than June 1948. In fact, Mountbatten accomplished his task with impressive speed, having persuaded Congress to accept the principle of partition.

The Indian Independence Act was passed in August 1947, when the separate states of India and Pakistan came into being. Pakistan was composed of two areas separated from each other by one thousand miles of Indian territory. They were West Pakistan, formed by the union of Frontier Province, Sind, Baluchistan and West Punjab, and East Pakistan, which was allocated East Bengal and part of Assam. The Indian princes were urged to join either India or Pakistan, and only two did not do so almost immediately. The Nizam of Hyderabad, reputed to be the richest man in the world, hoped to maintain his state's independence, but when law and order began to crumble in his territory, India seized the chance to annex it in September 1948. The other state was Kashmir, which was claimed by both India and Pakistan.

The Kashmir problem

The Maharajah of Kashmir and the ruling class were Hindu, but the population was predominantly Muslim and anxious for union with Pakistan. As the Maharajah hesitated, undecided what to do, the small territory of Poonch tried to break away in October 1947. Muslim tribesmen from Pakistan invaded Kashmir, and the ruler appealed to India for help. Nehru agreed on condition that Kashmir should associate itself with the Indian Union, and Indian troops were sent just in time to save the capital, Srinigar, from capture.

Muslims head for refugee camps in Pakistan.

Although Nehru promised that the people of Kashmir would be allowed to vote on their political future when law and order had been restored, Pakistan accused the Indian government of using the tribal invasion as an excuse to annex the province. Nehru, on the other hand, believed that Pakistan had secretly planned to seize it, hoping to present India with a *fait accompli*. War broke out between the two countries in 1948, and India referred the dispute to the United Nations Security Council which succeeded in arranging a ceasefire for January 1949.

Relations between India and Pakistan steadily deteriorated, and all attempts to solve the Kashmir problem failed. The Maharajah was deposed in 1949, but the promised plebiscite was never held. As tens of thousands of Muslims fled from Kashmir into neighbouring Pakistan, to be replaced by an influx of Hindus from India, so the structure of society was transformed in India's favour. A new constitution, based on the expectation that Kashmir would eventually form part of the Indian Union, was introduced in 1953, when the pro-Indian chief minister of Kashmir declared that his country was part of India and would remain so.

The Kashmir dispute became part of the Cold War in 1954, when Pakistan joined the South East Asia Treaty Organisation (SEATO), an alliance created by the United States as part of its world-wide strategy to contain communism (see Chapter Nineteen). Nehru, resenting the way in which the Western powers had strengthened India's chief enemy, withdrew his promise to hold a plebiscite in Kashmir, and established closer constitutional ties between it and India. Pakistan asked the United Nations to declare the new arrangements null and void, but the Soviet Union supported India and vetoed the resolution.

India became finally convinced that Pakistan would not accept a peaceful settlement of the Kashmir problem when Pakistan made a border agreement with China, following the brief Indo-China War over their disputed frontiers in 1962 (see Chapter Twelve). When the United States and Britain sent military aid to India, a second Pakistani-Indian conflict became inevitable.

Fighting between the two countries broke out in August 1965. China showed its sympathy for Pakistan by massing troops on the Sikkim border, but the great powers acted quickly to prevent the conflict spreading. President Ayub Khan of Pakistan, and Mr Lal Bahadur Shastri (who became premier when Nehru died in 1964) agreed to a truce. In 1966 the Russian Premier, Alexei Kosygin, brought the two leaders together at Tashkent, in the Soviet Union. There they promised not to resort to war as a means of resolving the Kashmir dispute, while the Soviet Union for its part agreed to act as the guarantor of India and Pakistan's frontiers. It was not until 1972, however, that India and Pakistan agreed to a ceasefire line in Kashmir and the exchange of prisoners-of-war, and only in 1976 did the two countries resume diplomatic relations with each other. In the meantime Pakistan had been torn apart by civil war.

The establishment of Bangladesh

Although East and West Pakistan formed a single state during the period 1947–71, it was only their fear of India which kept them united, for they had little else in common except the Muslim religion. Jinnah, who had immense prestige as the founder of Pakistan, might have succeeded in overcoming the fears and prejudices which divided the two communities, but his death in September 1948 deprived the new state of a great leader. His successor, Liaquat Ali Khan, was unable to achieve a constitutional settlement in the face of religious animosities between devout and moderate Muslims before he was assassinated in October 1951, and agreement on a constitution was not reached until 1956. After various short-lived governments had failed to promote political stability, martial law

was imposed upon the country in 1958 by General Ayub Khan.

The excessive political and economic influence of West Pakistan was fiercely resented by the predominantly Bengali population of East Pakistan, which had been most vociferous in demanding secession from India in 1947. During the 1950s East Pakistan became steadily poorer in comparison with its western counterpart, which spent most of the foreign aid received by the government and achieved some economic growth. The favoured treatment of West Pakistan was highlighted in 1960 by the agreement with India. The latter was given permission to draw off water from the eastern Punjab rivers, while Pakistan received massive financial help for building the Mangla and Tarbela Dams on the river Indus, to provide irrigation for agriculture and hydro-electric power for industry.

In 1968 there was widespread dissatisfaction with Ayub Khan's rule, and he was forced to hand over power to the commander-in-chief of Pakistan's armed forces, General Yahya Khan. The General reimposed martial law, preparatory to holding elections to an assembly which would draw up a fresh constitution for Pakistan. As a result of the elections the Awami party in East Pakistan which wanted independence, with the sole exception of foreign policy, emerged with a clear majority.

When Yahya Khan suspended the new assembly before it could draft a constitution, Sheik Mujib, leader of the Awami party, ordered a general strike in East Pakistan, where the President's authority to govern was completely rejected. Yahya Khan was determined to crush Bengali nationalism, and in March 1971 West Pakistani troops launched a ruthless military operation to crush the revolt.

Thus began a bitter civil war in which terrible atrocities were committed. Mujib was arrested, but some of his colleagues escaped into India, where they proclaimed themselves the government-in-exile of the new state of Bangladesh ('Bengal State'). India, which strongly favoured the separatist movement, invaded East Pakistan in December 1971, and rapidly defeated the West Pakistani army. In January 1972 Mujib became

Prime Minister of Bangladesh, the third independent state in the India sub-continent. At the Simla Conference in the same year, Mrs Indira Gandhi, the Indian Prime Minister, and Zulfiquar Ali Bhutto, the new President of Pakistan, agreed to withdraw their troops behind their countries' pre-war frontiers.

Bhutto's downfall

Bhutto was President of Pakistan until 1973, when he became Prime Minister under an amended constitution. He withdrew Pakistan from the Commonwealth in 1972, but faced severe problems at home, with a tribal revolt in Baluchistan in 1973 and violent unrest in the North West Frontier Province in 1975. Bhutto banned the Awami party, which he accused of encouraging parts of Pakistan to break away, and in the 1977 elections his party (the Pakistan People's party) won 155 of the 200 seats in the Assembly. Bhutto was immediately accused by his opponents of rigging the elections, and in July 1977 he was deposed by a military coup led by General Mohammed Zia ul Haq. In September 1977 Bhutto was arrested and charged with conspiring to murder a political opponent. He was found guilty and, despite world-wide pleas for clemency, was hanged in April 1979.

India's role in world affairs

The three wars with Pakistan were, in an important sense, uncharacteristic of India's foreign policy, which was an extension to international affairs of Gandhi's philosophy of non-violence. Their causes may be attributed to the circumstances in which independence was granted, rather than to fear of attack or desire for territorial aggrandisement. Certainly, with

Not all problems are solved by independence. This camp in Bangladesh gives some idea of the conditions under which people are still living.

the defeat of Germany and Japan in 1945, the Indian government felt it had nothing to fear from any of the great powers. For Britain, India had only a warm regard, and its decision to stay in the Commonwealth when it became a republic in 1950 was important for the future development of the Commonwealth. Nehru believed that the Russian threat to India, which had loomed so large in the minds of British statesmen and soldiers concerned with their responsibilities for British India, had never been real. Even if it had been, he thought, it had disappeared when the British left. India regarded China as an equal and, of the non-communist states, it was preceded only by Burma in recognising the People's Republic of China.

India therefore followed a policy of non-alignment, carefully refusing to take sides in the Cold War which had developed between the two superpowers after the Second World War. Nehru strongly opposed colonialism, and tried to form an Afro-Asian bloc of countries which could act as a third force in world affairs. He accepted Soviet military aid during India's dispute with Pakistan, and American aid following the border dispute with China in 1962, but avoided making military commitments to either great power. Although the genuineness of India's neutralism has sometimes been suspect (as, for example, when it seized the Portuguese possession of Goa in 1961) events since 1947 have given proof of India's determination to remain aloof from the struggle between the communist and non-communist camps.

Burma

From 1886 until 1937, when it was given a measure of self-government, Burma formed part of British India. During the Second World War the Burmese at first regarded the Japanese invaders as liberators, but having no wish to exchange British control for Japanese, they helped British forces to drive the Japanese out of Burma. The Union of Burma was proclaimed in 1948, when it immediately withdrew from the Commonwealth. Despite its dislike of the Western world, arising largely from experience of colonial rule, Burma has maintained a neutralist policy since independence, resisting communist influences from China, with which it shares a common frontier.

Ceylon

Ceylon (renamed Sri Lanka in 1972), a densely populated area of 24,000 square miles, gained independence along with India and Pakistan in 1947, when it became a Dominion within the Commonwealth. Britain remained responsible for the island's defence until 1956, when Ceylon became a republic, though it kept its membership of the Commonwealth. It joined the Colombo Plan in 1951, whereby twenty-one governments agreed to cooperate in promoting the economic development of Asian countries that needed aid. Ceylon refused to join SEATO however, for like its powerful continental neighbour, it had no wish to be involved in Cold War rivalries.

At the end of the Second World War Britain occupied a predominant position in the Middle East. Both France and Italy ceased to be Middle Eastern colonial powers; the promise of independence given in 1941 by General de Gaulle to the French mandates of Syria and Lebanon was confirmed in 1946. Italy also was forced by the peace settlement of 1947 to surrender its African empire. Neither the United States nor the Soviet Union, which was preoccupied with establishing its control over Eastern Europe, wished to become directly involved in Middle Eastern affairs.

The British government was aware that not all Arabs welcomed its influence, but it was not prepared to sacrifice vital interests in the oil-producing states of the Persian Gulf and in the Suez Canal. Sensibly, however, in its relationships with the Arab countries, Britain relied less upon military power than upon sponsorship of Arab unity; this it was hoped, would foster friendship between Britain and the Arab rulers. Thus Britain welcomed the Alexandria Conference on Arab Unity in 1944, which led to the creation of the Arab League in 1945. Its founder members were Egypt, Iraq, Transjordan, Syria, Lebanon, Saudi Arabia and Yemen.

The Arab League, however, did not become Britain's ally, since Arab nationalists were united in their determination to expel Western European influence from the Middle East. Although the Arab League was weakened by its internal rivalries and tensions, the unifying factor was a detestation of Zionism. In particular, the Arabs blamed Britain for the creation of Israel in 1948.

The end of the Palestine mandate

The Jews rallied strongly to the Allied cause during the 1939–45 war, although they distrusted the British government, which they considered had broken the promise made in the Balfour Declaration (1917) to establish a Jewish National Home in Palestine. As evidence of Nazi atrocities against the Jews accumulated after the war, Zionist pressure increased for unlimited Jewish immigration into Palestine and the transformation of Palestine into a Jewish state. Although there was much sympathy for the Jewish survivors in liberated Europe, the British government kept its promise to the Arabs to halt Jewish emigration to Palestine in 1944. Thousands of Jews who sought to enter the 'promised land' were intercepted by the British navy and denied admission.

Jewish extremists in their frustration resorted to violence, and militant organisations such as the Stern Gang and the *Irgun Zwei Leumi* (National Military Organisation), launched a campaign against the British in Palestine. In 1946 Jewish terrorists placed a bomb in the King David Hotel in Jerusalem, headquarters of the British administration. Many senior British officials were killed and a pattern of guerrilla attacks, sabotage and reprisals quickly developed. When Jewish extremists hanged two British soldiers in retaliation for the execution of three terrorists, British public opinion turned from sympathy for the Jewish cause to revulsion. In February 1947, the recommendations of a joint Anglo-American commission on Palestine were rejected by both Arabs and Jews and Ernest

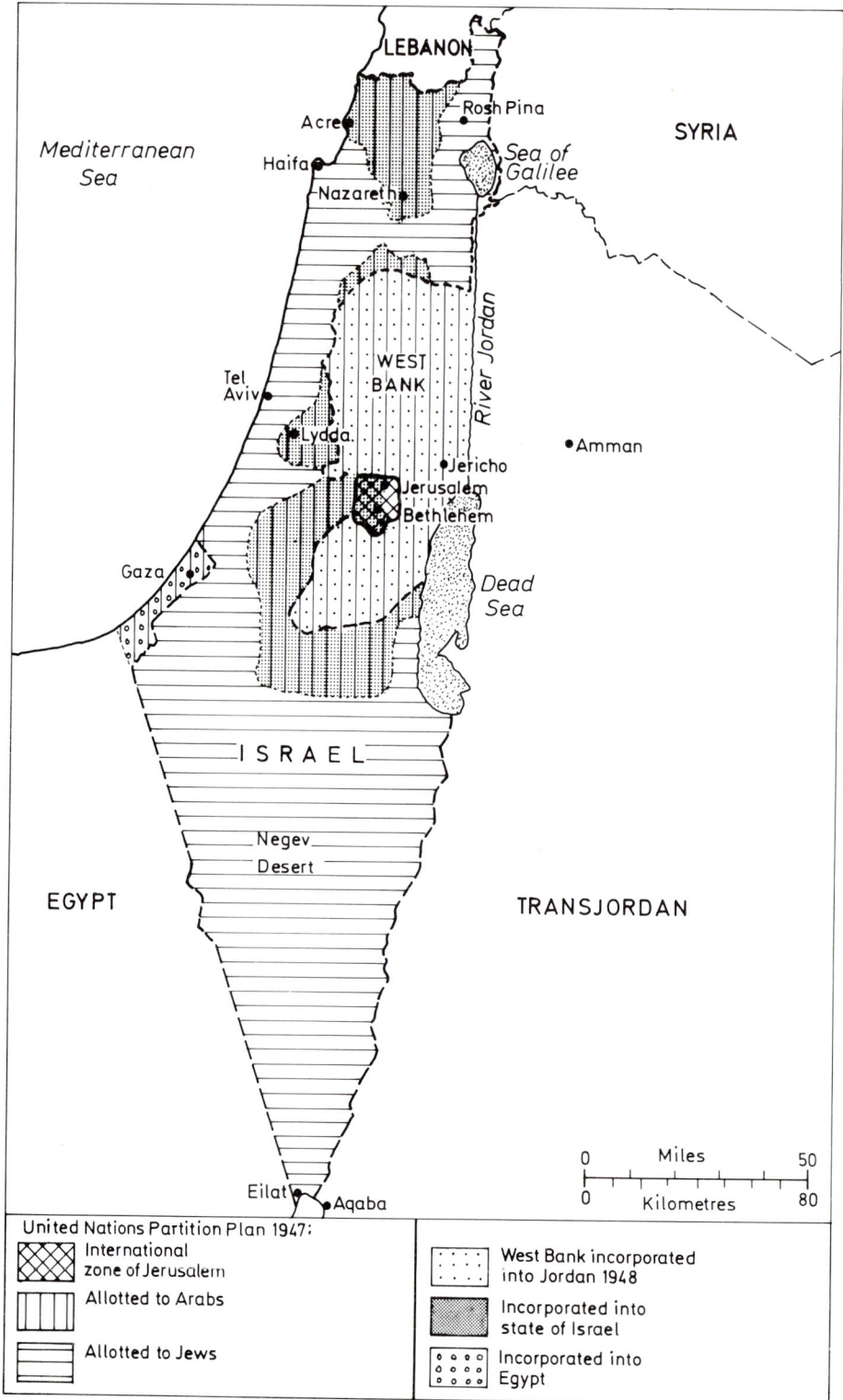

LEBANON

Acre

Rosh Pina

SYRIA

Mediterranean
Sea

Haifa

Sea of
Galilee

Nazareth

WEST
BANK

River Jordan

Tel
Aviv

Amman

Lydda

Jericho

Jerusalem
Bethlehem

Gaza

Dead
Sea

I S R A E L

Negev
Desert

EGYPT

TRANSJORDAN

0   Miles   50

0   Kilometres   80

Eilat
Aqaba

United Nations Partition Plan 1947:

International
zone of Jerusalem

West Bank incorporated
into Jordan 1948

Allotted to Arabs

Incorporated into
state of Israel

Allotted to Jews

Incorporated into
Egypt

22   *The making of Israel, 1947–48*

Bevin, the British Foreign Secretary, handed over responsibility for the Palestine mandate to the United Nations. A deadline was fixed for the withdrawal of British troops on 14 May 1948.

The UN set up a special commission on Palestine, which recommended its partition into separate Arab and Jewish states, with Jerusalem under international trusteeship. The Jews were overjoyed, but the Arabs were bitterly hostile to the proposed amputation of part of Palestine in order to create a Jewish state. Nevertheless, the General Assembly approved the plan by thirty-three votes to thirteen. Britain, having declared that it would only support proposals acceptable to both sides, abstained, but both the United States and the Soviet Union voted in favour of partition. Palestine sank into anarchy as Arab extremists joined the struggle. The British troops maintained a precarious neutrality, seeking only to prevent Jewish forces from capturing territory allocated to the Arabs by the UN partition plan.

In January 1948 Arab guerrillas entered Palestine, where they attacked Jewish settlements and blockaded the Jewish quarter of Jerusalem. Jewish reprisals were savage and indiscriminate as Arabs and Jews tried to win as much territory as possible before the British troops left. Horrified by the scale of guerrilla warfare, the United States asked the British government to keep its troops in Palestine, but it refused, and on 14 May 1948 the Palestine mandate expired.

The foundation of the state of Israel

On the same day the state of Israel was proclaimed by David Ben Gurion in Tel Aviv. The next day the armies of the Arab League invaded Israel, but the *Haganah* (originally a Jewish militia formed to protect Jewish settlements from terrorist raids) proved more than a match for the Arabs. Well-trained and completely dedicated, the Jews won considerably more territory than had been allocated to them by the UN partition plan. On the Arab side only the British-trained Arab Legion of Transjordan emerged from the struggle with credit, as elsewhere the badly-led Arab armies suffered a series of humiliating defeats.

The armistice agreement which ended the First Arab-Israeli War left Israel with the lion's share of Palestine, including the New City of Jerusalem, parts of Galilee and the Negev. The West Bank of Jordan, with the Old City of Jerusalem, was annexed by Transjordan, thereafter renamed Jordan. Egypt acquired the Gaza Strip, a narrow belt of land bordering the Mediterranean.

The Zionists had triumphed in their aim of creating a Jewish state. An immigrant population had been permitted to build up its numbers in an Arab country (at a time when the Arabs had been prevented by the British mandate from taking any action except to protest) and had seized its independence by armed force. An independent Palestinian state, proposed in the UN partition plan, never came into existence. Instead, nearly one million Palestinian Arabs fled from their homeland into neighbouring Arab countries.

Peace talks on the island of Rhodes dragged on until they broke down in deadlock in 1951. The Arabs refused to make peace until all the Palestinian refugees had been reinstated, while the Israelis refused to discuss this matter until the Arabs recognised Israel and the ceasefire lines developed into Israel's unofficial frontiers. Meanwhile the Arab League intensified its boycott of Jews. After 1950 all ships bound for Israel were blacklisted and banned from calling at Arab ports. Soon the boycott was extended to airspace, and in 1955 Egypt warned the Israeli airline that if its planes flew over the Tiran Straits they would be fired upon. In an attempt to reduce the chances of another war breaking out, Britain, France and the United States signed the Tripartite Agreement in 1950, whereby sales of armaments to Middle East countries were restricted.

The decline of British and French influence

Arab nationalism, intensified by the 1948–9 war, soon clashed directly with Western European imperialism. In April 1951, under the leadership of Dr Mussadeq, Iran nationalised the Anglo-Iranian Oil Company. Britain protested and referred the matter to the UN Security Council, which ruled that the dispute came within the domestic jurisdiction of Iran. Had it not been for the rapid exploitation of Kuwait's oilfields, petrol rationing would have resulted in Britain.

In October 1951 the Egyptian government denounced the Anglo-Egyptian Treaty of 1936, and demanded the evacuation of British troops from the Canal Zone and the Sudan. Britain refused to accept that Egypt could tear up a treaty of its own accord, and held on to its base, despite

the protests of Egyptian nationalists. In July 1952 King Farouk of Egypt was deposed by a military coup headed by Colonels Neguib and Nasser and the Anglo-Egyptian dispute cooled as they consolidated their revolution. The two countries reached agreement over the Sudan, which was given the right to choose either to join Egypt, or become independent. (It chose the latter in 1956.) By the Cairo Agreement (1954), Britain undertook to withdraw its forces from the Canal Zone in 1956, while Egypt promised Britain military facilities in the event of one of the Arab League states, or Turkey, being

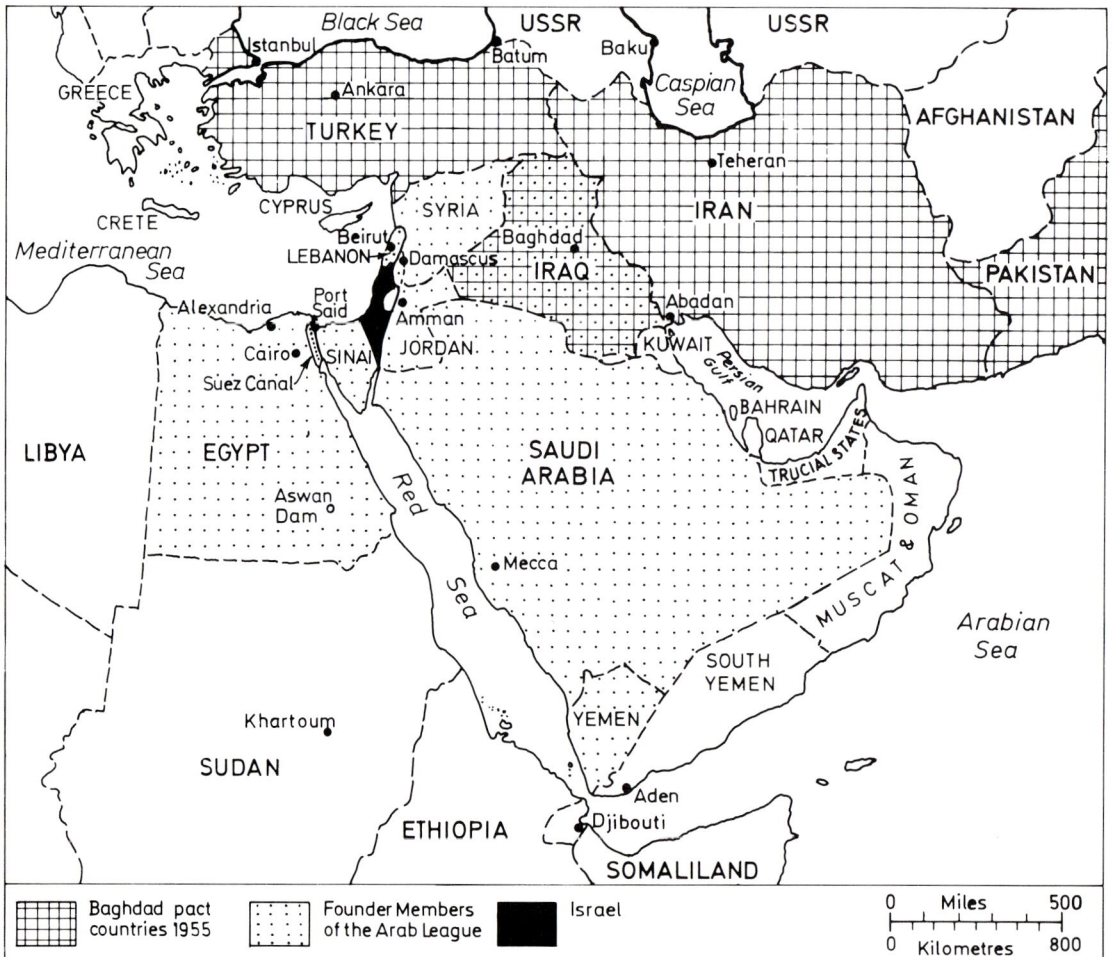

23   *The Middle East, 1955*

attacked. Nasser (who had deposed Neguib as President in April 1954) agreed that the Suez Canal Company, whose shares were owned by the British and French governments, should continue to operate the Canal. Ships of all nations could use the Canal in time of peace or war (as laid down by the Constantinople Convention of 1888), except that the ban on Israeli shipping, imposed in 1948, would be maintained.

The Baghdad Pact

Although John Foster Dulles, the American Secretary of State, regarded Britain as more of a liability than an asset, he was aware that the withdrawal of its troops from Egypt would weaken Britain's military influence in the Middle East. He wished to contain Russian communism, and in particular, to prevent the Soviet Union gaining influence in the Mediterranean area. Dulles therefore organised the Baghdad Pact in 1955, a defensive league of Middle Eastern states (Iraq, Iran, Turkey and Pakistan), along with Britain, to form a barrier against Russia. The Baghdad Pact was renamed the Central Treaty Organisation (CENTO) when Iraq withdrew from it in 1959.

Nasser denounced the Baghdad Pact, since he wished to build a league of Arab states under Egypt's leadership, which would dominate the Middle East and North Africa. Moreover, the Arab states which enlisted in the Baghdad Pact would not be available for the renewal of the struggle with Israel. On the other hand if Egypt joined in order to qualify for a supply of arms from the West, as Pakistan did, it would be restricted as to their use. In particular, Nasser singled out Iraq, Egypt's rival for the leadership of the Arab world and now to be strengthened by American arms, as a traitor to the Arab cause.

Nasser's diplomacy in other directions also irritated the French and British governments. When Britain tried to persuade its ally Jordan to join the Baghdad Pact, Nasser stirred up Arab nationalist feelings – to such an extent that in March 1956 King Hussein of Jordan was forced to dismiss Glubb Pasha, the British Commander

of the Arab Legion. The British government regarded this as a blow to its prestige in the Middle East.

This incident followed closely upon Nasser's success in obtaining arms from the communist bloc. France had been selling arms to the Israelis, thus undermining the Tripartite Agreement, in retaliation for Egyptian assistance to the Algerian nationalists who were struggling for independence from French rule. Since the Western powers refused to supply arms to Egypt, Nasser negotiated with the Iron Curtain countries in order to redress the imbalance.

The Soviet Union seized the opportunity to assume the role of protector of Arab nationalism, and in September 1955 Egypt purchased Czechoslovakian arms in return for the Egyptian cotton crop. The West now faced the alarming prospect that the Soviet Union might establish a foothold in the Middle East. Nasser was idolised by the Arab nationalists for having outwitted the Western powers, who would now be forced to compete with the Soviet Union for Egypt's friendship.

In December 1955 Dulles offered American aid to finance the construction of the Aswan Dam, but Nasser delayed accepting it, hoping for a better offer of Soviet aid which he felt sure would be made. Then in June 1956 Egypt announced its recognition of communist China. Such independence, in American eyes, was carrying neutralism too far and the United States withdrew its offer of aid in order to teach Nasser a lesson.

Although the French ambassador warned the British government that Nasser would solve his financial difficulties by seizing the Canal, the announcement in July that Egypt had nationalised the Canal took the Cabinet by surprise. Nasser declared that the Canal dues, which amounted to thirty-five million pounds per year, would finance the Aswan Dam.

Both the British and the French governments believed that their countries' vital interests were threatened by the nationalisation of the Canal. Over eighty per cent of the oil used by Western Europe was imported from the Middle East, the greater part of it in tankers which used the Canal. Anthony Eden, the British Prime Minister, claimed that Nasser's move was an act of plunder, as a result of which Western Europe could be blackmailed by the interruption of the free flow of oil upon which industries depended.

Eden mistakenly saw Nasser as another Hitler and declared that the West should not repeat the mistake it made in the Thirties by appeasing a dictator. He argued that:

The seizure of the Suez Canal is the opening gambit in a campaign designed by Nasser to expel all Western influence and interest from Arab countries. He believes that if he can get away with it, his prestige in Arabia will be so great that he will be able to mount revolutions of young officers in Saudi Arabia, Jordan, Syria and Iraq. These new governments will in effect be Egyptian satellites, if not Russian ones. When that moment comes Nasser can deny oil to Western Europe and we shall be at his mercy.

The Israelis had more cause for alarm, since their security was endangered as a result of Egypt's recent arms deal. They secretly discussed plans with the British and French governments for a combined attack on Egypt, so that negotiations to resolve the Canal dispute peacefully had little hope of success.

The Suez War 1956

On 29 October 1956 Israeli forces launched a lightning attack upon the Egyptian army in the Sinai peninsula and drove rapidly towards the Canal. The following day the British and French governments issued ultimata to Egypt and Israel, ordering both sides to withdraw ten miles from the Canal. Israel readily agreed, for its forces had not yet reached the vicinity of the Canal, but Egypt refused since it was not the aggressor. Five days later British and French aircraft bombed Egyptian airfields, and paratroops captured Port Said. The British and French governments claimed that they had acted to protect the Canal.

World reaction to these moves was almost uniformly hostile. The Soviet Union threatened rocket attacks on London and Paris. The United States refused to support its allies, and deplored Anglo-French 'gunboat diplomacy' as a relic of nineteenth century imperialism. The Commonwealth was divided, as were the British and French peoples, and a sterling crisis developed. The UN passed a resolution ordering a cease fire. Under these pressures the British yielded,

Work in progress on the diversion channel outlet of the Aswan Dam.

Israeli troops poised for attack in their Sherman tanks.

and when the French and Israelis were forced to follow suit the humiliation of Britain and France was complete.

A UN Emergency Force was despatched to Egypt in November to supervise the ceasefire. In March 1957 the Israelis reluctantly withdrew from the Gaza Strip and the Gulf of Aqaba coastline, for possession of these territories might have prevented the resumption of border raids upon Israel and would have opened up the Gulf to Israeli shipping. Once more the Arab states refused to make peace and Egypt resumed the blockade of Israel. For the next ten years an uneasy peace reigned on the Gaza-Eilat armistice line.

The Suez War proved beyond doubt that the special relationship between Britain and the United States no longer existed. Some British politicians felt that the latter was prepared to sacrifice Britain's interests for the sake of its world-wide objectives. The Western alliance system was strained, but Russia's ruthless suppression of the Hungarian Revolt, from which the world's gaze had been diverted by events in the Middle East, quickly restored its unity.

The United Nations, which had reacted decisively to the attack upon Egypt, the United States and the Soviet Union, all emerged with increased prestige in the Afro-Asian countries. The United States had lived up to its reputation as an opponent of colonialism, while Soviet propaganda stressed the part played by the Kremlin in bringing about an end to the war.

For Nasser, despite the defeat of the Egyptian army, the Suez affair was a diplomatic triumph, and he became a hero of the Arab world. He had defied the forces of Western imperialism and had emerged supreme in the eyes of his countrymen. Meanwhile, Eden and Mollet, the architects of the Suez venture, faded into the political background.

The Eisenhower Doctrine 1957

The Middle East had been relatively free from communist influence, but with the decline of British power in the region the United States feared that the Soviet Union would exploit its friendship with Egypt. President Eisenhower, therefore, offered American economic aid and military protection to any Arab government which requested help.

The pro-Western governments of Iraq and Lebanon welcomed the American offer, while King Hussein of Jordan dismissed his ministers, who had insisted that it should be rejected. Only Egypt and Syria stuck firmly to their neutralist policies.

The United Arab Republic (UAR)

To the Arab masses Nasser was the symbol of Arab nationalism, which meant freedom from Western imperialism. In Syria the Ba'athist party, which was socialist and nationalist, supported Nasser's plans to unite the Arab world and with the approval of the Syrian army it negotiated the federal union of Egypt and Syria. Though the Ba'athists disliked Nasser's insistence on a one party state, they were confident that they could assert their influence in the National Union, the only political organisation tolerated in Egypt. Nasser's conditions, therefore, were accepted, and the United Arab Republic was proclaimed in February 1958.

This event awakened extraordinary enthusiasm in the Arab populations. In Iraq a military coup overthrew the pro-Western government of Feisal and his Prime Minister, Nuri es-Said, who was lynched by the mob. General Kassem came to power and withdrew Iraq from the Baghdad Pact, declaring Iraq part of the Arab nation. Arab nationalists were jubilant over the destruction of a pro-Western monarchy. In the Lebanon popular disturbances forced President Chamoun to appeal for American aid, and marines from the US Sixth Fleet landed in Beirut to prop up his tottering regime. At the same time British troops were flown from Cyprus to Jordan to support Hussein's government.

The Arab world divided

Despite Kassem's pronouncements on Arab unity, relations between Iraq and Egypt remained cold. Kassem encouraged the formation of a so-called Palestinian Army as a means of embarrassing Egypt and Jordan. Both of these countries had ruled parts of Palestine ever since the end of the 1948 Arab-Israeli War. Nasser in turn encouraged the Kurds in the Mosul region to revolt against Iraqi rule. When Kassem claimed Kuwait immediately after it had been granted independence by the British in June 1961, Nasser supported Kuwait's claim to stay independent. Kassem's death during a military coup in 1963 did little to heal the divisions within the Arab world, for by that time the UAR had collapsed, and Egypt was involved in the civil war in the Yemen.

The collapse of the UAR, 1961

The Syrians were soon disillusioned by their new relationship with Egypt. The Communists were suppressed, and the Ba'athists resented the authoritarian nature of Nasser's government. Syria was exploited to benefit the Egyptian economy, and its inhabitants were treated as second class citizens. Moreover, the Iraqi revolution in 1958 removed Syria's fear of attack by Iraq, and lessened its dependence upon Egyptian support. In September 1961 a military *coup* in Damascus overthrew the pro-Nasser administration, and Syria's withdrawal from the UAR was announced.

The civil war in the Yemen

Yemen was one of the most backward countries in the world, but there was fierce opposition to the regime, and in 1962 Abdullah as Sallal overthrew the Imam's feudal government. Royalist forces in the north, however, rallied to the Imam's cause, and a full-scale civil war broke out. The rulers of Saudi Arabia and Jordan supplied the Yemeni royalists with money and arms, while Nasser sent Egyptian troops to help the republicans. In 1963 UN intervention failed to halt the fighting, which spread to the neighbouring South Arabian Federation. There rebel tribesmen threatened to overthrow the sheiks with whom Britain had made alliances. The security of Aden, Britain's strategic base on the route from the Persian Gulf to Europe, was threatened by these developments and Britain was drawn into the fighting.

Egypt's involvement in the Yemen proved an expensive drain on its economy, and after the Six Day War in 1967 the Egyptian government cut its losses by withdrawing its troops. The royalists failed to exploit their advantage, however, and the republicans, helped by a massive airlift of Soviet military equipment, gradually asserted an uneasy control over the country. In 1968 the civil war petered out.

Before then Britain had retreated from South Arabia. The importance of Aden had been diminished by the closure of the Suez Canal as a result of the Six Day War and the British government wisely decided that further military resistance to Arab nationalism was useless. British troops were withdrawn from the Aden Protectorate in August 1967 and the South Arabia Federation became independent as the People's Republic of South Yemen.

The Six Day War (5–10 June 1967)

Meanwhile the struggle for Yemen had been overshadowed by the Six Day War, for the 1956 war had resolved nothing. Indeed, thousands of Palestinian refugees living in makeshift camps scattered over the Gaza Strip, Syria, Lebanon and Jordan, made willing recruits for the various terrorist organisations. Jordan could do little to stop Palestinian guerrilla raids on Israeli settlements being organised on its territory. The Israelis retaliated by attacks of their own, such as that on the Jordanian town of Es Samu, which killed many troops and civilians. Syria openly sympathised with the Palestinians, and Syrian artillery lobbed shells from the Golan Heights on to the construction works connected with the Jordan river irrigation project.

In 1967 events moved rapidly towards war after a major skirmish between Syrian and Israeli

forces. Nasser reacted strongly to what he considered Israeli aggression by supporting Syria. He demanded the evacuation of the UN peacekeeping force stationed along the Gaza-Eilat armistice line; since the UN troops were only on Egyptian soil with Cairo's consent, U Thant, the UN Secretary General, had no choice but to agree. Their withdrawal left Egypt in control of the Gulf of Aqaba. Four days later Nasser closed the Straits of Tiran to Israeli shipping, an act which the Israeli government had already stated would be a sufficient cause for war. Nasser also moved Egyptian troops up to the Israeli frontier, while Jordan and Egypt signed a military alliance which was soon joined by Iraq.

Faced with these alarming developments the Israelis believed that their survival was at stake, and they decided on a pre-emptive strike to destroy the Arab armies gathering on Israel's frontiers. On 5 June Israeli forces suddenly struck. Within hours of the war breaking out, Egypt's airforce was destroyed and Israel won total air supremacy. Israeli tanks, with air cover, dashed into the Sinai peninsula, and rapidly drove the demoralised Egyptians back to the Suez Canal, capturing immense quantities of equipment. Simultaneously, the Israelis seized the West Bank of Jordan, and the Old City of Jerusalem. With Jordan and Egypt virtually knocked out of the war, Israeli forces attacked the Syrians on the hills above Galilee. When the fighting stopped on 10 June Israel had achieved all its military objectives.

The Six Day War, however, only heightened Arab-Israeli tension. In the West Bank Arab villages were destroyed to prevent their inhabitants returning, despite the UN plea that the refugees should be encouraged to return. Furthermore, the Israelis now regarded Jerusalem, a Muslim as well as a Jewish holy city, as a permanent possession.

Arab terrorist organisations such as *Al Fatah* ('the Fatherland'), and the Palestine Liberation Organisation (PLO) headed by Yasser Arafat, ensured that the Palestinian problem was kept in the forefront of the news. In 1970 a terrorist group called *Black September* attracted worldwide publicity to Palestinian claims by hijacking several airliners. During the 1972 Olympic

Jews gather together to celebrate a holy day at the Wailing Wall in Jerusalem, watched over by an armed Israeli soldier.

Games in Munich eleven members of the Israeli team were kidnapped and killed by terrorists. Israeli officials and embassies in foreign countries were also targets for the terrorist groups. The Israelis countered terror with terror. In December 1968 they attacked Beirut Airport since Lebanon was harbouring guerrillas, while in April 1973 Israeli agents killed three terrorist leaders in their hotel bedrooms in Beirut.

The Yom Kippur War (October 1973)

The fourth Arab-Israeli war began on 6 October 1973, which was Yom Kippur (the 'Day of Atonement') in the Jewish calendar. No public or private business was conducted, and all public services closed down for the day. Signs of an impending Arab attack were disregarded by Israeli Intelligence as another bluff in the war of

nerves. At mid-day, in a carefully planned and co-ordinated assault, Egyptian troops crossed the Suez Canal under the protection of anti-air-craft missiles supplied by the Soviet Union, and Syrian forces attacked Israeli strongpoints in the Golan Heights.

By 10 October, when Iraq joined the war, Israel's mobilisation had been completed, and Arab advances were being halted in the greatest tank battles the world had seen. Both Jordan and Saudi Arabia sent troops to the Syrian front, but did not open up fronts on their own frontiers. The turning point in the war came when a column of Israeli tanks crossed the Suez Canal near the Great Bitter Lake, and established a bridgehead on the other side. When Israeli forces trapped an Egyptian army in the port of Suez the end of the war was in sight. Negotiations for a ceasefire were finally concluded on 18 January 1974.

For Israel the cost of the war was heavy, for nearly 2500 soldiers had been killed. Even after the ceasefire had been agreed the Israelis dared not demobilise, and the strain on the nation's economy was severe. In November 1974 the government was forced to devalue the Israeli pound by forty-three per cent, and to increase taxes and restrict imports.

Terrorist activity had not been curtailed. The Popular Front for the Liberation of Palestine (PFLP) announced through a news agency:

Through violence alone the revolutionaries have won world-wide recognition as the representatives of the Palestinians. Only a determination to continue the struggle by violent means will enable us to consolidate our position. We will go to Geneva for peace talks when we have destroyed the state of Israel.

Israeli confidence that any Arab attack could be rapidly defeated was damaged by the Yom Kippur War. Moreover, the Israelis were uncomfortably aware that in cutting oil supplies to the Western world, the Arabs had discovered a powerful weapon to assist their cause. In October 1973 the Persian Gulf states increased their oil prices by seventeen per cent. In December they placed an embargo upon oil deliveries to the United States and the Netherlands as friends of Israel, reduced oil supplies to Western

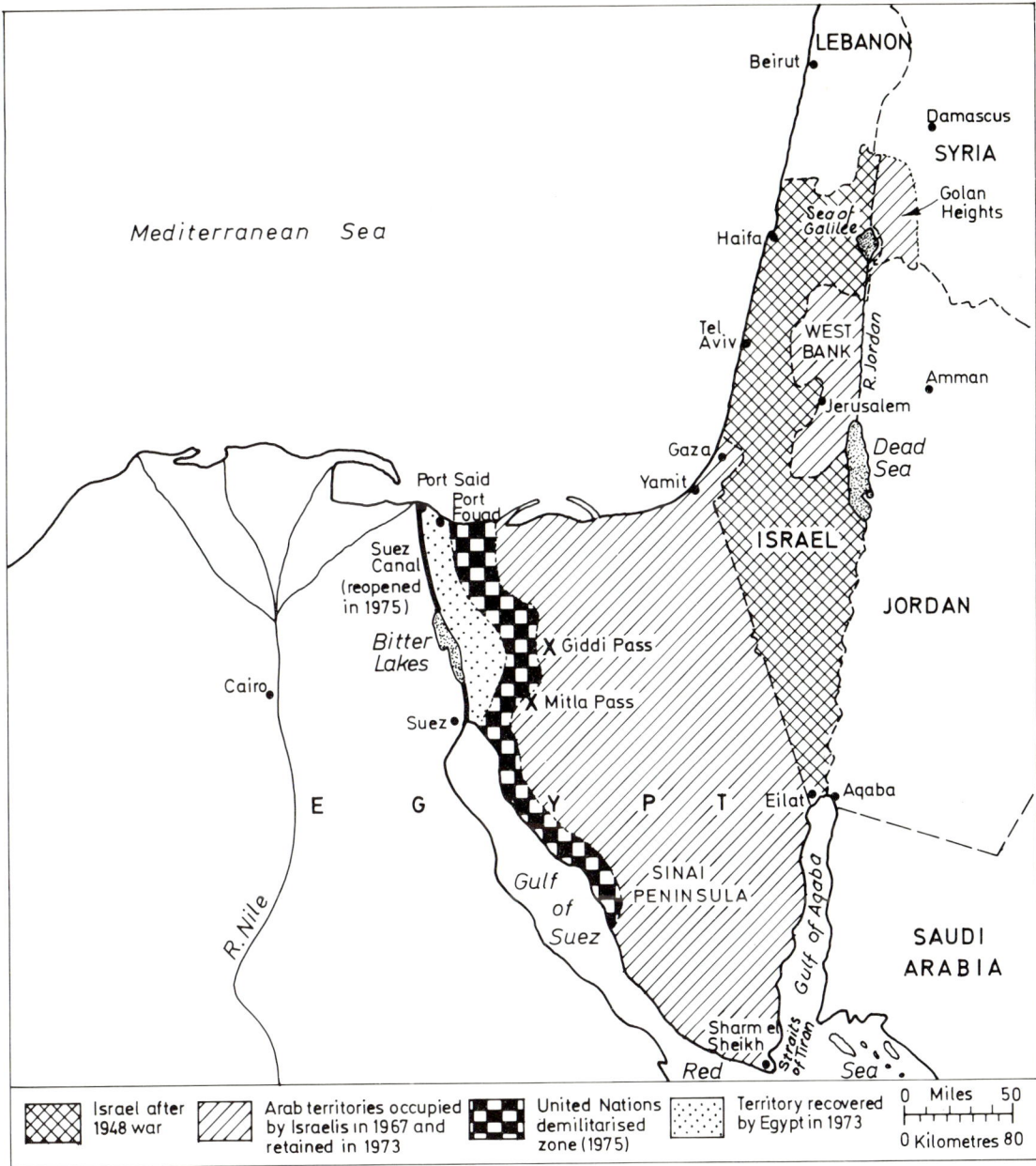

LEBANON
Beirut •

Damascus •
SYRIA

Mediterranean   Sea

Golan
Heights

Sea of
Galilee

Haifa •

Tel
Aviv •

WEST
BANK

R. Jordan

Amman •

• Jerusalem

Gaza •

Dead
Sea

Port Said
Port
Fouad

Yamit •

ISRAEL

Suez
Canal
(reopened
in 1975)

JORDAN

Bitter
Lakes

X Giddi Pass

Cairo •

X Mitla Pass

Suez •

E   G   Y   P   T   Eilat • • Aqaba

Gulf
of
Suez

SINAI
PENINSULA

SAUDI
ARABIA

R. Nile

Gulf of Aqaba

Sharm el
Sheikh

Straits of Tiran

Red   Sea

▨	Israel after 1948 war	▨	Arab territories occupied by Israelis in 1967 and retained in 1973	▨	United Nations demilitarised zone (1975)	▨	Territory recovered by Egypt in 1973	0 Miles 50

0 Kilometres 80

24   *Israel and its Arab neighbours after the Yom Kippur War, 1973*

Europe and Japan, and raised further the price of oil, from 5.10 dollars to 11.65 dollars per barrel. This decision to more than double the price of oil had very grave consequences for the balance of payments of oil importing countries; it was an important factor in causing very high rates of inflation throughout the world in the next two years. So far as the Israeli government was concerned, it was forced to recognise that there were clearly limits to the friendship and aid Israel could expect from the Western countries, whose economies depended upon imported oil.

The Rabat Conference 1974

The Rabat summit conference of Arab states supported the decision of Egypt and Syria to recognise the PLO as the representative of all the Palestinians. King Hussein of Jordan, who earlier in the year had stated his intention to recover the 'lost territory' of the West Bank, occupied by Israeli forces ever since the 1967 war, was forced to surrender any claim to the West Bank as part of his kingdom. The PLO hoped that eventually the West Bank would form the basis of a Palestinian state.

The international status which the PLO had won was again confirmed in November when the UN General Assembly also recognised the PLO as the mouthpiece of the Palestinian people. Yasser Arafat, who addressed the UN Assembly on the Palestinian problem, was surrounded by the protocol normally reserved for heads of governments.

The Civil War in Lebanon

In April 1975 violence convulsed the tiny state of Lebanon, as right wing Christian gunmen set up road blocks in parts of southern Lebanon to 'check' the identity of passing motorists. Over one hundred Muslims were dragged from their vehicles and shot in cold blood; Palestinian refugee camps were also attacked. In their turn Muslim gunmen sought revenge by attacking Christian settlements. The outbreak of civil war was a direct consequence of Lebanon's unwilling involvement in the Middle East conflict.

The pro-Western attitude of successive Lebanese governments since 1945 could not be reconciled with the growth of Arab nationalism among the Muslims, who constituted half the population. In 1958 only American intervention saved the government when Muslim nationalists, dazzled by Nasser's success in withstanding the combined assault of Britain, France and Israel, attempted to overthrow President Chamoun.

Much against the will of its government, Lebanon became a haven for Arab terrorists and refugees from the Middle East fighting. Since no Arab state after 1948 was prepared to accept responsibility for resettling hundreds of thousands of refugees, their camps became breeding grounds for various Palestinian terrorist organisations. The threat to Lebanon's stability was magnified in September 1970 ('Black September'), when King Hussein forced many Palestinians out of Jordan where they were threatening to break down law and order. Most of them fled into neighbouring Lebanon. Syrian-backed Arab commandos also moved into southern Lebanon. By the end of 1972 over 5000 *Fedayeen* ('freedom fighters') were reported to be in Lebanon, which had become known as *Fatahland*. After the Yom Kippur War the Palestinians, with their military bases, became virtually a separate state inside Lebanon.

From the relative security of neutral Lebanon Arab guerrilla bands waged unofficial war on Israel. The Palestine Liberation Organisation, which had its headquarters in Beirut, announced that all tourists to Israel were potential targets.

For the first time, a fence had to be built on the border between Israel and Lebanon in 1975 after the continual skirmishes in the area.

This was the background to terrorist attacks upon unsuspecting travellers at Athens and Rome airports in August and December 1973 respectively. Terrorist groups infiltrated Israel from southern Lebanon and attacked Israeli settlements. In one such raid on Kiriyat Shemona in April 1974 eighteen Israelis were killed. In another the following month, twenty school children died and many more were wounded when terrorists deliberately chose a school at Ma'lot as their target.

The Israelis retaliated by bombing Palestinian bases in southern Lebanon. Condemned by the UN, the Israeli raids reinforced the extremists in Lebanon, both those who supported and those who opposed the Palestinians. The Christians bitterly resented the Palestinians for involving neutral Lebanon in their struggle with Israel; both Christians and Muslims alike blamed the government for its failure to protect villages in southern Lebanon from Israeli aggression.

The division between Muslims and Christians was accentuated by inflation, which emphasised the differences between the low living standards of the poor, who were often Muslims, and the prosperity of the middle classes, who had become rich on the proceeds of Lebanon's commercial success. In 1975 these tensions brought about civil war, which claimed over five thousand lives before the end of the year. Although the civil war brought some respite to Israel from guerrilla raids, Syria's involvement in the Lebanon in 1976 was yet another complication in the tangled web of Arab-Israeli relations.

The Sadat peace initiative, 1977

In 1977, after many years of bitter Arab-Israeli hostility, Anwar el-Sadat (President of Egypt since 1970) announced that he was willing to visit Israel in order to put forward peace proposals. The first Arab leader to set foot on Israeli territory since 1948, Sadat addressed the Knesset, or Israeli parliament, in November, making a moving appeal for a Middle East peace settlement. Sadat's action was condemned by virtually every other Arab leader, but it raised hopes that an end to the state of war between Israel and

its Arab neighbours could somehow be achieved.

Sadat's mission at first seemed to have failed, for the Israeli Prime Minister, Menachem Begin, did not respond with any constructive proposals of his own. Several months later in September 1978, however, the two leaders met the American President Jimmy Carter at Camp David, Maryland, where they agreed to a framework for Middle East peace. Sadat and Begin promised that they would not use force to settle disputes between their two countries, and that they would enter into negotiations to solve the Palestinian problem. In March 1979 the two leaders signed a peace treaty.

The rest of the Arab world, however, was strongly opposed to the idea of a separate peace treaty between Egypt and Israel. The Ninth Arab Summit Conference held at Baghdad in November 1978 declared that: 'The struggle to recover Arab rights in Palestine and the occupied Arab territories is a responsibility in which all Arabs must join.' In April 1979 Egypt was expelled from the powerful Organisation of Petroleum Exporting Countries (OPEC), and at home Sadat faced opposition to his policy. So long as the abolition of the Zionist state and its replacement by a multi-racial state of Palestine remained the objective of the Arab nations, peace in the Middle East was certain to be fragile.

The resurgence of Islam

The Arab-Israeli struggle was only one source of tension in the Middle East during the 1970s, for of even greater significance in world affairs was the gradual revival of Islam, a culture and religion which rejected many Western values. By generating intense feelings of national pride in millions of Muslims, Islam represented a potential challenge not only to the West, but also to the Soviet Union, whose population in the republics adjoining Iran and Afghanistan contained several million Muslims.

For decades the Arab countries had been dominated by the Western industrialised nations, whose superiority had only been emphasised by the willingness of Arab governments to sell their oil cheaply. The three-fold increase in oil prices in 1973, however, proved conclusively that Western Europe's prosperity depended upon OPEC oil. This sudden realisation radically altered the relationships between the Arab oil-producing states and their Western customers.

At the same time many Muslims found it impossible to reconcile Islamic culture and laws with Western technology and customs which they had inherited from the period of European colonialism. In all twentieth-century Western societies the influence of the Churches had declined, but devout Muslims believed that God's laws, as laid down in the Qu'aran, were the basis of the Islamic state. They argued that in the Western world material progress had been accompanied by the erosion of spiritual values, while the need to maintain high living standards had forced many women into employment, with consequent harm to family life. Their resistance to Westernisation, and their desire to rebuild a new social order in which the Islamic faith was supreme, were the underlying reasons for the revolution in Iran in 1979.

Iran (formerly called Persia until 1935) lies between the Soviet Union and the Indian sub-continent, a British imperial possession until 1948. From the early nineteenth century Britain and Russia competed with each other for political and economic advantages in Persia until 1907, when they agreed to divide the country into two exclusive zones of influence, separated by a neutral, or 'buffer', zone. Although Russia's influence receded temporarily following its defeat in the First World War and revolution in 1917, Britain's interest in Persia was heightened by the discovery of oil and the creation of the Anglo-Iranian (Persian) Oil Company in 1909. Reza Khan, (a Cossack officer who seized power in 1921 and eventually declared himself Shah, or ruler, in 1925) tried to reduce British influence by using German officers and specialists to help with his modernisation programme. Iran's neutrality in the Second World War was not respected, however, for Britain's dependence on Iranian oil and the fear that Iran might fall under the control of Nazi Germany, led to the country's occupation by Britain and the Soviet Union in 1941. The Shah was then forced to abdicate in favour of his son, Muhammed Reza.

Britain withdrew its forces at the end of the Second World War, and the Soviet Union, rather more reluctantly, in 1946. Pent-up resentment against foreign intervention and exploitation of Iran's oil revenues led to the election of a nationalist government headed by Dr Mussadeq, which nationalised the Anglo-Iranian Oil Company in 1951. This action was very unpopular with the multi-national oil companies, and they intrigued to bring about Mussadeq's downfall. In 1953 Mussadeq lost a struggle for power with the Shah, and was overthrown by the army. Political and social unrest continued, however, caused by inflation, corruption and the agitation of the illegal communist Tudeh party. At one extreme it tried to exploit the grievances of the poverty-stricken peasants, and at the other, the unwillingness of the powerful property-owning class to give up any of their land.

In 1961 the Shah began to rule by decree, and in 1963 assumed full control of the government. He set out to overcome Iran's problems by modernising the country along Western lines, using the oil revenues to promote industrial development. At the same time he introduced reforms to stamp out corruption, improve tax collection, strengthen the powers of the provincial governors and redistribute the land. This was the beginning of the 'white' (or 'bloodless') revolution. In north-western Iran, where peasant unrest was widespread, the government confiscated lands belonging to the great landowners, and redistributed them among half a million peasants. The landowners received one fifth of the value of the land in cash, the rest in shares in state or industrial enterprises. Next the smaller landowners were compelled to lease or sell their holdings above 200 hectares.

Although these measures won the Shah the support of the peasants, opposition to his rule gradually intensified. The mullahs, or religious leaders, sided with the great landowners, claiming that the redistribution of land was contrary to the teachings of Islam. Their anger increased in 1963 when women were given the vote, and in 1964 the Ayatollah Khomeini, the Shi'i* Muslims' leader, was exiled. Merchants were alienated by higher customs duties, students by regulations whereby their grants depended upon successful examination results, and officials by the drive against corruption. Having failed to gain acceptance of his measures by persuasion, the Shah was forced to adopt a policy of repression. Political opponents were imprisoned for long periods without trial, and many were tortured by the *Savak*, or secret police. Finally, in 1975, Iran became a one-party state, when all pretence of democracy disappeared.

Smouldering opposition to the Shah's rule burst into flames at the beginning of 1978 with strikes and riots, while from Paris the exiled Khomeini demanded a return to Islamic principles. Martial law was introduced, and a military

* Shi'ism is the official creed of Iran. Its followers believe that the Imam, or religious leader of the community, is chosen by God and is infallible. According to Shi'ite doctrines, the Imams are descended from Ali, the son-in-law and cousin of prophet Mohammed (who died in 632 AD), and his eleven male descendants.

government under General Azhari was established. In January 1979 the Shah tried to mollify the opposition by the appointment of Dr Bakhtiar, who formed a new government. He supported the Palestinian movement, banned exports of oil to Israel and South Africa, and abolished the secret police. These measures, however, failed to silence the opposition, and the Shah left the country, officially for a long holiday. (He died in July 1980 after a long illness.)

Meanwhile, the Ayatollah formed an Islamic Revolutionary Council in Paris, and returned to Iran in February 1979. Dr Bakhtiar was replaced by Dr Bazargan, but real power rested with the secret Islamic Revolutionary Council. Anti-western feeling was shown by Iran's withdrawal from CENTO, and by the seizure of fifty American embassy officials and their families who were held as hostages until January 1981, despite protests by President Jimmy Carter of the United States.

Shi'ite Muslims gather against the railings outside the occupied US embassy in Tehran, hoping to catch a glimpse of the hostages.

Soviet military intervention in Afghanistan 1979–80

The Middle Eastern situation was further complicated in 1978 by developments in neighbouring Afghanistan, where the government of General Daoud, who had deposed King Zahir five years previously in a military *coup*, was himself overthrown. Daoud and many of his family were killed, and Nur Taraki, leader of the People's Party, became President. Taraki enjoyed the support of the Soviet Union, but he was opposed by many Afghan Muslims, who objected to his land reforms, plans to improve the status of women and executions of thousands of political opponents. Taraki was overthrown in September 1979, but his successor only lasted until December 1979, when Soviet troops occupied Afghanistan, and installed Babrak Karmal as President.

Soviet military intervention, for the first time in a country outside Eastern Europe, precipitated a dangerous East-West confrontation. As well as arousing fears in China, Iran and Pakistan about Soviet motives in the Middle East, it seemed to many Western leaders to be an advance towards Soviet control of the Persian Gulf, through which Western Europe received its vital oil supplies. Amidst widespread criticism of the Soviet occupation a number of countries decided to boycott the 1980 Moscow Olympics. Certainly the immediate consequence of the Soviet action was the heightening of international tension, for it reversed the progress towards *détente*, which had been a feature of the 1970s. In this respect at least the world at the beginning of 1980 moved a little closer to nuclear war.

CHAPTER SIXTEEN:
Black Africa North of the Equator

For too long excluded from free human enterprise, and relegated to the sidelines of history, Africa has become fully aware of the needs of its future, and refuses henceforth to trail in the wake of history, or to allow the sacrifice of generations of its people to continue indefinitely.

> 'African Freedom is Indivisible' Sekou Touré, President of the Republic of Guinea, in his Address to the General Assembly of the United Nations, November 1959.

The legacy of European colonial rule in Africa

The frontiers of modern African states are an inheritance from the days of colonial rule. The European powers partitioned Africa for their own convenience, by a process of bargaining which avoided war among themselves, but which had little regard either for natural features* or existing territorial or tribal boundaries. Hence the European possessions had no unity except that imposed by foreign rule. Tribal lands were often divided arbitrarily between two powers. Inter-tribal warfare disappeared as the Europeans established peace throughout a continent as large as North America and Europe combined, but fierce tribal loyalties remained

---

* One important exception was the Caprivi Strip in South West Africa, so-called after the German Chancellor who negotiated an agreement with Britain in 1890, whereby German South West Africa was given access to the Zambesi river via a narrow strip of land.

unaffected and tribal rivalries re-asserted themselves as soon as the Europeans withdrew.

The early European settlements were coastal. As their hinterlands were developed, roads and railways were built primarily to link ports with the interior of the country, in order that its raw materials and foodstuffs might be exploited. Only rarely were communications across colonial frontiers developed, since the colonial powers had little interest in promoting balanced economies.

Thus the chief difficulties confronting African states as they achieved independence were artificial frontiers, tribalism (loyalty to one's tribe rather than country), poor communications and economic backwardness. Also problematic was the lack of skilled workers resulting from inadequate provisions for education, and a very low standard of living for the African peoples. In these circumstances it is not surprising that many African leaders were forced to concentrate upon the tasks of defending the territorial integrity of their states and of maintaining themselves in power, instead of reforming conditions. Civil wars and military dictatorships, therefore, became a familiar part of the African scene.

The 'wind of change' in Africa

To African nationalists the continent of Africa during the first half of the twentieth century seemed like an imprisoned land, controlled by the Europeans almost exclusively for their own benefit; only three African countries were independent in 1939. Liberia on the west coast, originally established as a homeland for freed slaves,

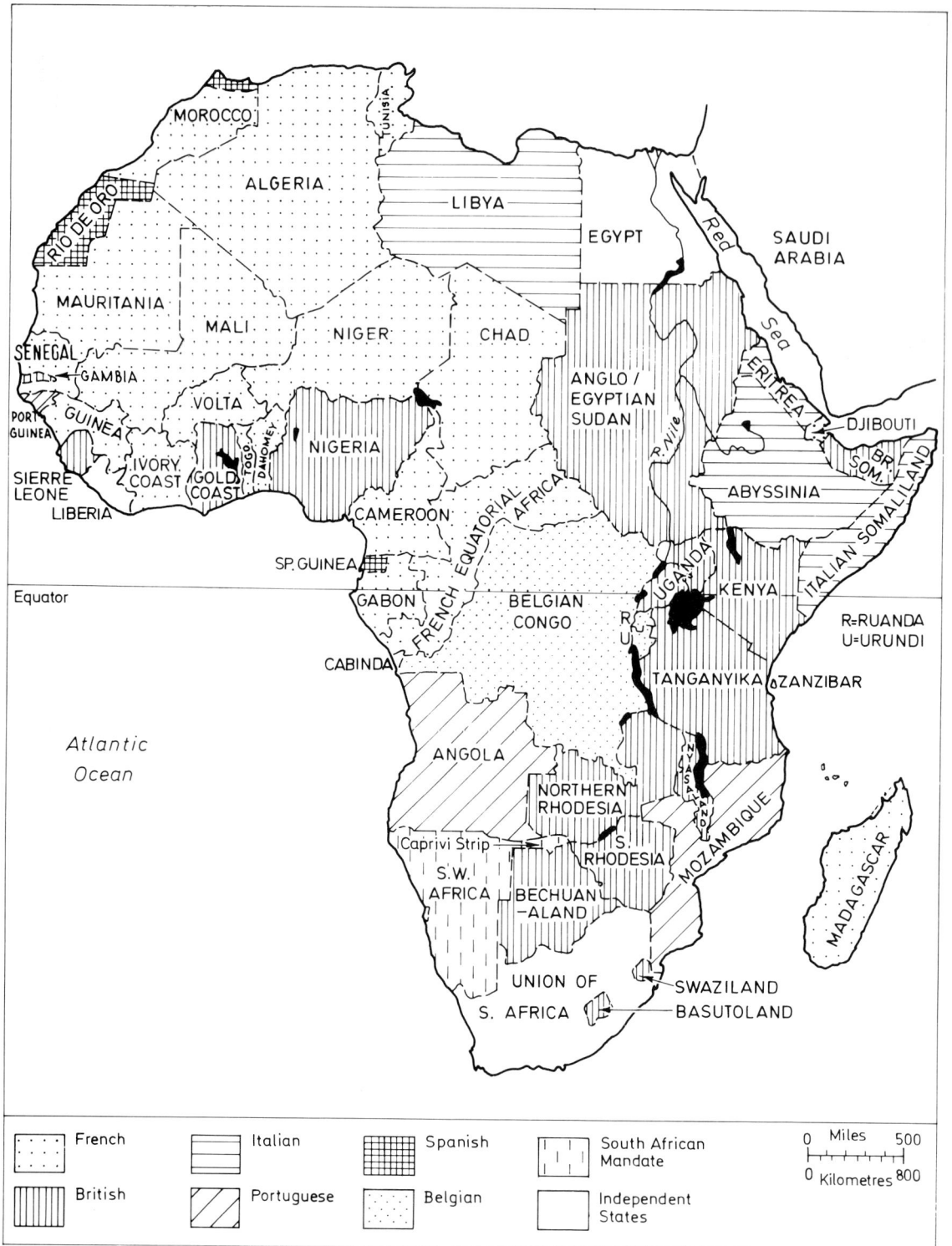

MOROCCO
TUNISIA
ALGERIA
LIBYA
EGYPT
RIO DE ORO
SAUDI ARABIA
Red Sea
MAURITANIA
MALI
NIGER
CHAD
ANGLO / EGYPTIAN SUDAN
ERITREA
DJIBOUTI
SENEGAL
GAMBIA
VOLTA
R. Nile
BR. SOM.
PORT GUINEA
GUINEA
DAHOMEY
NIGERIA
ABYSSINIA
ITALIAN SOMALILAND
SIERRE LEONE
IVORY COAST
GOLD COAST
TOGO
CAMEROON
FRENCH EQUATORIAL AFRICA
LIBERIA
SP. GUINEA
Equator
GABON
BELGIAN CONGO
UGANDA
KENYA
R. U
R=RUANDA U=URUNDI
CABINDA
TANGANYIKA
ZANZIBAR
Atlantic Ocean
ANGOLA
NORTHERN RHODESIA
NYASALAND
MOZAMBIQUE
MADAGASCAR
Caprivi Strip
S. RHODESIA
S.W. AFRICA
BECHUAN-ALAND
UNION OF S. AFRICA
SWAZILAND
BASUTOLAND

Legend	
⋯ French	South African Mandate
British	Italian
Portuguese	Spanish
Belgian	Independent States

0 Miles 500
0 Kilometres 800

25   *Colonial rule in Africa, 1939*

had always been so. Egypt's independence was recognised by the Anglo-Egyptian Treaty of 1936 (although since Britain retained the right to garrison the Suez Canal Zone, the Egyptians did not regard themselves as being fully independent until their victory in the Suez War in 1956). The Dominion status of the Union of South Africa was formally recognised by the Statute of Westminster in 1931. In addition to these three countries Southern Rhodesia became self-governing, though not fully independent, in 1923.

Even before the Second World War Africa had been infected by a spirit of nationalism. After it, African opposition to colonial rule became a formidable force, which within the space of one generation transformed the face of Africa. In 1978 only three countries, South West Africa (Namibia), Rhodesia (Zimbabwe) and the Republic of South Africa were not under independent black African or Arab rule. This was the consequence of the famous 'wind of change' Harold Macmillan referred to in 1960, when he said:

In the twentieth century and especially since the end of the war, the processes which gave birth to the nation states of Europe have been repeated all over the world. We have seen the awakening of national consciousness in peoples who have for centuries lived in dependence upon some other power.

Fifteen years ago this movement spread through Asia. Many countries there of different races and civilisations pressed their claim to an independent national life. Today the same thing is happening in Africa. . . .

The wind of change is blowing through this continent and whether we like it or not, this growth of national consciousness is a political fact. We must all accept it as a fact, and our national policies must take account of it.

Among the first countries to appreciate the strength and implications of African nationalism and to come to terms with it was Britain, which during the 1950s prepared its African colonies for independence. Its motives however, were not always fully trusted.

Ghana

In 1957 the Gold Coast and Togoland became the first British colonies in Africa to achieve independence when they were combined to form Ghana, named after an ancient West African kingdom. Dr Kwame Nkrumah (1909–72), leader of the Convention People's party which he had established in 1949, became the country's first Prime Minister and its President in 1960 when Ghana was declared a republic.

A keen supporter of pan-Africanism, or the unity of all African peoples, Nkrumah believed that strong rule was needed to prevent the new state lapsing into tribalism. After 1959 political opponents were imprisoned, and the constitutional experiment in the two-party system of government favoured by Britain ended in 1964; in this year all organised opposition to Nkrumah's rule was made illegal.

Nkrumah was eager to make Ghana a socialist state, but the programme of industrialisation and improvements he introduced was over-ambitious and financed by borrowed money from foreign countries. When the price of cocoa, Ghana's chief export, fell in the 1960s, Ghana's burden of debt became a serious drain on its economy.

Although many schemes, such as the construction of the Volta River Dam, the building of roads, schools and hospitals, and agricultural improvements, were praiseworthy, much money was also squandered on prestige projects. Among these were the provision of expensive government buildings in the capital, Accra, and a motorway which carried very little traffic. As Ghana's economy deteriorated, with rising unemployment and inflation causing severe social problems, a group of army officers took advantage of Nkrumah's absence on a visit to China in 1966 to overthrow him. They established a military dictatorship of the National Liberation Council. Ghana eventually returned to civilian rule in 1969 when Dr Kofi Busia, leader of the Progressive party, became Prime Minister. He could find no cure for Ghana's economic problems, however, and in 1972 military rule was restored when Colonel Acheampong seized power.

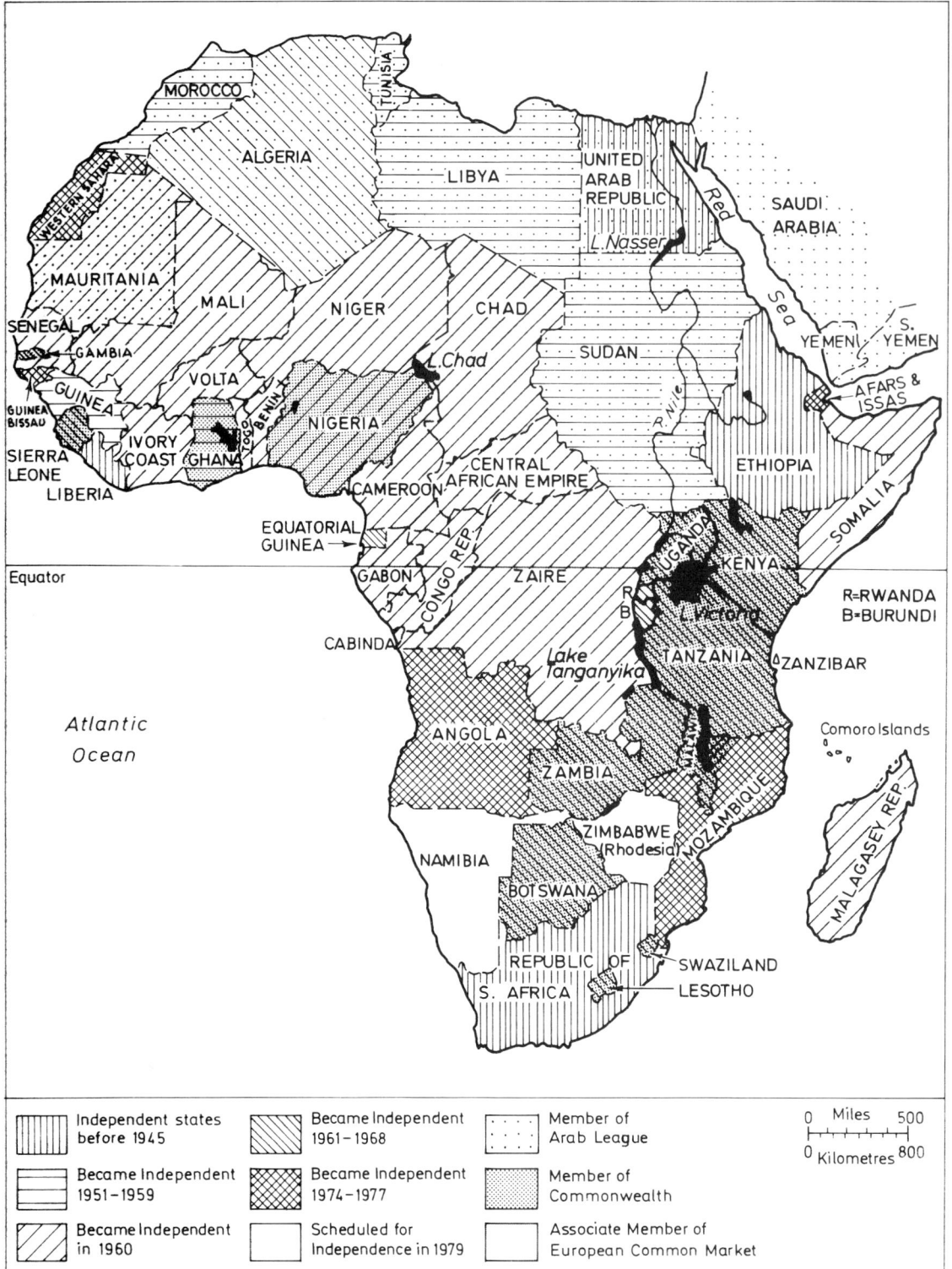

MOROCCO
TUNISIA
ALGERIA
LIBYA
UNITED ARAB REPUBLIC
L.Nasser
SAUDI ARABIA
Red Sea
WESTERN SAHARA
MAURITANIA
MALI
NIGER
CHAD
SUDAN
YEMEN
S. YEMEN
SENEGAL
GAMBIA
GUINEA
L.Chad
AFARS & ISSAS
GUINEA BISSAU
VOLTA
TOGO
BENIN
NIGERIA
SIERRA LEONE
IVORY COAST
GHANA
CENTRAL AFRICAN EMPIRE
ETHIOPIA
SOMALIA
LIBERIA
CAMEROON
EQUATORIAL GUINEA
GABON
CONGO REP.
ZAIRE
UGANDA
KENYA
R=RWANDA B=BURUNDI
R.Nile
L.Victoria
Equator
CABINDA
R B
TANZANIA
ZANZIBAR
Atlantic
Ocean
Lake Tanganyika
ComoroIslands
ANGOLA
ZAMBIA
MOZAMBIQUE
MALAGASEY REP.
NAMIBIA
ZIMBABWE (Rhodesia)
BOTSWANA
REPUBLIC OF S. AFRICA
SWAZILAND
LESOTHO

Independent states before 1945	Became Independent 1961–1968	Member of Arab League
Became Independent 1951–1959	Became Independent 1974–1977	Member of Commonwealth
Became Independent in 1960	Scheduled for Independence in 1979	Associate Member of European Common Market

0   Miles   500
0 Kilometres 800

26   *Independent Africa and its regional groupings, 1978*

Nigeria

The announcement of Nigeria's independence on 1 October 1960 was greeted with misgivings by many Nigerians, for the new state faced numerous problems. They included the political inexperience of its leaders, the rivalries of tribal groupings which competed with each other for power and influence in the central government, disagreement over regional shares of the country's oil revenues, and bribery and corruption at all levels of the administration. Corruption was commonplace, since it was customary practice for an African who became successful to look with favour upon the less fortunate members of his family, rewarding them with official posts or in some other way.

The most important problem, however, was tribalism. Nigeria was composed of over 250 tribes of which four were dominant – the Yoruba in the western region, the Fulani and the Hausa in the northern part (which contained half of Nigeria's population), and the Ibo in the east. In the years preceding independence various political parties were formed to protect regional and tribal interests. The Northern People's Congress (NPC) demanded at least fifty per cent representation, and fiercely opposed any plans which threatened the supremacy of Northern Nigeria. The Action Group, led by Obafemi Awolowo, confident in the western region's prosperity resulting from the boom in cocoa prices, pressed for regional self-government and the creation of more regions in order to break up the dominant position of the North. The National Council for Nigeria and the Cameroons, led by Dr Azikiwe, increasingly dominated by the Ibos, favoured the idea of a strong central government, with oil revenues shared in such a way as to benefit the poorer regions.

Under the 1954 federal constitution there were three regional governments, as well as the central, or federal, government for the whole of Nigeria. The eastern and the western regions became internally self-governing in 1956; the northern in 1959, when they were responsible for such matters as agriculture, education and economic development. The federal government was left in control of defence, international trade, customs duties, currency and banking, thereby ensuring that it would exert a powerful influence in national affairs.

The first Prime Minister of Nigeria was Sir Abubakar Balewa, leader of the NPC, the largest party, who formed a coalition government with Ibo support and ruled the country for six years until he was killed in 1966. Awolowo's Action Group representing Yoruba interests emerged as the official opposition party, and when Nigeria became a republic in 1963, Dr Azikiwe was appointed its first President.

Signs of unrest soon appeared, however, for both the Yoruba in the west, and the Ibos in the east, disliked Hausa domination of the federal government. The Yorubas in particular bitterly resented Balewa's action in arresting the western region's Prime Minister, Awolowo, on a charge of treason, and taking over the administration of the province for six months.

The Nigerian civil war 1967–70

The growing hostility between Northern Nigeria and the rest of the country culminated in January 1966, when Balewa and the Prime Ministers of the western and northern regions were overthrown and killed by a group of Ibo army officers. A military government was formed by Major General Ironsi, but as the full extent of Ibo involvement in the events of January was realised, he was killed in July 1966 along with a number of Ibo army officers. General Gowon now assumed full control of the federal government. He released Awolowo from prison, but failed to stop the killing of thousands of Ibos living in the northern region. The Ibos retaliated by killing Hausas in the eastern region.

As the crisis escalated Gowon introduced military rule, and announced plans for the creation of twelve states, in the hope of preserving Nigeria's unity. The Ibos' hatred of Hausa supremacy, and their fear that they would never be safe within a united Nigeria, were now too great, however. Under the leadership of Colonel Ojukwu, the eastern region thus declared itself the independent state of Biafra in May 1967. All attempts at reconciliation proved useless, and civil war began in July.

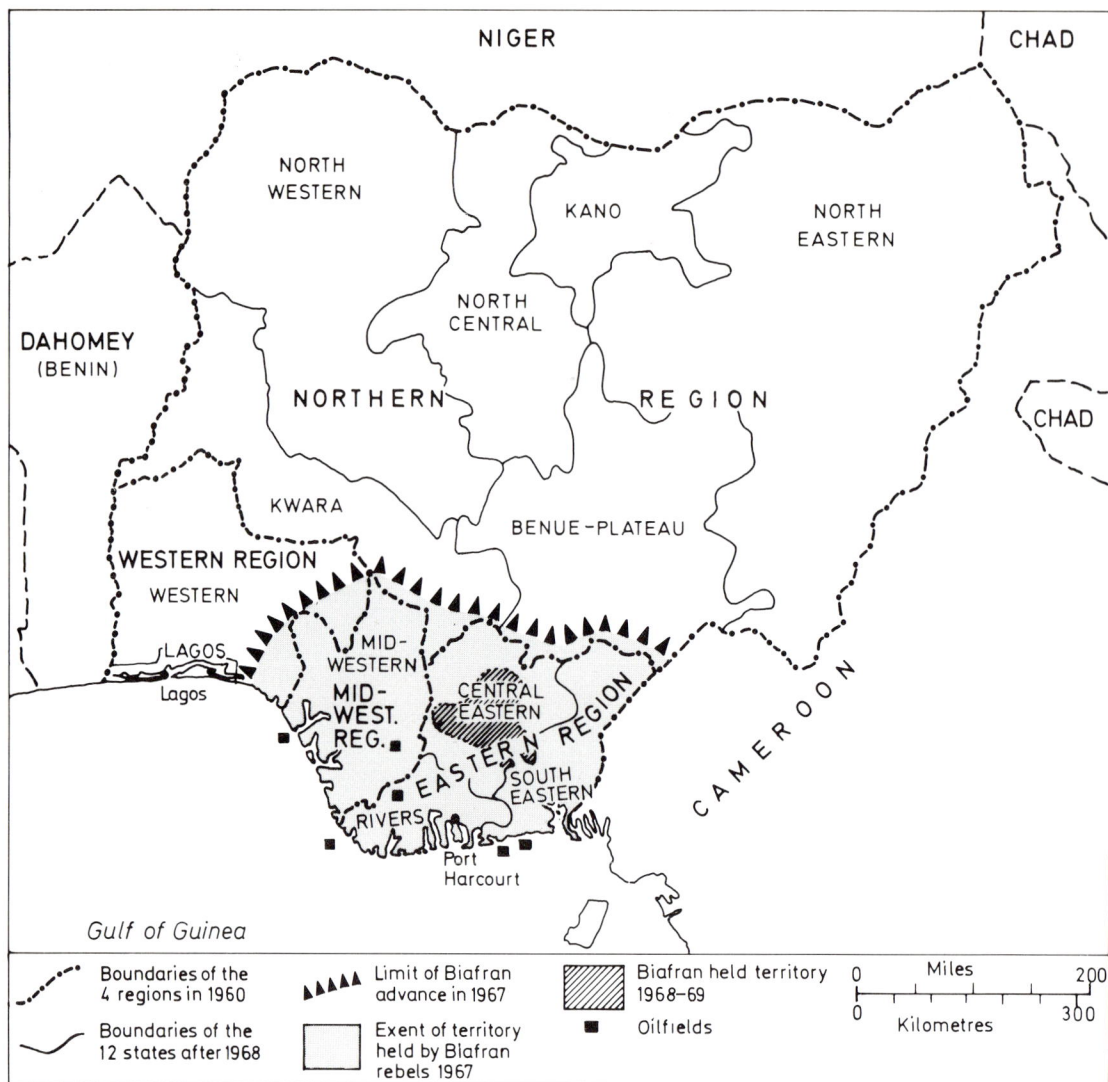

27   *The Nigerian Civil War*

Although Biafra was recognised by Presidents Nyerere of Tanzania and Kaunda of Zambia, and received encouragement from several countries, including France, Portugal, South Africa and Rhodesia, the self-proclaimed state had few friends. The Organisation for African Unity, concerned lest the secession of Biafra might encourage similar breakaway movements in other African states, supported Nigeria by a vote of thirty-three states to four, while both Britain and the Soviet Union supplied arms to Nigeria.

By early 1968 Biafra had become land-locked, but the Biafrans, fearful of wholesale massacres if they surrendered, struggled against overwhelming odds until they were confined to a pocket of territory 1500 square miles in extent. Eventually lack of military supplies, starvation and disease forced them to surrender in January 1970.

Biafra's attempt to secede failed primarily because the rest of Nigeria patched up its differences, in the realisation that the collapse of the

A woman Ibo refugee, carrying her dead child, is ordered to a compound in Biafra by a Federal Nigerian soldier.

federation would cause more problems than it would solve. Gowon immediately recognised the urgent need to heal the scars caused by tribal warfare. There was no witchhunt to punish those considered responsible for the civil war, or for committing atrocities during the fighting. The twelve states had already come into existence in 1968, and Biafra resumed its rightful place within Nigeria. Relief was brought to the devastated areas and roads, bridges, schools and hospitals were repaired. Gowon also restored good relations with those countries which had supported the Biafran rebels, and within a few years Nigeria was firmly set on the road to becoming one of the most important and prosperous states in Africa.

French West Africa

During the Second World War, French West Africa was a major source of raw materials and recruits for de Gaulle's Free French Movement, which opposed the Vichy regime in France. In recognition of the important role the French African colonies had played in support of the Allied cause, de Gaulle summoned representatives of all the territories in January 1944 to the Brazzaville Conference, where proposals for wide-ranging reforms were outlined. Accordingly, in 1946, French possessions in Africa were given the status of overseas territories of France. As members of the French Union, the territories had African representation in the National Assembly, the Senate and the Assembly of the French Union, and until 1960 large sums of money were spent by France in promoting their economic development.

Nevertheless, the French possessions in West Africa were influenced by rapid political development after 1950 in the neighbouring British colonies, which led to Ghana's independence in 1957. The French government tried to stave off demands for independence by passing the *loi cadre* in 1956, an enabling law allowing its overseas territories a considerable degree of local self-government. Many African politicians remained dissatisfied, however, and they accused the French government of seeking to balkanise French West Africa so as to keep control of it.

In 1958 President de Gaulle tried to solve the problem by a new constitution, whereby the theoretically indivisible Union of France and its overseas territories in Africa were given full self-government, apart from matters of foreign policy, defence and economic planning. Only Guinea voted against the scheme, and was given independence 'with all its consequences', which meant that it was immediately deprived of all French aid and technical assistance.

The African members of the French Community, however, soon became discontented with less than complete sovereignty, and in 1960 the French agreed to their independence. French influence in the new states remained strong, nevertheless, and many of them became associate members of the EEC by the Yaoundé Convention of 1963.

The Congo

Until 1908 the Belgian Congo, an enormous area three times the size of Western Europe, was the private possession of King Leopold II of Belgium. Not satisfied with being simply the ruler of a tiny European kingdom, Leopold II was a man of boundless ambition who dreamed of building a great overseas empire. He realised that H. M. Stanley's expedition to the river Congo in 1876 had made it possible to open up Central Africa to European trade and further exploration. In 1879 Leopold formed the Congo Association, and appointed Stanley as his chief agent in establishing a chain of trading posts in the Congo. Six years later, when this had been achieved, Leopold reached agreements with the European powers and the United States through skilful diplomacy and secured international recognition of his right to be sovereign of the Congo Free State.

For several years Leopold's vast African estate did not produce the wealth its owner had anticipated, until it was saved from bankruptcy by the world-wide demand for rubber (a result of the remarkable growth of the motor car industry after 1891). The methods employed by many Belgian officials to obtain their quotas of rubber

(such as flogging or mutilation of Congolese who failed to collect sufficient quantities) were inhumane, and reports of Belgian atrocities in the Congo shocked world opinion. By the early twentieth century the demand that Leopold should not be allowed to continue as ruler of the largest European possession in Central Africa was irresistible, and in 1908 the Belgian government took control of the Congo Free State. It was regarded as a point of national honour to bring to an end the evils for which Leopold II was held responsible.

Belgium, therefore, however reluctantly, became a colonial power. At the end of the First World War Rwanda and Urundi, two provinces which had formed part of German East Africa, were added to the Congo Free State as Belgian mandates. Successive Belgian governments raised the living standards of the Congolese, but opposed any advance towards self-government, since the powerful Belgian mining companies, the *Union Minière*, did not wish to lose their stake in the Congo's mineral wealth.

Congolese resistance to Belgian rule grew strongly after 1945, although most political parties reflected tribal rivalries. The only truly national party was the Congolese National Movement, led by Patrice Lumumba who had managed to win widespread support in four of the six provinces in the Congo. Lumumba wanted one government for the whole of the Congo, but other leaders preferred a federal system of government, in which each of the six provinces would keep a large measure of control over its affairs.

The Congolese were encouraged by the progress being made towards independence by neighbouring territories, while the Belgians realised that neither Britain nor France, the chief colonial powers, were prepared to offer much resistance to African demands for self-government. Thus when serious riots occurred in the Congo in 1959 the African leaders were summoned to a conference in Brussels in January 1960. There it was agreed that the Congo should become independent almost immediately. After elections had been held in the Congo, Joseph Kasavubu was installed as President, and Patrice Lumumba became Prime Minister.

Tshombe at a press conference, two weeks after declaring the independence of Katanga.

The Congo was ill-prepared for independence, however, and in July 1960, the Congolese army mutinied against its European officers. As law and order broke down, African resentment against colonial rule was expressed in attacks upon white settlers, and in the ensuing panic a mass exodus of Europeans from the country began. The Belgian government sent 5000 paratroopers to Leopoldville in order to protect Belgian nationals and property. Meanwhile, fresh problems arose for Lumumba's government when Moise Tshombe (1918–69) proclaimed Katanga province to be the independent state of Shaba, and asked for Belgian protection.

Lumumba requested United Nations' help in restoring order and expelling the Belgian troops, and within two weeks 10,000 UN troops from countries such as Sweden, India and Ethiopia, had arrived. They restored order, but the problem of Katanga's secession remained, since it was not clear whether the UN's responsibilities included the subjection of the Katangese to the authority of the central government. This confusion was made worse in September when President Kasavubu and Prime Minister Lumumba quarrelled with each other. Both men claimed to lead the rightful government of the Congo, and for several weeks it was impossible to tell who was actually in control of the country. This dilemma was eventually resolved by Colonel Joseph Mobutu, the commander of the Congolese army, who declared his support for Kasavubu. Mobutu's troops clashed with those who had remained loyal to Lumumba, who fled from Leopoldville. In January 1961 Lumumba was captured by Congolese soldiers and taken to Katanga, where he was murdered in mysterious circumstances.

Lumumba's supporters, led by Antoine Gizenga, tried to form a government of their own in Stanleyville, the capital of Orientale province. They were supported for a time by the Russians, who resented Western influence in the Congo. The Russians supplied arms to the Lumumbists, but soon alienated the Africans, who welcomed their interference no more than they had done that of the Belgians. After negotiations lasting several months Gizenga's party came to terms with the New Prime Minister of the Congo, Cyrille Adoula.

Katanga's break with the rest of the Congo was illegal, but it had the support of Belgian troops, who restored order in the province, and of the Belgian mining companies, which financed the recruitment of foreign mercenaries. These soldiers enabled Tshombe to defy the Congolese government for over two years. The UN, however, refused to recognise Katanga's secession, since it would have deprived the Congo of the mineral wealth upon which its prosperity depended. Moreover, Katanga's example might have been copied in many other African states.

The UN did not find it easy to resolve the conflict. In September 1961 Dag Hammarskjöld, the UN Secretary General, was killed when the aeroplane in which he was flying to meet Tshombe for peace talks crashed *en route*. U Thant, his successor, realised that the reunification of the Congo was essential; not only to guarantee the future prosperity of the Congo, but also to uphold the prestige of the UN itself as an international peace-keeping organisation.

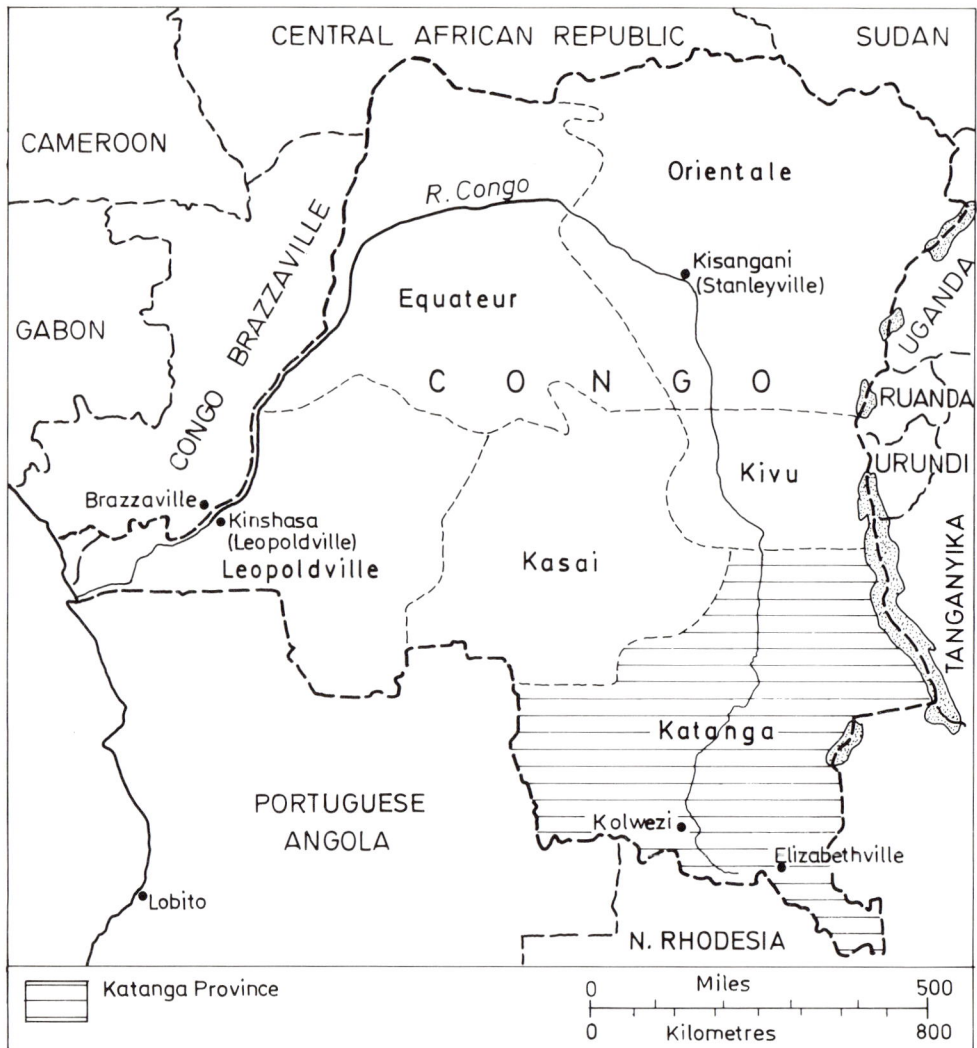

28   *The Congo, 1961*

The UN force in the Congo was therefore authorised by the Security Council to expel the mercenaries from Katanga. After some inconclusive fighting Tshombe agreed to meet Adoula in December 1961, when he renounced Katanga's secession.

This was not an end to the matter, however, for a final settlement was not so easily achieved and a genuine reconciliation was only reached after negotiations lasting more than two years. In June 1964 Tshombe returned to the Congo

from Europe (where he had been living in temporary exile), just as the last UN troops were leaving the country. He was invited by Kasavubu to become Prime Minister, and accepted.

Tshombe faced an uphill task, as fighting had broken out again in various parts of the Congo. His acceptance of United States and Western European aid in the struggle against the rebels, moreover, had made him suspect in the eyes of many Africans; in October 1965 he was dismissed by Mobutu, who was now the real ruler in the Congo. Disgraced, Tshombe fled from the country, and in his absence was sentenced to death. In 1967 he was imprisoned in Algeria, after his aircraft had been hi-jacked. He died in 1969.

Mobutu made himself President in November 1965. He nationalised the European mining companies in 1966 and set up the Popular Movement of the Revolution, the only party to be allowed in the Congo (soon to be renamed

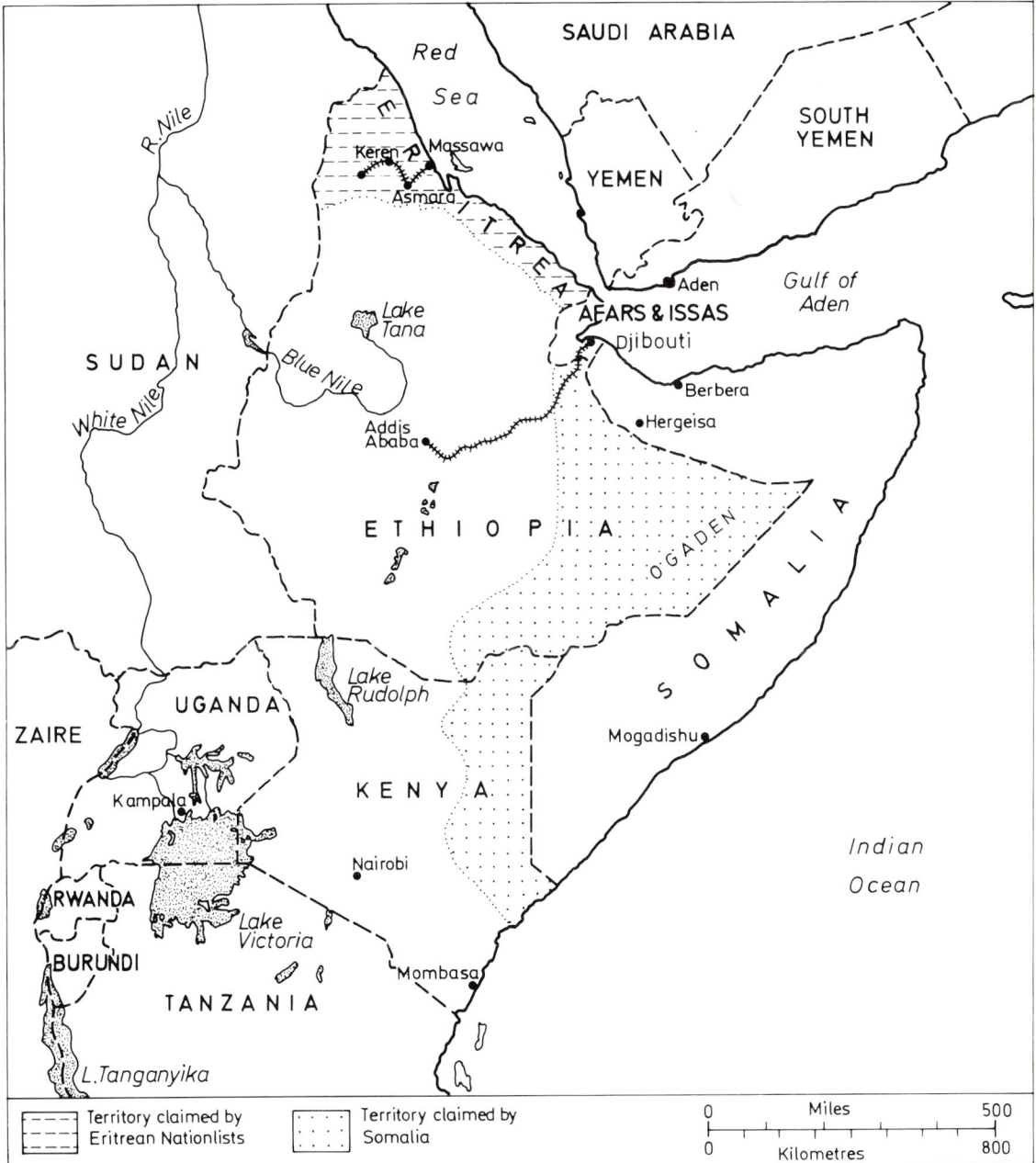

Territory claimed by Eritrean Nationlists

Territory claimed by Somalia

| 0 | Miles | 500 |
| 0 | Kilometres | 800 |

29 *East Africa, 1976*

Zaire, the old Portuguese name for the Congo river). Mobutu's firm rule brought a long period of stability to Zaire, troubled only by an invasion of the country in March 1977 by Katangan exiles living in Angola. Their attack on Kolwezi, one of the main centres of the copper industry, was repulsed when Morocco responded to Mobutu's appeal for help by sending troops. The invaders were driven out of Zaire, but the ever-present dangers of tribal conflict had once again been sharply emphasised.

Ethiopia

Ethiopia was the last African country to be conquered by the Europeans. After only five years of rule by fascist Italy, however, in 1941 British and South African troops expelled the Italian forces from the territory and from neighbouring Italian Somaliland and Eritrea. The Emperor Haile Selassie (1891–75) returned from exile and secured his country's independence in January 1942, although British troops remained in the province of Ogaden until 1954.

There was much sympathy for Haile Selassie on the part of the United States and the Western powers, who had failed to help Ethiopia resist Italian aggression in 1935. Addis Ababa became the headquarters of the UN Economic Commission for Africa and of the Organisation for African Unity, founded in 1963, when Haile Selassie was made its first president. He mediated in the dispute between Algeria and Morocco in 1963, in the Nigerian (Biafran) War, 1968–9, and in the Sudanese civil war in 1972.

The Emperor's keen interest in African affairs contrasted with his lack of interest in Ethiopia's domestic affairs, which contributed to his downfall. In February 1974, after his government had failed to cope with a disastrous drought and famine in which an estimated 400,000 people died, he was deposed by a group of army officers, who formed a Provisional Military Government.

Although civilian ministers remained in office, real power was vested in the *Dergue*, a committee of 102 elected army officers, which soon came to be dominated by Major Mengista

Haile Mariam, who became head of state. He dealt ruthlessly with political opponents and made Ethiopia a socialist state, nationalising all land in 1975. The close links with the United States were gradually cast off, as the new regime turned to communist countries for aid. Close ties were developed with the Soviet Union, and in March 1977 Fidel Castro of Cuba visited Addis Ababa. In the meantime, however, Ethiopia had been threatened with disintegration, as parts of the country tried to break away.

The secession movement in Eritrea

By the terms of the 1947 peace treaty Italy surrendered all its African colonies, and in 1950 the United Nations decided that Eritrea should be federated with Ethiopia. In 1962, amid allegations of bribery and corruption, the Eritrean assembly voted for full union with Ethiopia. This decision was challenged by Eritrean nationalists, who had formed the Eritrean Liberation Front to resist such a move.

Although the ELF won publicity for its cause by a series of successful hi-jackings in 1969, the movement at first made little headway. In early 1975, however, the ELF attacked the Eritrean capital, Asmara, which they nearly succeeded in capturing. The guerrillas' successes won concessions from the Ethiopian government, which offered Eritrea self-rule. Nevertheless, the rebels, confident that they were heading for victory, refused to accept anything less than complete independence. This proved to be a mistake, for by the end of 1978 the Ethiopian army, with the help of Cuban volunteers and Soviet military equipment, appeared to have overcome the Eritrean rebels.

The conflict between Somalia and Ethiopia

When the Italians conquered Ethiopia in 1936 they joined the province of Ogaden, which was inhabited chiefly by Somalis, to their colony of Somaliland. During the Second World War

Somali nationalism grew and the Somalis, like the Eritreans, were promised freedom from Italian rule after the war.

In 1946 Ernest Bevin, the British Foreign Secretary, proposed that the Ogaden region of Ethiopia should become part of an independent Somalia, to be formed by the union of British Somaliland with the Italian Somaliland. This plan was resisted fiercely by Haile Selassie and opposed by Russia, so it was therefore abandoned. By the time Somalia became independent in 1960, Ethiopia had regained control of the Ogaden, following the departure of British troops in 1954.

Somalia's territorial claims, which included part of Kenya and French Somaliland (now Afars and Issas) as well as the Ogaden, made little progress, and the border fighting was temporarily halted in 1968, when Somalia reached an agreement with its two powerful neighbours, Ethiopia and Kenya. In 1974 Mohammed Siad Barre, who had seized power in 1969 and made Somalia a socialist state, joined the Arab League, hoping that it would support Somalia's renewed claim to the Ogaden.

The quarrel between Somalia and Ethiopia developed into an open war in June 1977, when Somali troops cut the important railway link between Addis Ababa and the port of Djibouti and occupied the greater part of the Ogaden. Their success was short-lived, however, for the Soviet Union supported Ethiopia, having been denied the prospect of a naval base on Somalia's coast.

Kenya

Kenya, a British possession since 1895 and a Crown Colony since 1920, became independent on 12 December 1963. Unlike many African states it has enjoyed a stable government since becoming independent, largely owing to the firm leadership of Jomo Kenyatta.

The son of the leader of a small farming community, Kenyatta was a Kikuyu, the largest of the many tribes that live in Kenya. He joined the African nationalist movement in 1922, becoming secretary of the Kikuyu Central Association in 1927, and starting up a newspaper in the following year in which he publicised African grievances.

Africans were denied the vote, had few opportunities to acquire a good education and had a much lower standard of living than the rest of the population. Their chief discontent, however, concerned the shortage of fertile land available to them, since government policy confined the Africans to reserves, allowing white settlers to own the best land. Kenyatta also vigorously opposed the idea of the union of Kenya, Uganda and Tanganyika, which European settlers hoped would become the basis of a Dominion, similar to that of South Africa, in which white supremacy would be assured. The British government eventually abandoned the plan, but at the same time permitted very little progress towards independence.

In 1946 Kenyatta was chosen as leader of the Kenya African Union, a new party which campaigned for the principle of 'one man, one vote'. Acceptance of this principle would have ensured African majority rule, but the nationalists met with little success until the outbreak of the Mau Mau rebellion in 1952.

Mau-Mau suspects rounded up before being taken to court and tried for terrorist activities.

The Mau Mau was a Kikuyu secret society whose members practised a form of witchcraft. For a period of three years, during which time a state of emergency existed in Kenya, the Mau Mau terrorised the population by a series of murders of white settlers and Africans who worked for Europeans. Kenyatta, who was suspected of being the Mau Mau leader, was arrested and sentenced to seven years imprisonment. The extent of his involvement in Mau Mau activities is far from certain, however, since it was subsequently proved that some of the evidence offered at his trial was falsified. The state of emergency was ended in 1955, but only parties based on individual tribes were allowed until 1959, when the British government decided to grant Kenya independence without delay. National parties were permitted, so long as they were multi-racial, and in 1960 Africans were given the vote.

Released from detention in 1961, Kenyatta became president of the Kenyan African National Union (KANU), formed by Tom Mboya and Oginga Odinga. This party formed the provisional government in May 1963, when it defeated its rival, the Kenyan African Democratic Union (KADU) at the polls. When Kenya became independent at the end of the year Kenyatta was made Prime Minister and in 1964 President when his country became a republic. Kenyatta remained in office until his death in 1978.

Uganda

There was no need for a nationalist party to struggle for Uganda's freedom, since by 1950 it was clear that Britain intended it to become an African country. Nevertheless, there were fierce arguments over the form the new state should take, since the protectorate consisted of four African kingdoms, which were jealous of each other's influence. When Milton Obote took office as Prime Minister as the country achieved independence in 1962, his most difficult problem was how to unify tribal loyalties.

Obote tried to solve this problem by making the ruler of the most important tribe, the Buganda, President when Uganda became a republic in 1963. This arrangement did not work out very well and opposition to Obote's rule grew. In 1966, after an unsuccessful attempt had been made to overthrow him, Obote made himself President, destroyed the privileged status of the four kingdoms within the state of Uganda, and abolished all political parties. He survived several assassination attempts, and remained in office until 1971, when General Idi Amin seized power while Obote was absent from the country, attending the Commonwealth Conference in Singapore.

Amin stifled opposition by abolishing freedom of the press and association, and by giving the army powers of arrest and search and permission to shoot armed robbers. At the same time the police and the army were purged of members whose tribal loyalties cast any doubt on their allegiance to President Amin. During the next few years thousands of Ugandan citizens were imprisoned and killed on Amin's orders.

Amin quarrelled with Britain in 1972, when he expelled all Asians with British passports, giving them ninety days in which to leave Uganda. Most were forced to leave their property behind them. When Britain suspended all economic aid to Uganda, Amin retaliated by seizing British property and investments in Uganda and expelling British citizens.

In 1972 Amin also broke off diplomatic relations with Israel, and expressed approval of the murder of several Israeli athletes at the Munich Olympic Games. These gestures of anti-Zionism gained him the friendship of a number of Arab countries, which was further demonstrated when Amin visited several Arab states during the October War in 1973. Israel gained a measure of revenge when it mounted a commando raid on Entebbe airport in June 1976 in order to rescue over eighty Israelis who had been hijacked, and were being held as hostages for the release of fifty-three Palestinian terrorists from prisons. Most of the Ugandan air force was destroyed during the raid, which demonstrated the country's vulnerability to a foreign attack. Amin's regime was eventually overthrown in April 1979, when Tanzanian troops supported a Ugandan uprising.

European influence in South Africa can be traced back to 1488, when Bartholomew Diaz, a Portuguese explorer, rounded the Cape of Good Hope in his search for a sea route to the Far East. It was not until 1652, however, that the Dutch, who captured the monopoly of the Indian Ocean trade from the Portuguese at the end of the sixteenth century, founded a permanent European settlement at Cape Town. During the Napoleonic and Revolutionary Wars with France (1793–1815), Britain seized the Dutch colony in 1806, and established a foothold in South Africa. Cape Town was of great strategic importance, since it lay on the route to India. Britain therefore retained possession of the colony at the end of the war, giving Holland six million pounds as compensation.

The inhabitants of the colony were Boers (a word which means 'farmers'), a strongly religious people of Dutch descent. Relations between the British and the Boers were never cordial, for British rule threatened to undermine the Boers' way of life without, it seemed, offering in return adequate protection against African attacks. When slavery was abolished in the British Empire in 1834 the Boers received poor compensation for the slaves they owned, and many decided to leave Britain's jurisdiction altogether, by settling fresh lands beyond the borders of Cape Colony. This migration (1836–38) was called the Great Trek, when the Boers established themselves in lands which they called Natal, the Orange Free State and Transvaal.

They were not, however, left undisturbed for very long. Worried in case the Boer states should develop friendly relations with a foreign power which might acquire a naval base on the Indian Ocean, Britain assumed control of Natal in 1843

and the Orange Free State in 1848; only to return the Free State to Boer rule in 1854. There matters rested until 1877, when the Transvaal, bankrupt and threatened by the Zulu military confederacy, was taken temporarily under British protection. When the defeat of the Zulus did not result in the restoration of independence, war broke out between the British and the Transvaalers, in which the British were defeated in a skirmish at Majuba Hill (1881). At this juncture the Transvaal was granted its independence.

At the end of the nineteenth century the clash of interests between British imperialism and Afrikaner (Boer) nationalism led to the Boer War (1899–1902). As a result of the war, the two Boer Republics, Transvaal and the Orange Free State, were annexed by Britain. In an attempt to win the goodwill of the Afrikaners, the British government granted self-government to the newly annexed colonies in 1907. This was followed two years later by the formation of the Union of South Africa: when Cape Colony, Natal, the Orange Free State and Transvaal were joined together by a British Act of Parliament, and became a Dominion alongside Canada and Australia.

Afrikaner nationalism

During the nineteenth century the Boers developed their own distinctive language, at first called 'Cape Dutch' and later, 'Afrikaans', and by the end of the century the Boers regarded themselves as Afrikaners, or 'Africans'. Up to 1902 the Boer Republics fought stubbornly to maintain their independence. After their defeat, however, far-sighted Boers realised that the creation of an Afrikaner state had been made possible by annexation of the Orange Free State and the Transvaal. Afrikaners outnumbered the rest of the white population of South Africa, so that in an electoral system where the overwhelming majority of non-Europeans was disfranchised, the principle of 'one man one vote' guaranteed Afrikaner supremacy.

In the Transvaal the two war leaders, Louis Botha and Jan Christian Smuts, formed an Afrikaner party called *Het Volk* (The People), whose aim was responsible government. A similar organisation led by James Hertzog, the United Party, sprang up in the Orange Free State. In Cape Colony Afrikaner interests were represented by the Afrikaner Bond. Within each of these parties the moderates believed that they should work closely with the British, when the two white nationalities together constituted only a fraction (seventeen per cent) of the whole population. They were therefore supported by some British settlers, on the condition that the imperial links with the Crown were kept intact.

This harmony of purpose, however, did not last very long, for many Afrikaners fiercely resented their association with Britain. Louis Botha (who became Prime Minister of the Union of South Africa in 1910) was able to form a Union government in which the ministries of all four former colonies were represented, and the *Het Volk* and the United Party merged to become the South Africa party; but divisions soon appeared. In 1913 Hertzog and his supporters, who wanted the Afrikaners to develop separately from the rest of the white population, broke away and formed the Nationalist Party. The rifts widened with the outbreak of the First World War.

Botha persuaded the South African Parliament by a small majority to declare war on Germany, and even agree to the invasion of German South West Africa by South African volunteers. This was more than many Afrikaners could tolerate, and nationalists who saw the war as an opportunity to get rid of British influence rebelled. The rising was easily crushed, but the strength of Afrikaner nationalism increased during the war.

When Botha died in 1919 he was succeeded by Smuts, one of the founders of the League of Nations. Like Botha, Smuts wanted reconciliation with Britain, whereas Hertzog wanted a separate Afrikaner nation. In 1924 Smuts lost the general election, and the Nationalist Party took office. Hertzog, however, refrained from breaking the links with Britain, which was South Africa's most valuable trading partner, and was content with Balfour's★ definition of Dominion status in 1926. By this definition Britain and the Dominions regarded themselves as:

autonomous communities within the British Empire, equal in status, in no way subordinate to one another, though united by a common allegiance to the Crown, and freely associated as members of the British Commonwealth of Nations.

After 1929 economic problems caused by the world trade depression brought about a steep decline in the popularity of the Nationalist Party. Smuts put aside the temptation to exploit South Africa's difficulties by ousting Hertzog from power, and offered to serve under him in a coalition government. In 1934 the Nationalist and South Africa Parties combined to form the United Party. The more extreme Nationalists, however, broke away and founded the Afrikaner Nationalists, led by Dr Daniel Malan and committed to the maintainance of Afrikaner supremacy in South Africa.

In 1939 the South African Parliament narrowly voted to join Britain in the war against Germany. Hertzog resigned and joined the Nationalist Party, while Smuts succeeded him as Prime Minister. Many Afrikaners, who regarded themselves as protectors of European civilisation in South Africa, sympathised with Nazi 'master race' theories. They joined the militant Afrikaner organisation called the 'ox wagon sentinels' (*Ossewabrandwag*), which criticised South Africa's involvement in the war. John Vorster, a future South African premier, was among those interned by the government for opposing 'England's War'.

The popularity of Smuts' government declined rapidly after the end of the Second World War. White South Africans were worried by the determination of the colonial peoples to win their freedom, especially when India was

★ The Earl of Balfour was Lord President in Stanley Baldwin's second Conservative cabinet.

granted its independence in 1947. During the South African elections of 1948 Dr Malan urged voters to defend white supremacy against the threat of black African nationalism. Malan's solution to South Africa's problems was *apartheid*, or the 'separate development' of the black and white races.

Apartheid in action

Apartheid was not a new idea. From the earliest days of the Union, blacks had been effectively deprived of the vote. In European residential areas Africans were regarded as foreign visitors, welcomed as cheap labour but restricted in their numbers and length of stay. A Native Trust and Land Act of 1936 gave the government powers to remove African families living on European farms and return them to tribal reserves. After 1948, however, successive Nationalist governments tried to reduce to an absolute minimum contact between the different racial groups.

A Mixed Marriages Act (1949) prohibited inter-marriage between whites and non-whites. The repatriation of Asians to India was encouraged, a policy which deeply offended the Indian government. A Population Registration Act (1950) compelled individuals to carry identity cards on which were entered details of their race and job classification. The notorious pass laws were among the most detested aspects of *apartheid*.

The Group Areas Act (1950) set aside parts of towns and the countryside where only blacks or whites were permitted to live or to own property. The act was retrospective, so that over the years, as different areas were brought within its scope, large numbers of people were forced to sell up and move to another district. Other laws gave the government powers to force Africans to live in a particular township, thus restricting their liberty of movement.

In 1953 a Bantu Education Act brought all African schools under government control. The architect of this act, Dr Hendrick Verwoerd,

A park reserved for whites in Johannesburg. The bench is labelled 'Europeans only'.

believed that the kind of education offered to the Africans should be shaped by consideration of the sort of jobs they would be allowed to hold in a white-dominated society. Most African schools were run by missionary societies or by the Churches, which were too dependent upon government grants to offer much opposition. Even so, many schools were closed by the Churches rather than aid a law of which they disapproved. In 1959 the principle of segregation was applied to higher education by the Separate Universities Act. Other laws segregated the races on public transport and beaches, and reserved the more highly paid occupations for whites. Even racially mixed political parties were made illegal in 1968.

The Bantustans

Carried to its ultimate conclusion, *apartheid* meant the complete separation of the different racial groups into territories called 'homelands', where each race would be free to develop its own individual culture. In the case of the Africans these territories were later known as 'Bantustans' ('Bantu' being the term applied by the government to all blacks). This constructive side to *apartheid* might have been acceptable had the different races been allocated territories in proportion to their numbers. As only fourteen per cent of South Africa was designated to become 'homelands' for the non-Europeans, however, who constituted over eighty per cent of the population, it was generally regarded as a device for maintaining white supremacy.

The Tomlinson Commission was set up in 1950 by Dr Malan to inquire into the development of 'homelands'. In 1956, it optimistically reported that even by the end of the twentieth century only sixty per cent of the black population could be accommodated in 'homelands', and then only if the government promoted substantial industrial development in these areas.

The government was unwilling, however, to finance industrial growth in the 'homelands', which were intended eventually to become independent black states. Instead, it pursued the alternative policy of border industries, whereby new industries were established on the borders of the 'Bantustans', whose populations lived there, but worked in the white areas. Such a policy relegated the Bantustans to the status of labour reserves; Nelson Mandela, a black nationalist leader sentenced to life imprisonment by a South African court for his revolutionary activities, was prompted to declare bitterly that:

The few scattered African Reserves in various parts of the Union, comprising about thirteen per cent of the least desirable land area, represent the last shreds of land ownership left to the African people of their original ancestral home. After the encroachments of generations of European land sharks had turned the once free and independent peasant farmers of this country into a nation of landless outcasts and roving beggars, humble 'work seekers' on the mines and the farms where yesterday they had been masters of the land, the new white masters of the country generously presented them the few remaining miserable areas as reservoirs and breeding grounds for black labour. These are the Reserves.

African resistance to *apartheid*, and government repression

Black nationalists objected not so much to the theory of *apartheid* as to the injustices in society created by laws intended not merely to separate the different races, but also to reinforce white supremacy by denying black people the opportunity to improve their conditions. In one important sense, therefore, the more the South African government succeeded in separating the races, the more it divided them into friends and foes. When Chief Buthelezi of Kwazulu homeland declared that people who discriminate against each other are at war with each other, he could not have been more explicit on the divisive nature of *apartheid*.

In 1952 the African National Congress (ANC), founded in 1912, organised a widespread passive resistance campaign when many blacks and whites openly defied the pass laws and allowed themselves to be arrested. The protest fizzled out after several thousand objectors had been imprisoned, and sentences of whipping carried out. In 1953 the courts were given powers to punish severely the offence of inciting other people to break the law, so that the organisers of both peaceful and violent means of resisting government measures risked stern penalties. A Public Safety Act also empowered the government to declare a state of emergency, when it could suspend laws and rule by emergency decree.

In 1955, 3000 delegates from the various opposition groups held a rally at Kliptown, near Johannesburg, where they drew up a Freedom Charter, demanding votes for all adults. Soon afterwards, 156 organisers of the meeting were arrested on charges of plotting to overthrow the state. The so-called Treason Trials dragged on until 1961, when all the accused were acquitted, but the government had succeeded in neutralising their influence for several years. In the meantime, however, many ANC supporters, deprived of their leadership, broke away to form the more extreme Pan African Congress (PAC), led by Robert Subukwe.

Violence erupted in 1960. Nine policemen were murdered at Cato Manor, near Durban, and in East Pondoland a terrorist movement gained control over the local population, by the expedient of burning the huts of Africans who stayed loyal to the government. Eventually the area was sealed off by the army, which used helicopters and armoured cars to quell the disturbances. The most tragic incident, however, took place at Sharpeville in the Transvaal, when several thousand peaceful demonstrators marched on the local police station to hand in their identity cards. The police panicked and fired on the crowd, killing sixty-nine and wounding eighty men, women and children. As the news of the Sharpeville Massacre spread, riots broke out in many towns and cities, and thousands of Africans burned their passes. Abroad, South Africa's reputation was tarnished, and many countries condemned the killings.

In the aftermath of the Sharpeville affair, the ANC and PAC were banned, thus depriving the Africans of any legal form of political action to

Police move in at Sharpville.

change laws which they considered unjust. Many Africans were now convinced that violence alone would secure concessions, and some went to neighbouring black states where they received training in guerrilla warfare.

Faced with the threat of growing terrorism, the government tightened its security system. It passed a Sabotage Act in 1962, which laid down a minimum of five years' imprisonment for committing acts of sabotage. Restrictions on individual liberty were increased; political opponents could be placed under house arrest, banned from social gatherings, or forbidden to communicate with other banned people. In 1963 police were empowered to detain suspected terrorists for up to ninety days, when the detention could be renewed. A Terrorism Act of 1967 enabled the police to detain suspected 'freedom fighters' indefinitely, without trial. The Bureau of State Security (BOSS), a secret service organisation whose task was to ferret out terrorist groups, was created in 1969. These measures succeeded in preventing outbreaks of serious violence in South Africa until June 1976, when 10,000 African students in the township of Soweto, a suburb of Johannesburg, rioted in protest against the use of Afrikaans in African schools.

South Africa's foreign relations since 1945

Apart from internal dissent, successive Nationalist Prime Minsters Dr Daniel Malan (1948–54), Jan Strijdom (1954–58), Dr Hendrik Verwoerd (1958–66) and John Vorster (who took office after Verwoerd's assassination) had to contend with hostile public opinion abroad. *Apartheid* went against the mainstream of development not only in South Africa itself, but also in the world at large, where the coloured races were determined to achieve their equality with the white races. Nowhere was this process more clearly reflected than in Africa. Whereas in 1954 eighty per cent of Africans were subject to white rule, ten years later eighty per cent of Africans were under African governments. South Africa opposed the decolonisation movement until it

became obvious that the emergence of independent states could not be checked.

South Africa's problems multiplied as the former African colonies of the Western countries took their places in the United Nations Assembly. In 1960, for example, no fewer than sixteen African states were admitted as new members of the UN. As early as 1946, in the UN Assembly's opening session, South Africa's racialist policies had been strongly criticised, but the growth of an influential bloc of Afro-Asian countries in the UN, supported by the votes of the communist states, greatly increased the pressure on South Africa to change.

Many African countries demanded the imposition of economic sanctions against South Africa, to force it to abandon the policy of 'separate development'. Some closed their airports to South African aircraft, and refused them permission to fly over their territory. The neighbouring African countries, however, were too dependent upon trade with South Africa for sanctions to be very effective, especially as neither the British nor the American government was willing to impose trade sanctions, even though they both disapproved of South Africa's policies.

Some attempts to isolate South Africa, however, were more successful. By stages it was forced to withdraw from various international organisations, such as UNESCO and the Independent Labour Organisation, while its virtual expulsion from the British Commonwealth in 1961 was part of the same process of boycott. When South Africa became a republic in October 1961 it applied to remain in the Commonwealth, but hostility on the part of many members was so strong that Verwoerd decided to withdraw the application. Disapproval of South Africa's policies even extended to sport, and many countries refused to allow their national teams to play South African sides. South African athletes were also banned from the Olympic Games.

Fresh dangers for South Africa developed when nationalist revolts against Portuguese rule in the neighbouring territories of Angola and Mozambique began in 1961 and 1964 respectively. The total collapse of Portuguese rule in

Africa in 1974, and the establishment of communist governments in Angola and Mozambique, created a potentially dangerous situation for the Afrikaner government. One more bastion of white supremacy was removed and South Africa's frontiers were exposed to invasion by nationalist guerrillas.

In Rhodesia, the Unilateral Declaration of Independence (UDI) in 1965 (see below) at first seemed to offer South Africa a valuable ally against black nationalism. Unfortunately, the establishment of an illegal white government under Mr Ian Smith not only focussed attention on the race problems of southern Africa, but also, by retarding peaceful development towards majority (black) rule in the colony, brought nearer the terrible prospect of racial conflict.

Vorster responded to these dangers by trying to create friendly links with the other African nations. In 1967 he formed diplomatic ties with Malawi, although Malawi's action was bitterly criticised by the Organisation for African Unity (OAU), which had been formed to promote the interests of the emerging African nations. Vorster emphasised that South Africa was an African state, anxious to contribute towards the prosperity and peaceful development of the whole continent. He visited the Ivory Coast in 1974 and Liberia in 1975; the rulers of these countries had decided that conciliation might succeed in modifying South Africa's policy of 'separate development' where hostility had previously failed. In an historic meeting in August 1975 with President Kaunda of Zambia on the Victoria Falls Bridge, Vorster pledged his support for reaching a negotiated settlement on black majority rule in Rhodesia. Unfortunately, Vorster's 'good neighbour' policy was strained by the problem of Namibia, and growing racial violence in South Africa and Rhodesia after 1976.

Namibia

Namibia (South West Africa) is a vast area of 800,000 square kilometres with an estimated population of three quarters of a million. The territory was colonised by Germany in 1884 dur-

ing the 'scramble for Africa' by the European powers. In 1919 it was awarded to South Africa as a League of Nations mandate. When the UN came into existence in 1946 South Africa refused to agree that its mandate, which was valued for security reasons, should become a UN Trust Territory, and it rejected the UN's right of supervision.

In 1966 the UN Assembly resolved that South Africa had not fulfilled the conditions of the mandate, which was terminated. A Council for Namibia, as South West Africa was renamed, was set up to administer the territory, which was to become independent as soon as possible. South Africa, however, refused to admit a UN Commission sent in 1967, and despite the ruling of the International Court of Justice in 1971 that its presence in Namibia was illegal, continued to administer the country.

In 1975, when Angola and Mozambique became independent, and the end of white minority rule in Rhodesia looked inevitable, Vorster decided that a friendly black state on South Africa's north west border was desirable. He therefore set up the Turnhalle Conference at Windhoek, the capital of Namibia, to prepare the country for independence under a federal constitution on 31 December 1978.

The Turnhalle proposals, however, were rejected by the UN and by the South West Africa People's Organisation (SWAPO), a nationalist movement led by Sam Nujomo which had been excluded from the conference, but which claimed that it alone was entitled to negotiate with the South African government on the future of Namibia.

In 1977 Vorster was persuaded to abandon the Turnhalle plan and agree to free elections to an assembly, which would draft a constitution for a united Namibia. Vorster, however, refused to evacuate South African troops stationed in Namibia, on the grounds that this would allow SWAPO guerrillas to seize control of the country. A second obstacle to an agreed settlement was Walvis Bay, the only suitable site for a deepwater port. South Africa wanted to keep possession of the port, but SWAPO, supported by the UN and the Western powers, insisted that it should belong to Namibia.

Rhodesia

Southern Rhodesia, called Zimbabwe by the African nationalists, became a self-governing colony in 1923, but Britain remained legally responsible for the colony's foreign affairs. This explains why successive British governments refused to recognise the Unilateral Declaration of Independence made by the Rhodesian Premier, Mr Ian Smith, in November 1965. The British government was not prepared to use force to overthrow Mr Smith's illegal regime, however, and it was only after eleven years of protracted negotiations that in September 1976 the Rhodesian government declared its readiness to accept black majority rule, with certain safeguards.

The origins of 'black consciousness' in Zimbabwe

One of the chief causes of African unrest was a shortage of land. Although only a fraction of the population was white, half the land area was allocated to European ownership. After the Second World War thousands of Africans were forcibly removed from their lands to make room for settlers from Britain. Many more lost their land in 1951 when communal ownership of land and restricted grazing rights were abolished in an effort to improve farming methods. Africans not actually farming their land at that time lost it. Those who were dispossessed had great difficulty in supporting themselves and their families outside the reserves, since few jobs were available. The contrast between the rich, white minority, entrenched in power, and the mass of impoverished blacks, bred fierce resentment.

The Central African Federation

In 1953 the British government combined Southern Rhodesia, Northern Rhodesia and Nyasaland, to form the Central African Federation which, it was hoped, would be a strong economic unit, and would promote the development of a multiracial society. The Federation,

however, was not a success, for it lasted a mere ten years before it was torn apart by internal stresses. The African chiefs were opposed to a federal form of government which posed a threat to their authority, while the mass of the black population feared that their rights to land would be undermined. It was soon clear that the whites chiefly benefited from the Federation, and after 1955 African leaders such as Hastings Banda, the first Prime Minister of Malawi, began to demand the vote for all adults and self-government.

The strength of African opposition to the Federation convinced the British government that it was unworkable, and new constitutions were granted to Nyasaland and Northern Rhodesia in 1961 and 1962 respectively. African governments were elected immediately, and the demands for separation could be denied no longer. In 1963 Northern Rhodesia became the independent state of Zambia, and Nyasaland became Malawi.

The Unilateral Declaration of Independence (UDI)

The white Rhodesians were bitterly disappointed by the failure to secure Dominion status for the Federation while it was still white-controlled. They were also exasperated by Britain's refusal to grant Southern Rhodesia its independence, unlike the other two components of the Federation, on the grounds that there was no agreement over the question of majority rule. A Rhodesia Front party, hostile to the idea of racial integration and the prospect of black rule, was formed in 1962 and, supported enthusiastically by white Rhodesians, immediately won sufficient votes to form a government. Three years later the Rhodesia Front, now led by Mr Ian Smith (who succeeded Winston Field as Prime Minister in April 1964) captured all fifty seats in parliament reserved by the 1961 constitution for white voters. During his election campaign Mr Smith promised that he would make Rhodesia independent if he was returned to office.

The break with Britain was now inevitable and in November 1965 Mr Smith announced

Rhodesia's independence. Attempts to negotiate a settlement of the problem by Mr Smith and Harold Wilson, the British Prime Minister, on board the British warships *HMS Tiger* in December 1966 and *HMS Fearless* in October 1968, were to no avail. Economic sanctions imposed on Rhodesia were largely ineffective, since Rhodesia was able to obtain outlets for its trade through Portuguese territory and through South Africa. In 1969 a new constitution, which ruled out the possibility of an eventual black government, was promulgated, and Rhodesia became a republic in 1970.

African nationalist movements in Rhodesia

The African National Congress was banned in 1959 and most of its leaders detained without trial or banished to remote areas. It was then immediately succeeded by the National Democratic Party, which wanted the recognition of the principle of 'one man, one vote'. This, too, was outlawed in December 1961, whereupon the Zimbabwe African People's Union (ZAPU) was founded by Joshua Nkomo; only for Nkomo to be gaoled in 1962 and his party banned. A breakaway movement, the Zimbabwe African National Union (ZANU), the rival to ZAPU, was formed by the Rev Ndabaningi Sithole in 1963. In 1964 this party was also made illegal and Sithole spent the next ten years in prison. In the meantime, Sithole's leadership of ZANU was challenged by Robert Mugabe, whose aim was to establish a socialist state in Zimbabwe.

Finally, a fourth nationalist movement, the African National Council, formed in 1969 and led by Bishop Abel Muzorewa, adopted the moderate stance of seeking to reach a negotiated constitutional settlement with the Rhodesian government. By the early 1970s the activities of Zimbabwe guerrillas, operating from bases in Tanzania, were threatening law and order in Rhodesia. It was the ending of Portuguese rule in Africa in 1974, however, which brought an entirely new dimension to the conflict, by enabling guerrillas to infiltrate Rhodesia through the neighbouring territory of Mozambique.

Soldiers of a crack fighting force, the Rhodesian African Rifles, searching for guerrillas in northern Rhodesia.

The collapse of Portuguese power in Mozambique

Mozambique became a Portuguese colony in the nineteenth century, and was incorporated into Portugal in 1951 by being designated an overseas province. Organised resistance to Portuguese rule began in 1962 when three revolutionary groups merged to become the *Frelimo*, the Mozambique Liberation Front, or *Frente de Libertacao de Mocambique*. The armed struggle started in 1964 and at its height, involved over 60,000 Portuguese soldiers before a ceasefire was arranged after the collapse of Dr Salazar's dictatorship in Lisbon in April 1974.

Samora Machel, the *Frelimo* leader in 1970, became President of an independent Mozambique in June 1975. All land, rented property, banks and insurance companies were nationalised without compensation, but economic difficulties forced Mozambique into close trade links with South Africa, despite Machel's dislike of *apartheid*. Two years later the *Frelimo* was reorganised along Communist party lines, with restricted membership, and Machel signed a twenty year treaty of friendship with the Soviet Union.

President Machel allowed Zimbabwe guerrillas to train on Mozambican territory, and the attempts of Rhodesian security forces to destroy the guerrilla training camps led to clashes with *Frelimo* troops. Following one such raid in March 1976, when twenty-four Mozambicans were killed, Machel closed Mozambique's frontier with Rhodesia and declared that a state of war existed between the two countries. In January 1977 he joined the Presidents of Angola, Botswana, Tanzania and Zambia in declaring support for the Zimbabwe Patriotic Front, an uneasy alliance of the two guerrilla wings led by Mugabe and Nkomo, who had been released from gaol in 1974.

The contest for power in Angola

The struggle for independence in Angola was complicated by the existence of three liberation movements, each supported by one of the three broad ethnic groups in Angola. Rivalry between these groups led to the outbreak of civil war as soon as the Portuguese left in 1975.

When the rebellion started in 1961 in Luanda, the Angolan capital, there were two nationalist movements. The first was the Union of the Peoples of Angola, founded by Holden Roberto in 1954. He was supported by his brother-in-law, General Mobutu, who later became dictator of Zaire in 1965. Roberto joined forces with another tribal movement to create the National Front for the Liberation of Angola in 1962, the *Frente Nacionale de Libertacao de Angola* (FNLA), and claimed that he headed the rightful government of Angola.

The second revolutionary movement was the MPLA (*Movimento Popular de Libertacao de Angola*), or the People's Movement for the Liberation of Angola, founded secretly in Luanda in 1956 by Aghostinho Neto. After winning independence, the MPLA intended to revolu-

tionise the old tribal structure of the country, and create a socialist state. In the power struggle between the MPLA and FNLA, the former was supported by the Soviet Union, while the latter had the backing of France and the United States.

The third party was UNITA, the Union for the Total Independence of Angola. It was founded in 1966 by Jonas Savimbi, who had left the FNLA in 1964 after holding the office of Foreign Minister in Roberto's revolutionary government-in-exile. The UNITA forces were allowed by the Portuguese to establish themselves near Luso, in Angola, since they opposed the MPLA.

When the Portuguese troops were evacuated from Angola in November 1975, the internal struggle between the three movements to form a national government intensified. The MPLA forces captured Luanda, and with the help of supplies of Soviet military equipment, managed to hold on to the city. The United States decided not to intervene in the Angolan civil war, and the FNLA and UNITA forces combined against the threat from MPLA.

UNITA invited the help of South African troops, who crossed from Namibia into Angola on the excuse of protecting the Cunene River hydro-electric scheme. By the spring of 1976, however, the MPLA (supported by Cuban troops despatched by Fidel Castro to aid the socialist revolutionary movement in Africa) had won a decisive victory over its opponents. In March the South African soldiers were withdrawn, after assurances from the MPLA that the hydro-electric plant on the Cunene river would not be harmed.

The approach of black rule in Rhodesia

The success of the revolutionary movements in Angola and Mozambique encouraged Nkomo and Mugabe in their belief that the guerrilla war would topple the illegal white Rhodesian government. The danger of Russian and Cuban military influence in Southern Africa alarmed the United States and prompted urgent diplomatic moves to produce a peaceful settlement of

30 *Southern Africa, 1976*

Map labels: Kinshasa, ZAIRE, TANZANIA, Dar es Salaam, Luanda, ANGOLA, ZAMBIA, MALAWI, Lusaka, Zomba, MOZAMBIQUE, Salisbury, RHODESIA (ZIMBABWE), NAMIBIA (SOUTH WEST AFRICA), BOTSWANA, Walvis Bay, Windhoek, Gabarones, Pretoria, Johannesburg, Maputo, Mbabane, SWAZILAND, Maseru, LESOTHO, Durban, REPUBLIC OF SOUTH AFRICA, Cape Town

Legend: 'Front line' States opposed to illegal White rule in Rhodesia / Commonwealth Members / Miles 0–250 / Kilometres 0–400

the Rhodesian problem. The Americans found an ally in Dr Vorster, who preferred to see a stable black government in Rhodesia to a precarious white rule threatened with guerrilla warfare. Vorster warned Mr Smith that the South African government would not help the white Rhodesians if a race war broke out, and advised him to reach a settlement.

During the summer of 1976 Henry Kissinger, the American Secretary of State, visited Southern Africa in order to discuss the developing crisis. After talks with Dr Vorster, Kissinger met the Presidents of Zambia, Tanzania, Mozambique and Angola (the so-called 'front line' states). Continuing his 'shuttle diplomacy' Kissinger met Vorster a second time and then Mr Smith, when it was announced that agreement had been reached on proposals for drawing up a constitution which would guarantee majority rule in Rhodesia. Unfortunately, misunderstandings over the precise nature of the proposals led to the failure of a conference in Geneva, attended by all the Rhodesian leaders. The British and the United States governments thereupon announced a fresh solution in September 1977.

The Anglo-American Plan envisaged an assembly composed of one hundred members elected by a simple majority vote. During the transition period a British Resident Commissioner would administer the country, and a United Nations Force would guarantee elections free from intimidation. The two guerrilla armies – Nkomo's Zimbabwe People's Revolutionary Army based in Zambia and Mugabe's African National Liberation Army based in Mozambique – and the Rhodesian security forces would be merged into a new Zimbabwean national army. The interests of the white population were to be guaranteed for ten years by twenty-eight specially elected members. At the end of this period the voting arrangements would be reviewed by parliament.

Mr Smith and the Rhodesian-based African leaders rejected the Anglo-American plan in November 1977 and made an internal settlement, i.e. one in which the Patriotic Front leaders, Nkomo and Mugabe, did not participate. The latter tried unsuccessfully to prevent Africans voting in the elections held in early 1979, as a result of which Mr Smith handed over power to Bishop Muzorewa. Not surprisingly, however, Nkomo and Mugabe denounced the new constitutional arrangements as a sham, and declared that unless fresh elections were held, in which Patriotic Front candidates could stand for office, they would overthrow Muzorewa's government by force. As the guerrilla war in Rhodesia escalated, lengthy talks took place at the Lancaster House Conference in London, where a new constitution and ceasefire arrangements were agreed in December 1979. Fresh elections were held in February 1980, at which ZANU won fifty-seven out of the eighty seats allocated to black voters. Robert Mugabe became Prime Minister and Joshua Nkomo, Minister for Home Affairs. In April the country became the independent state of Zimbabwe.

Tanzania

Tanganyika, formerly part of German East Africa, became a League of Nations mandate in 1919, administered by Britain. The Tanganyikan economy stagnated between the World Wars, for the German settlers were expelled and their estates allowed to decline. Attempts to diversify the economy after 1945 – notably the famous groundnuts scheme to provide cooking oil for British housewives, an expensive failure – all met with little success.

A large but very poor country, Tanganyika became independent in December 1961. Three years later it united with Zanzibar, when it was renamed Tanzania. Its President, Julius Nyerere (1921–) leader of the Tanzanian African National Union (TANU), was to give the country a long period of stable government.

Nyerere planned to build a self-reliant, socialist state. His ideas were the inspiration for the Arusha Declaration of 1967, which was intended

Votes rule over guns—a guerrilla loyal to Joshua Nkomo lays down his weapons to vote in the elections. (Weapons were forbidden in the polling booth.)

to provide the framework for a better social order, based upon the principles of equal opportunities and justice for all. Party leaders were expected to surrender private sources of income, schools were to be provided not just for a privileged minority but for all children, cooperative villages were to be promoted, and banks and many industries were nationalised. Since independence Tanzania has advanced far down the road to becoming a socialist state.

Nyerere opposed all forms of colonialism and racialism. This led to his quarrel with the British government over its failure to take strong action against Rhodesia's Unilateral Declaration of Independence in 1965 (see page 170). He sympathised with the African struggle for freedom from Portuguese rule in neighbouring Mozambique; in the 1970s he offered training facilities on Tanzanian soil for African guerrillas operating against Mr Ian Smith's regime in Rhodesia. Tanzania also developed friendly contacts with China, which provided the cash and skilled labour for the construction of the Tanzam railway between Lusaka in Zambia and the Tanzanian port of Dar es Salaam, completed in 1975. Relations with Zambia were strengthened after 1973, when Rhodesia closed its border with Zambia, causing the latter's trade to be re-routed through Dar es Salaam.

Tanzania's relations with Kenya and Uganda, however, were not always cordial. Antagonism arising from the socialism of Tanzania and the capitalism of Kenya was partly responsible for a quarrel between the two countries in 1977, which resulted in Tanzania closing its border with Kenya. Likewise, Nyerere made no secret of his dislike of General Amin of Uganda, and in 1971 Tanzania's action in giving political asylum to Milton Obote, the ex-Ugandan leader, soured relations between the two countries. Amin frequently accused the Tanzanian government of plotting to overthrow his regime, and major border clashes occurred between the two countries. As a result of these differences of opinion the East African Community, an economic union of Kenya, Uganda and Tanzania based upon the idea of the European Common Market, collapsed during the 1970s.

President Nyerere at the head of a queue to vote in the general election in 1965. His was the only party to vote for!

Zambia

Zambia's chief problem after becoming independent in 1964 was to free itself from the economic domination of South Africa. This was not
an easy task, since the Zambian economy suffered badly from the fall in copper prices during
the 1970s, and from Zambia's involvement in
the struggle for black majority rule in Rhodesia.
Consequently President Kenneth Kaunda
(1924–) followed a policy of Africanisation in
his country, so that commerce, industry and
administration were all placed in the hands
of Zambian citizens. At the same time,
however, Asians were assured that they
need not fear the threat of mass expulsion,
as had happened in Uganda. Economic
links with East Africa were strengthened,
particularly since the opening of the Tanzam
railway, but Zambia's prosperity was still
bound up with events in Rhodesia. There,
black majority rule was finally achieved in
1980.

Conclusion

The struggle for black supremacy in Rhodesia
and Namibia had serious implications for South
Africa which, with a 2,000 mile frontier across
a continent of potentially hostile neighbours,
wished to avoid a confrontation with Black
Africa. Already the three African governments
of Liberia, Senegal and the Ivory Coast had
abandoned their peaceful approach in 1978 – the
so-called 'dialogue' with the ruling white
minority in South Africa – and Liberia began to
finance guerrilla movements opposed to *apartheid*. South Africa's dilemma was, therefore, an
unenviable one. A refusal to alter the *status quo*
would offend international opinion. Yet to begin
dismantling the *apartheid* laws involved the
risk of inciting a revolution in which eighteen
million black people, supported by guerrilla
movements outside South Africa, could sweep
away not only the whole edifice of power upon
which the supremacy of four million whites
was based, but also law and order itself.

CHAPTER EIGHTEEN:
Central and Latin America

Ever since the Central and Latin American countries declared themselves independent of Spanish and Portuguese rule in the early nineteenth century, they have been of special interest to the United States; the latter warning the rest of the world against further interference in the western hemisphere. The American republics accepted gratefully the military protection afforded by the United States, but their economic dependence gave rise at times to strong resentment of 'Dollar Diplomacy' and 'Yankee Imperialism'.

Two chief characteristics of the republics have been deep divisions in society and political instability. In most of the countries a tiny minority owned more than half the nation's wealth. Many landowners left great estates uncultivated, while the mass of the peasants had to make do with small holdings hardly sufficient to support their families.

Industry was unable to flourish when the bulk of the population was too poor to buy its products, for the rich, who exported foodstuffs and raw materials, were able to purchase from abroad all the luxuries and manufactured goods they wanted. The slow pace of industrial progress had several important consequences. It stunted the growth of a middle class, thus creating a wide gulf between the rich and the poor. It failed to create a demand for skilled workers such as technicians and engineers, so that most people had only their manual labour as a means of earning their living. Most serious of all, the lack of industry meant a lack of jobs. With the population doubling every twenty-five years during the twentieth century, a shortage of land forced many peasants to drift into the towns in the hope of finding work, where they merely swelled the number of unemployed. All these conditions provoked intense social discontents and violent political upheavals.

The Latin American republics became notorious for revolutions and civil wars, political assassinations and short-lived constitutions. The wealthy elite constituted the ruling class, using their power to consolidate their privileges. In this process they were aided by the small middle class, which became an ally in repressing the rest of the population, and by the army, which looked upon itself as the guardian of the state. Because the South American countries faced no threat of attack by foreign powers, thanks to the protection of the United States, the armed services became chiefly concerned with domestic issues. They tended to perpetuate the traditional structure of society by supporting the government of the day or by replacing a grossly inefficient or corrupt government, in the conviction that they were acting in the national interest.

Both before and after the Second World War the United States intervened militarily in a number of Central and Latin American states in order to maintain political stability. In 1947, concerned over the development of the Cold War, the United States persuaded the American republics to sign the Treaty of Rio de Janeiro; by this, they agreed that an attack upon any American state would be regarded as an attack upon all. In the event of indirect aggression, however, such as the support of a revolution in one American state by another, they agreed to meet and consider what action should be taken. In 1948 all twenty-one republics signed the Charter bringing into existence the Organisation of American States (OAS), and by the Pact of Bogota they resolved to settle inter-American disputes peacefully.

31   *Central America, 1962*

The United States gave generous financial aid to all the American republics in order to promote economic growth and combat the spread of communism in the New World. It encouraged the formation of a Central American Common Market in 1960. In the same year President Kennedy promised massive dollar aid to encourage industry, education and measures to control the spread of disease. This aid was given with the proviso that the governments receiving aid must carry out extensive land and tax reforms in order to reduce poverty and social injustice. Details of this 'Alliance for Progress' were announced by the Inter-American Economic and Social Council at its meeting in Punta del Este, in Uruguay, in 1961. They reflected the United States' concern firstly, that communism might have a powerful appeal to the impoverished masses of the South American continent, and secondly, over the success of the Cuban revolution.

Cuba

Cuba's importance in world affairs in 1979 far exceeded that which one would have expected from its size and population. When Fidel Castro seized power in 1958 Cuba became the first communist state in the western hemisphere. The United States' campaign to eradicate communism from the island provoked a crisis with the Soviet Union, which for a short time seemed to threaten the start of a nuclear war. Meanwhile, Cuban support for left wing guerrilla movements in Latin America and Africa became an important factor in the world wide struggle between the forces of communism and capitalism.

Between 1934 and 1958 the Cuban people suffered under the dictatorship of Fulgencio Batista. Although Cuba was one of the richest countries in Latin America, its wealth was very unevenly distributed. The luxury hotels and gambling casinos of Havana, the capital, contrasted with the hovels of the poor, who formed the great majority of the population.

Fidel Castro became the leader of the Cuban revolutionary movement in the early 1950s. His melodramatic attack upon the Moncada barracks in Santiago de Cuba in 1953 earned him a two year prison sentence and was the origin of the 26 July Movement, as the anti-Batista movement came to be called. On his release in 1955 Castro went to Mexico. There he organised a group of eighty supporters, who sailed with him on the yacht *Granma* in 1956 to invade Cuba. Among them was an Argentine revolutionary, Ernesto 'Che' Guevara, who had been disillusioned by the collapse of a revolution in Guatemala in 1954, and was later to become a folk hero after his death in the Bolivian jungle in 1967. Batista's forces, however, were prepared for Castro's expedition, which shortly after landing was left with only fifteen men. They formed the nucleus of a guerrilla band which overthrew Batista two years later.

Batista's repressive rule drove many Cubans to support Castro as the means of ending a cruel dictatorship and by 1958 the guerrilla movement had gained control of the mountainous Sierra Maestra region of Cuba. In December Batista recognised that defeat was inevitable and fled, while on 1 January 1959 Fidel Castro's forces occupied Havana, amid scenes of wild rejoicing.

Castro's communist sympathies soon emerged when he quarrelled with his liberal supporters and appointed communists to posts in his government. All large businesses and farms over 150 acres in size were taken into state ownership. Castro obtained supplies of oil from the Soviet Union, and Guevara toured the communist countries of Eastern Europe seeking aid. When the United States-owned oil refineries refused to refine the Russian oil, Castro confiscated them. The United States retaliated with a trade boycott of Cuba, whereupon Castro sold his country's entire sugar crop to the Soviet Union, as a way of solving his economic difficulties. He was exchanging dependence upon the United States for close commercial ties with

Castro with Khrushchev, perhaps the most powerful man in the USSR at that time.

the Soviet Union. The latter supplied Cuba with military equipment, making it the most powerful state in Latin America.

The establishment of a communist regime so close to its shores alarmed the United States government, which backed a foolhardy attempt by 1400 Cuban exiles to invade Cuba and overthrow Castro in 1961. The Bay of Pigs invasion was a complete fiasco, and resulted in a secret attempt by the Soviet Union to exploit the Cuban revolution, by installing medium range nuclear weapons on the island. This provoked a dangerous confrontation between the two superpowers (see Chapter Nineteen).

Fidel Castro emerged from the crisis with his prestige higher than ever, despite the fact that Cuba was expelled from the OAS, and became economically dependent upon the Soviet Union. The United States broke off diplomatic relations with Cuba, but promised not to invade the island. It was only after more than a decade, in the improved atmosphere of East-West relations in the 1970s, that the OAS agreed to allow Latin American states to resume normal relations with Cuba after 1975. It was not until 1977, moreover, that the United States lifted travel restrictions to the island.

In 1976 a new socialist constitution came into force in Cuba. The Cuban Communist party was the only one permitted, and a National Assembly of People's Power, with 481 deputies elected by the town assemblies, was established. Real power, however, rested in the thirty-one member Council of State, presided over by Castro, who was therefore both Head of Government and Head of State.

The Dominican Republic

Dominica, a small republic of 19,000 square miles, occupies the eastern part of the former Spanish colony Hispaniola. During the twentieth century, apart from a period of direct rule by the United States (1916–24), and brief interludes of democratic government, the country has been ruled by dictators.

From 1930 until his assassination in May 1961 Rafael Trujillo was dictator, and his family was the Dominican government. Trujillo was forced to resign when the Organisation of American States imposed an economic blockade of Dominica, following his involvement in a plot to kill his enemy, President Betancourt of Venezuela.

Joaquin Balaguer succeeded Trujillo in name only, such was the power and influence of the Trujillo family until its forced exile following pressure from the United States. In 1962, Juan Bosch, leader of the Dominican Revolutionary party, was elected President. He was suspected by the rich of being a communist, however, and in September 1963 he was overthrown by a military coup and deported to Puerto Rico.

Bosch's Revolutionary party went underground, as a triumvirate dominated by Donald Reid was installed in office. Civil war broke out in 1965 when Reid tried to forestall an army plot to oust him by arresting its ringleaders. The Communists attempted to seize power but were foiled by President Johnson's prompt despatch of 20,000 marines to the country. The United States government was determined that Dominica should not follow Cuba's example by becoming a communist state.

The crisis ended when Joaquin Balaguer, leader of the Reformist party, became President in 1966. With the support of the Dominican army and the United States, Balaguer ruled until August 1978, when the first peaceful transfer of power in Dominica's history took place; Dr Antonio Guzman, leader of the Revolutionary party (now moderate in outlook), was inaugurated President.

Haiti

Haiti was the first Latin American country to win its independence (from the French) in 1804. In 1957 Dr Francois Duvalier ('Papa Doc') became President. He organised his own private police force, the *Tontons Macoutes*, who terrorised the largely illiterate population into making him President for life in 1964. Under his rule Haiti became a police state, with the Single Party for Revolutionary and Government Action founded by 'Papa Doc', being the only one permitted. When Duvalier died in 1971 he was succeeded by his son, who was also elected President during his lifetime.

Puerto Rico

By the Treaty of Paris (1899) which ended the Spanish-American War, Puerto Rico was annexed by the United States; its inhabitants were given American citizenship in 1917. During the 1930s the Nationalist party campaigned for complete independence, but the population was divided on the issue, since the country's prosperity was based upon its economic ties with the United States. Although Puerto Rico became a commonwealth in 1952, with internal self-government, a terrorist movement demanding full independence developed. In October 1977 Puerto Rican nationalists seized the Statue of Liberty, and held it for several hours, in an attempt to publicise their cause.

Mexico

The Mexican people developed a sense of national identity as a result of the Mexican Revolution (1910–17). During the inter-war period the government took the lead in promoting economic and social reforms: such as raising the status of labour by permitting the existence of trade unions, redistributing land and establishing a system of secondary education. With the formation of the National Revolutionary party in 1928 Mexico became a one-party state.

Mexico was content to remain a small power. It joined the Allies during the Second World War, but gave only token military help in the actual fighting; its main contribution to the Allied cause being the supply of raw materials to the United States. After 1941 Mexico entered an era of good neighbourliness with the United States, with which it shared a long, unfortified frontier.

By 1978, following the discovery of vast oil reserves far exceeding those of Saudi Arabia, Mexico had become a major producer of oil, and its international status had risen accordingly. An assortment of world leaders, ranging from President Carter of the United States to Fidel Castro of Cuba, courted its government in the knowledge that Mexico could shortly become the most important producer of oil in the West. In 1975 the EEC signed trade agreements with Mexico, which also strengthened its links with the Third World countries. Yet Mexico faced great problems, for oil had the power to revolutionise a society in which many people lived below the poverty line. Mexico City, with a population of thirteen million, was the largest poor city in the world, with almost half its adult population unemployed. The Olympic Games, which were held there in 1968, were accompanied by violent anti-government demonstrations, and it remains to be seen whether the benefits of prosperity can be extended to the poorer sections of the Mexican community before their grievances become intolerable.

Guatemala, El Salvador, and Honduras

In 1974 Guatemala threatened to invade the neighbouring British dependency of Belize (British Honduras). Although several Central American countries supported Guatemala's claim to the territory, it was opposed by Panama; an action which led to diplomatic relations between the two countries being severed. Britain sent troops to defend the colony, whose claim to independence at a future date was supported by the United Nations. The issue was still unresolved in 1978, when the Guatemalan President, General Garci, faced a growing problem of political unrest in his country.

Between 1969 and 1976 El Salvador was involved in a dispute with Honduras. Although its forces were largely successful in border clashes, El Salvador's economy was damaged by the expulsion of 50,000 illegal immigrants from Honduras, which also closed its border to trade with El Salvador. After 1972 El Salvador was troubled by urban guerrilla warfare. In April 1977 left wing terrorists killed the Minister for Foreign Affairs, while right wing terrorist attacks were aimed against Jesuit priests, who were accused of encouraging the peasants to demand land reform and higher wages.

Honduras came under military rule in 1972, but elections for a new government were promised for 1979. In 1974 Hurricane Fifi destroyed the greater part of the banana crop, causing a large trade deficit.

Armed Sadinista rebels stamp on a portrait of President Somoza, Managua 1979.

Nicaragua

Nicaragua, the largest state in Central America, is rich in natural resources, but only gold and copper are mined intensively. Its mainly rural economy is dependent upon exports of coffee and cotton, and hopes for future industrial development rest upon the possible construction of a trans-Nicaraguan canal. This would supplement the Panama Canal, which is unable to take modern oil tankers and container ships.

Nicaragua's politics were dominated by the Somoza family, which ruled the country from 1933 to 1979, apart from a brief interlude between 1963 and 1967. During the 1970s Somoza's rule was challenged by the Sandinista National Liberation Front (a left wing organisation named after Augusto Sandino, a Nicaraguan nationalist who was executed in 1934), whose guerrilla attacks forced President Anastasio Somoza to impose martial law upon the country between 1974 and 1977. In August 1978 a revolt was sparked off when Sandinista guerrillas captured the National Palace in the capital, Managua, and secured the release of over fifty political prisoners. The Sandinistas received encouragement and financial aid from many Latin American states, including Cuba, Panama (which sent a detachment of troops), Costa Rico, Mexico and Venezuela. After months of bitter fighting, in which government forces used tanks, rockets and aircraft in an attempt to overcome centres of resistance, Somoza acknowledged his defeat in July 1979 and fled to the safety of Miami, USA. In September 1980, however, he was assassinated in Paraguay by his enemies.

Costa Rica

Compared with most countries in Central and South America, Costa Rica has a high standard of living, thus justifying its name (which means 'rich coast'). Costa Rica benefited from its membership of the Central American Common Market, and from the construction of the Inter American Highway in 1955, which gave traders and businessmen access to the Panama Canal and to Guatemalan ports.

After the Second World War and particularly during the terms of office of José Figueres, elected President three times between 1948 and 1970, Costa Rica made great advances towards democratic government. The army was abolished in 1948, when it was replaced by a civil guard with police duties. In 1978 Figueres was replaced by Rodrigo Caraza.

Panama

The idea of a canal across the isthmus connecting the Atlantic and Pacific Oceans was first conceived by the Spanish in the sixteenth century, but it was not until 1880 that Ferdinand de Lesseps, the French engineer who had built the Suez Canal, began work on the project. The difficulties encountered were enormous and ten years later the French Panama Company went bankrupt. Although work on the canal restarted in 1894, little progress was made until 1903, when the Panamanians declared their independence of Colombian rule. Meanwhile, in 1902, the United States government had acquired the rights to build the canal. Eventually the eighty-two kilometre canal, linking Balboa on the Pacific coast with Cristobel on the Caribbean, was completed in August 1914.

The strategic value of the canal was most evident between 1941 and 1945, when the USA was at war with Japan and Germany. Its commercial importance for North America is equally great, since most ships using the canal are bound for, or have left, North American ports. Yet relations between the Panamanian and United States governments were not always smooth, since only a small proportion of the canal revenues was handed over to the Panama government. In 1977, however, two new treaties regarding the canal were signed. They assured the Panama government of an average annual income of eighty million dollars from the canal, which would be administered by the United States until the end of the twentieth century.

The states of Latin America

Colombia

Colombia's politics since 1945 have been punctuated by short-lived authoritarian governments and outbreaks of extreme violence, in which over 200,000 people have died. The rivalry between the liberal and conservative parties became a savage feud in 1948, following the murder of Jorge Gaitan, a leading left wing politician, as he was walking down a street in the capital, Bogota, in broad daylight. Riots in protest against the killing broke out, resulting in a nation-wide orgy of destruction of property known as the *bogotaza*.

Maracaibo Lagoon

TRINIDAD

CARACAS
VENEZUELA
GEORGETOWN
GUYANA
FRENCH GUIANA
SURI- NAM
BOGOTA
COLOMBIA
QUITO
ECUADOR
PERU
BRAZIL
LIMA
BOLIVIA
LA PAZ
BRASILIA
Pacific Ocean
PARAGUAY
ASUNCION
Rio de Janeiro
ARGENTINA
URUGUAY
Valparaiso
SANTIAGO
Punta del Este
BUENOS AIRES
MONTEVIDEO
Atlantic Ocean
FALKLAND ISLANDS
(British, but claimed by Argentina)

0 Miles 500
0 Kilometres 800

32   *South America*

Under the presidency of Laureano Gomez (1950–3) Colombia began to develop into a fascist state, but in 1953 Gomez was overthrown by Rojas Pinillo, who promised to abolish the privileges of the wealthy minority, and established a dictatorship based upon the support of the masses. Pinillo's popularity, however, declined when Colombia's economy was severely damaged by a fall in the price of coffee. He was removed from office in 1958 when the conservative and liberal parties ended their feud and formed a National Front, whereby they agreed to take it in turns to rule the country for four years at a time.

Colombia's economy benefited from the stability created by this experiment in power sharing, but many problems remained unsolved. With less than a quarter of the population receiving a formal secondary education, skilled labour was in short supply, and attempts to diversify the economy were not very successful. Moreover, with one of the fastest-growing populations in Latin America the problem of unemployment in the cities steadily worsened.

Venezuela

Venezuela owes its name to the first Spanish explorers who, on seeing a South American Indian village with huts built on stilts, were reminded of the Italian city of Venice and called the country 'Little Venice'.

The discovery of oil in the Maracaibo lagoon in 1917 transformed the Venezuelan economy. By 1928 Venezuela was the leading exporter of oil after the United States, and the country prospered despite the trade depression of the 1930s. The government paid off its entire foreign debt, built a network of roads and railways and constructed ports and harbours. In the 1970s Venezuela still ranked as one of the most important oil-producing and natural gas-producing regions in the world, enabling the country to enjoy the highest income per head of the population in the whole of Latin America. The wealth, however, was very unevenly distributed, the greater part being concentrated in the hands of a tiny minority and over half the population of thirteen million living in poverty.

Venezuela benefited from the demand for petroleum products generated by the Second World War, and Romulo Betancourt became President in 1945 at a time of rising prosperity. His plans for reform, however, were distrusted by the rich, and in 1948 he was overthrown by a military coup, which installed Marcos Perez Jimenez as dictator. Jimenez attempted to stifle opposition to his regime by outlawing political parties, repressing the trade unions, closing down universities and censoring the press.

Ten years later Jimenez was replaced by Betancourt, who became the first Venezuelan President to complete a term of office, despite an attempt by Dominican agents to assassinate him in 1960. Betancourt's policies of redistributing wealth and creating a balanced economy through state ownership of the most important industries, were copied by succeeding governments. Inflation was thus kept largely under control and a favourable balance of trade was maintained. Nevertheless, the continuation of Venezuelan democracy into the 1980s is not assured, for the pressures of social and economic discontents, combined with a long tradition of government by dictatorship★ may prove too strong to resist.

Ecuador

Ecuador has been at peace with its neighbours for many years, apart from a brief war with Peru in 1941 over a disputed area of the Amazon basin. Ecuador was defeated and at the peace conference held in Rio de Janeiro in 1942, surrendered its claims to the territory. Like many countries in Latin America, Ecuador faced great problems in the 1970s, caused by the rapidly growing population, an economy dangerously dependent upon a single crop (bananas), a low *per capita* income and glaring inequalities of wealth between the rich and the poor. Ecuador lacked sufficient capital and the skilled manpower needed for developing industry and communications. The growth of political parties since 1945 was also a slow process, owing to the popular appeal of José Velasco, who became President of Ecuador five times.

★ Venezuela has had only thirty-four years of democracy in its 168 years of independence.

Peru

Peru is the third largest country in Latin America, being exceeded in size only by Brazil and Argentina. During the Second World War and the Korean War, Peru benefited from the United States' demand for minerals to sustain its war effort.

Until 1968 Peru was technically a democracy, but political power was wielded by a tiny minority, and little progress was made towards overcoming the country's problems. These were caused mainly by the Andes mountains and the rivers and jungles of the Amazon basin, which made transportation expensive and arduous. As a consequence, many parts of Peru were isolated, and lacked facilities such as schools, hospitals, adequate housing, and communications. More than half the population could neither read nor write, and earned less than fifty pounds per year.

In 1963 Fernando Belaunde-Terry was elected President. Uncultivated land was seized by the state and redistributed to the peasants while the Indians were encouraged to colonise the foothills east of the Andes. A network of roads was planned, and education was expanded in an effort to reduce illiteracy.

A mountain village in the Andes.

These reforms were costly, however, and Belaunde-Terry was overthrown in 1968 by a military junta led by General Juan Alvorado. In his seven years as President, Alvorado carried out a vigorous programme of 'peruvianisation' (economic nationalism). The government nationalised many foreign-owned companies and plantations, and insisted that a majority of shareholders in firms should be Peruvian citizens. Alvorado also tried to assert Peru's independence of the United States by developing diplomatic relations with a number of communist countries. In 1976 he was replaced by another general, Morales Bermudez, when plans for a return to democratic government in 1980 were announced.

Bolivia

In the course of the last hundred years Bolivia has been involved in two wars. As a result of the War of the Pacific (1879–84) it lost its Pacific coastline to Chile, and became a land-locked state. In the Chaco War with Paraguay (1932–35) defeats and territorial losses led to a ten year period of military rule before this was ended in 1946 by a revolution, during which the President, Villaroel, was lynched by the mob.

Six years of political violence followed, as the Communists and the supporters of the Nationalist Revolutionary Party (formed during the Second World War) fought each other. In 1952 the struggle developed into the Bolivian National Revolution, when the Nationalists armed the peasants and workers, who proceeded to destroy the army. The new Nationalist government introduced universal suffrage in 1953 and granted lands to the Indian peasants, who were freed from compulsory labour services and given arms in order to defend the revolution. One of the chief reasons for the failure of the communist guerrilla movement in the 1960s (led by the Argentinian revolutionary, Ernesto 'Che' Guevara, until he was killed in 1967 by Bolivian soldiers) was that it failed to enlist the support of the peasants.

Despite considerable financial aid from the United States, successive Bolivian governments failed to solve the country's economic and social problems. Economic progress was hampered by a lack of outlets to the sea for Bolivian trade, and by the difficulties of transport and communications in a country dominated by the Andes mountain range, in which few passes are below 15,000 feet. During the 1970s communism remained a threat in a society with one of the lowest standards of living in South America. Only time will tell whether favourable conditions can be created for Bolivia's great natural resources to be developed.

Brazil

One of the largest countries in the world, Brazil comprises one half of the total area of South America. Formed in 1823 by the union of all the former Portuguese colonies in the western hemisphere, its frontiers touch ten countries. The population, which has increased ten-fold during the last hundred years, more than doubled between 1945 and 1978 when it grew from 46 to 110 millions. The population, however, is unevenly distributed, for the vast interior is very sparsely populated by Indian tribes in contrast to the densely populated coastal cities.

After the Second World War the Brazilian economy expanded greatly, but at the cost of a very high rate of inflation. Between 1956 and 1961 the foreign debt doubled, while the cost of living soared by 300 per cent. During the 1970s Brazil became one of the world's leading producers of coffee, cocoa, sugar, cattle, bananas, tobacco, asbestos and manganese. Three quarters of its exports were agricultural products, with coffee accounting for one third of its overseas earnings. Brazil, however, was unable to solve the urgent problems it shared in common with most countries of the Third World – rapid population growth, lack of industry and capital equipment, a low standard of living and a dependence upon exports of primary products. Successive post-war governments grappled with these difficulties, with varying degrees of success.

In 1945 Getulio Vargas, who had seized power in 1930, was overthrown in a bloodless revolution. A new constitution was drawn up, providing for a Senate whose members were appointed for eight years, and a Chamber of Deputies elected every four years. Presidential elections were to take place every five years, with the right to vote restricted to adults who could read and write (about one third of the population). Installed in office again in 1951, Vargas held power for another three years before he committed suicide after being accused of corruption and forced to resign by a group of army officers.

His successor, Juscelinio Kubitschek had the backing of an active but illegal Communist party and followed a policy of economic nationalism. Kubitschek set out on an ambitious programme of increasing the output of coal, petroleum, iron and steel, and initiated expensive hydro–electric power schemes. In an effort to reduce his country's economic dependence on the United States he made a trade agreement with the Soviet Union in 1959. Construction began on a brand new capital, Brasilia, which was intended to be a symbol of Brazil's future greatness, as well as focusing attention upon the need to develop the nation's great natural resources.

Modern flats contrast with shanties in Brazil.

In 1961, the year in which Brazil became a founder member of the Latin American Free Trade Area, Kubitschek was succeeded briefly by Janio Quadros. He was followed by Joao Goulart, regarded by many people as a communist. Under Goulart's leadership inflation was rampant, while economic growth stagnated. This was despite American dollar aid in the form of President Kennedy's 'Alliance for Progress', which financed measures designed to combat poverty, such as the provision of houses, schools and hospitals. As Brazil's economic difficulties multiplied, so the army became more and more disillusioned with the existing political system. In an effort to counteract the growing influence of the army Goulart tried to win popular support by promising land reforms and the nationalisation of the privately owned oil companies. The army, however, reacted strongly against this, and Goulart fled into exile in 1964.

By this time the army regarded itself as the guardian of the state and therefore responsible for ensuring efficient government, even though it might be seen to be acting against the expressed wishes of the electorate. The army officers therefore brought pressure to bear upon the new government, headed by Castello Branco, to introduce legislation to eliminate malpractices in administration. The First Institutional Act (1964) gave the government powers to dismiss or arrest officials guilty of misusing public funds or acting against the interests of the state. A Second Institutional Act (1965) set out to promote more responsible government by suspending the existing political parties, and replacing them by two new organisations. These were the National Renewal Alliance, which supported the government, and the Brazilian Democratic Movement, which was to be the official opposition party. A new constitution was introduced in 1967, whereby the President acquired powers to rule by emergency decrees if he considered it necessary, while offences against national security were to be tried by military, not civilian, courts.

After 1964 the army was the strongest political force in Brazil. Its stated aims were to return to responsible, democratic government as soon as conditions permitted and to make Brazil a powerful, industrial nation. Brazil's programme of developing nuclear power for industry led to strained relations with the United States, however, which did not welcome the idea of Brazil eventually possessing the capacity to develop nuclear weapons.

Paraguay

Politics in post-war Paraguay were dominated by General Alfredo Stroessner, who ended a period of great instability, which followed a civil war in 1947–8, by seizing power in 1954 and ruling the country for over a quarter of a century. Stroessner's strong rule, under which left wing opposition groups were banned, gave Paraguay a long period of peaceful development, and unlike many Latin American countries, it did not suffer from communist guerrilla campaigns. The trade union movement was state-controlled, while membership of the ruling Colorado party (so-called because it used the colour red in its early days to distinguish it from other factions), was an essential qualification for many occupations. These measures, combined with military rule, press censorship and detention of political opponents, effectively controlled the population of three million.

Despite American aid Paraguay's economy stagnated until 1970, when construction began on the world's largest hydro-electric station at Itaipu, on the frontier with Brazil. The remarkable economic progress during the 1970s began the process of transforming Paraguay from a poor, backward society into a modern industrial state.

Uruguay

Uruguay, with a territory of 72,000 square miles, is the smallest republic in South America. Almost half the population of three million in 1978, which is mainly of European descent, lived in the capital Montevideo. During the 1970s Uruguay's political stability was threatened by the *Tupamaros*, urban guerrillas named after Tupac Amaru, an Inca chief who rebelled against Spanish rule in the eighteenth century.

Uruguay benefited from the Second World War, when demand soared for livestock, its chief export; it also enjoyed a brief economic boom during the Korean War. Since the late 1950s, however, it suffered from severe inflation, which caused considerable social discontent.

Chile

Chile, with its 2700 mile Pacific coastline, is a long narrow country, for its average width is only 110 miles. Most of its eleven million inhabitants live in central Chile, for the northern part is largely desert, and the southern part is cold and inhospitable. Although it has a mainly agrarian economy, Chile is also a major exporter of nitrates and copper.

American investment in Chile increased after the Second World War, but a succession of right wing governments failed to solve the country's basic economic problems. Under the Presidency of Gonzalez Videla from 1946 to 1952 social discontent caused the emergence of a Communist party, which was outlawed in 1948. One of Videla's positive achievements, however, was to give women the vote in 1949.

His successor, General Carlos Ibanez, ruled with the support of the middle class, which was anxious to defend its privileged position. Ibanez provided strong government, but blocked any attempt to introduce social reform. In 1958 he was succeeded by Jorge Alessandri Rodriguez, who tried to solve the unemployment problem by a public works programme. Although Rodriguez managed to reduce the annual rate of inflation from sixty to thirty per cent, wages did not keep pace, and popular discontent resulted in widespread support for the Communist party, which had been legalised in 1958.

Eduardo Frei, leader of the Christian Democrat party formed in 1957, was elected President in 1964 on a programme of 'Revolution in Freedom', in which he promised Chileans a better deal. The government obtained control of the copper mining industry by purchasing fifty-one per cent of the shares of the American mining companies in Chile, thus enabling it to use the profits from copper exports to finance industrial development.

The government also established cooperative farms, in which the peasants were taught modern farming techniques. An Agrarian Law (1967) gave the government powers to confiscate uncultivated land, and limited individual land ownership to 190 acres. Agrarian reform proceeded very slowly, however, due to the reluctance of the wealthy classes to part with their land, to lack of finance, and to the difficulties of developing an efficient system of irrigation.

The peaceful revolution Frei hoped to accomplish was not to be, however. His policies raised the expectations of the great mass of the people, whose disappointment with the slow pace of social reform led to the growth of a revolutionary guerrilla movement in the late 1960s, and a fierce demand that the country's wealth should be more evenly shared. The result of these developments was the election of Salvador Allende (1908–73) in 1970, who became the world's first communist ruler to be freely chosen by popular vote.

Allende ruled with the help of a combination of Communists, Socialists and the break-away Christian Democrats who had deserted Frei, called Popular Unity. Many industries were taken into public ownership. The American mining companies were nationalised without compensation, on the grounds that they had already extracted sufficient wealth from the country. The American government retaliated by cutting off foreign aid to Chile and attempting to prevent the sale of Chilean copper exports in world markets. Allende responded by forming closer relations with the Soviet Union and other communist countries.

Allende, however, faced great problems in his attempt to establish socialism in Chile peacefully. The Movement of the Revolutionary Left (MIR), the urban terrorist organisation during Frei's Presidency, emerged into the open. By encouraging the peasants to occupy land illegally, it challenged the authority of the government. In 1971 5000 women demonstrated in Santiago, the capital, during the 'March of the Empty Pots', a protest against food shortages. In 1973 protracted strikes by truckdrivers and copper workers, secretly supported by the US

Central Intelligence Agency (CIA) which plotted to bring about the downfall of Allende's government, cost the government millions of dollars in lost revenues. Inflation soared to the dizzy level of 300 per cent in the first six months of the year.

President Allende's last day.

On 11 September 1973 Allende's rule ended in bloodshed when his government was attacked by Chile's armed forces, led by General Augusto Pinochet. The Chilean Navy seized the port of Valparaiso, while troops supported by tanks and aircraft attacked the Presidential palace. By the end of the day Allende lay dead in the ruins of his palace, and hundreds of his supporters had been killed in street-fighting. Chile's experiment with socialism was over.

Pinochet took office as President and ruled the country by military law. Political parties were banned, and the secret police rounded up opponents. Although most political prisoners had been released by 1977, allegations of the use of torture by the government to gain information persisted, and in the meantime many prisoners mysteriously disappeared. After Allende's death relations between Chile and the United States improved, and in 1977 plans for a return to lim-

ited civilian rule in 1981 were announced. The brutal circumstances in which Allende's government was terminated, however, lingered in people's memory.

Argentina

For over thirty years since the end of the Second World War Argentinian political life was dominated by the Peron family. Juan Peron (1895–1974) became Minister for Labour in 1943. For the next three years he used his office as a means of winning the support of the working classes by helping them to win favourable wage settlements. He became so popular with the working classes that when he was dismissed in 1945 demonstrations in his favour brought about the downfall of the government. Peron immediately organised a Labour party, and was elected President in 1946 by a narrow majority.

In office Peron strengthened his position by repressing opposition to his rule; he nationalised the public services and taxed the rich heavily. In 1952 he secured an amendment to the constitution, allowing him to become President for a further term, but his popularity was already on the wane. The death of his first wife, Eva Peron, was a serious blow as she had done much to organise the support of the trade unions. Moreover, the Church was hostile to Peron's efforts to undermine its authority, while the army opposed his policy of redistributing wealth to the working classes. In 1955 Peron was overthrown by a military coup which eventually brought General Pedro Aramburu to power. He banned Peron's party and crushed a revolt by the *peronistas*, shooting many of their leaders.

Nevertheless, the influence of the *peronistas* remained strong, and in 1962 the ban on Peron's party was revoked. Ten years later Peron returned from exile, to become President once again shortly afterwards. Argentina, however, was suffering from the ravages of inflation, and although Peron was succeeded on his death in 1974 by his second wife, *Senora* Martinez Peron, she remained in office for two ineffective years only, before the army lost patience with inefficient civilian rule and resumed control of the country in 1976.

One million workers mass to support President and Eva Peron.

It is neither easy nor wise to generalise about an area the size of Europe, containing twenty states which have little in common except their economic under-development, a tradition of authoritarian governments, and great tensions within society. The revolutionary, Ernesto 'Che' Guevara, however, believed that revolutionary warfare in Latin America was inevitable, for there:

two circumstances are joined: under-developed industry and an agrarian system of feudal character. That is why no matter how hard the living conditions of the urban workers are, the rural population lives under even more horrible oppression and exploitation. But, with few exceptions, it also constitutes the majority,

sometimes more than seventy per cent of the Latin American population . . . this great mass earns its livelihood by working on plantations earning miserable wages, or they till the soil under conditions of exploitation no different to those of the Middle Ages. These circumstances determine that the poor rural population constitutes a tremendous revolutionary force.

The answer to the question: will the South American continent be the stage for a violent struggle between the privileged classes and the great mass of the unprivileged? depends upon a variety of factors. Not the least of these are the speed of future economic progress and the governments' reactions to changes brought about by industrial growth.

In 1945 the United States was alone among the great powers in having no formal alliances; it had only signed executive agreements with its wartime allies, which did not require a two thirds majority of the Senate for approval. When the obligations of the Declaration of the United Nations (1942) ceased at the end of the war, the American people confidently expected a return to normal peacetime conditions and the withdrawal of American troops from Europe. This was not to be, however, since the spirit of wartime cooperation between the Soviet Union and its allies was replaced by mutual recriminations and hostility. By the end of 1946 there existed a state of 'Cold War', or 'non-shooting war', between the two superpowers.

In one sense the origins of the Cold War may be traced back to the establishment of a communist system of government in Russia in 1917. In Stalin's view the German invasion of the Soviet Union in 1941 was only the culmination of Western, capitalist, efforts to destroy the Bolshevik Revolution. Once victory in the Second World War was assured, Stalin was determined to achieve complete security for the Soviet Union by making Central and Eastern Europe a communist sphere of influence which would act as a barrier between the Soviet Union and Western Europe.

The imposition of Soviet-controlled governments in that region, however, disregarded the agreement reached at Yalta by the Big Three that its peoples should have the right to choose the form of government under which they would live. It also created fears that the Red Army would overrun Western Europe if American troops were evacuated. Russia's overwhelming superiority in terms of conventional land forces led the United States to rely on its monopoly of atomic weapons to deter aggression. This policy, together with a refusal to share its atomic secrets with the Soviet government, alarmed Stalin. He feared that the United States might seek to destroy Russia in a pre-emptive war (a possibility which was almost certainly discussed, but rejected, by the Allied leaders). This impression was reinforced by the decision to maintain American forces in Europe.

President Truman hoped that the problems arising from the dissolution of the wartime Grand Alliance and the growing distrust between the superpowers, would be overcome by the achievement of a lasting peace settlement under the auspices of the United Nations. Truman had inherited Woodrow Wilson's faith in national self-determination as a formula for peace and stability. At the same time he was nevertheless a realist, and was not prepared to risk war in order to free Eastern Europe from communist control.

Truman, however, resisted communist encroachments on territory belonging to the so-called 'free world'. He insisted that Soviet troops should be withdrawn from Iran in 1946. In the following year the United States helped the Greek government to overcome a communist rebellion, and gave financial aid to Turkey. In outlining his policy of containment to the American people Truman declared that the United States government would not allow 'changes in the *status quo* by such methods as coercion, or by such subterfuges as political infiltration'. In December 1947 he reinforced his global pledge to contain communist aggression with the offer of Marshall Aid, to promote the economic recovery of Western Europe (see Chapter Six).

When the Soviet Union imposed the Berlin Blockade in 1948 (see Chapter Five) Truman responded by ordering a massive airlift of supplies into the Western sectors of the beleaguered city, until Stalin conceded that his attempt to drive the Allies from Berlin had failed. In the meantime, Congress passed the Vandenberg resolution which authorised the President to make agreements with other countries in order to safeguard the United States. This made possible the formation of the North Atlantic Treaty Organisation in April 1949.

Important changes also took place in the Far Eastern policy of the United States. Shocked by the communist victory in China in 1949, and by the Russo-Chinese treaty of friendship signed in 1950, Truman decided to convert Japan from an ex-enemy state into an ally. A generous peace treaty, concluded in 1951, was accompanied by an alliance which permitted the United States to maintain military bases in Japan. The governments of Australia and New Zealand, fearing a possible revival of Japanese militarism, were reassured by the ANZUS pact which guaranteed them American support in the event of Japanese aggression.

The United States refused to recognise the legality of the People's Republic of China, preferring instead to support the exiled Nationalist government of Chiang Kai-shek in Taiwan (Formosa). American involvement in the Korean War in 1950 extended the policy of containment to the Far East, despite the danger that the resources of the United States might be overstrained by unlimited commitments to resist the advance of communism, wherever it appeared.

Readjustment and the 'Fair Deal'

Truman's achievements on the home front were less obvious than his foreign policy successes, but nonetheless real. He presided over a difficult period of transition from a wartime to a peacetime economy. After the defeat of Japan the American people wanted the return of millions of service men and women to civilian life, and a relaxation of wartime restrictions. By the end of 1947 the armed forces had been reduced from twelve million personnel to under three million, but the demand for more consumer goods was not so easily satisfied, and prices rose rapidly. The inflationary process was fuelled by wage demands from the trade unions, which had refrained from strike action during the war in return for a government promise to keep wages in line with prices.

A series of bitter confrontations took place between industrial workers and employers, in which Truman set out to protect the public interest. He defeated a strike of transport workers by threatening the train drivers with conscription, and resolved the miners' dispute by obtaining a court order forcing the coalminers to remain at work. He reluctantly accepted the Taft-Hartley Act of 1947, which restricted trade union powers and enforced a three month 'cooling-off' period in industrial disputes likely to lead to a national emergency. At the same time Truman tried to improve working conditions and the system of social security.

Truman's efforts to extend Roosevelt's New Deal programme, however, were rebuffed by Congress, where the Republicans had won majorities in both Houses in the 1946 elections. After his unexpected return to power in 1948 for a second term of office, however, Truman was in a stronger position to demand a Fair Deal for the American people. He persuaded Congress to raise the minimum wage from forty cents to seventy-five cents an hour, to extend social security benefits and to authorise a building programme to provide cheap housing for lowly-paid workers. Although his achievements in social engineering were modest in comparison with those of his Democratic successors, he certainly made their task easier by weakening the suspicion which accompanied any attempt to interfere with the principle of unfettered private enterprise.

The 1952 Presidential election

In choosing General Dwight D. Eisenhower as their Presidential candidate the Republicans acted wisely, for the General enjoyed great prestige and popularity as the organiser of victory in Europe in 1945, and as the first Supreme Commander of NATO. Eisenhower also capitalised on the disenchantment with the Korean war by promising to visit Korea in a personal attempt to bring about peace. The election campaign resulted in a substantial victory for Eisenhower over Adlai Stevenson, his Democratic opponent. Stevenson's defeat dismayed many Europeans, for he was internationally respected not only for his keen intellect, but also as a devoted supporter of the United Nations.

Eisenhower and Cold War problems

Shortly after his election victory Eisenhower visited Korea, where he realised that a conventional war against China would be a long and costly struggle. Nevertheless, he firmly rejected the doctrine of 'massive retaliation', which meant using atomic weapons to defeat a numerically superior enemy. His efforts to achieve a peace settlement were helped by Stalin's death in 1953, which caused uncertainty over the direction the Soviet Union's foreign policy would take. Eventually, after protracted negotiations at Panmunjon, the division of Korea along the thirty-eighth parallel was agreed.

Eisenhower refused to be drawn into the conflict in Indochina, where the French faced defeat by Ho Chi Minh's communist armies. At the same time he was determined to resist further communist encroachments in South East Asia; after the formation of North and South Vietnam in 1954, the United States sent economic aid and military advisers to South Vietnam, to enable it to resist pressures from the communist government of North Vietnam.

The events in South East Asia strained the United States' relations with its European allies, who were not prepared to go to the 'brink of war' in order to prevent a communist victory in Indochina. John Foster Dulles, the American Secretary of State, tried to strengthen the policy of containment by persuading the governments of Britain, France, Australia, New Zealand, Pakistan, Thailand and the Philippines to join the United States in signing the South East Asia Treaty Organisation (SEATO) in September 1954.

Unlike NATO, however, SEATO did not involve military commitments, since the signatories only agreed to consult each other if the peace of the region was endangered. Hong Kong and Taiwan were excluded from the terms of the treaty, while India, Burma and Indonesia insisted on maintaining their neutral attitude towards the Cold War. Not surprisingly, therefore, SEATO was not very effective; during the 1960s the British government refused to become involved in the Vietnam war, while France withdrew from the organisation altogether.

In 1954 another crisis arose over Taiwan, when the Chinese threatened to invade the offshore islands of Quemoy and Matsu, which were held by the Nationalists. Eisenhower refused to follow Dulles to the edge of a third world war by supporting the Nationalists whole-heartedly, and he defused a dangerous situation by persuading Chiang Kai-shek to evacuate the islands, which were very close to mainland China.

The Geneva Summit Conference 1955

The possession of the hydrogen bomb by both superpowers made 'brinkmanship' more perilous than ever, and Eisenhower hoped that a personal meeting with the Soviet leaders, Nikolai Bulganin and Nikita Khrushchev, would reduce East-West tension. The summit conference, attended also by Anthony Eden, the British Prime Minister, and Edgar Faure, the French Premier, was convened in Geneva in July. There Eisenhower unveiled his 'open skies' plan, whereby the Soviet and American governments would allow unlimited aerial inspection of their military establishments. The possibility of a surprise attack by either power would thus be minimised and steps could be taken towards nuclear disarmament. The proposal was rejected by Khrushchev, but Eisenhower won world-wide acclaim for his statesmanship.

Middle East tensions 1955–60

The Baghdad Pact, consisting of Iraq, Iran, Turkey, Pakistan and Britain, was inspired by Dulles in 1955 in an effort to contain growing Soviet influence in the Middle East, without committing the United States to direct military involvement. It failed, however, to achieve stability in the region. The Egyptian ruler, Colonel Nasser, bitterly criticised Iraq's membership of the pact as a betrayal of Arab unity. When Egypt became friendly with the Soviet Union, the United States withdrew its offer of economic aid for the construction of the Aswan Dam, causing Nasser to nationalise the Suez Canal (see Chapter Fifteen). These events formed the background to the combined Anglo-French-Israeli attack on Egypt in October 1956. Eisenhower refused to support England and France, who were soon forced to withdraw their troops from Egypt. In the meantime, Soviet troops crushed a Hungarian uprising against a repressive communist regime while the Western powers were divided amongst themselves.

The decline of British influence in the Middle East led Congress to authorise the President to give aid to any Middle East country threatened by communist aggression. The Eisenhower Doctrine, as it was called, was implemented in 1958. This was a result of the overthrow of the pro-Western government in Iraq and attempts to force Lebanon and Jordan to join the United Arab Republic (a federation of Egypt and Syria formed earlier in the year). Eisenhower supported President Chamoun of Lebanon by sending several thousand US marines to the capital, Beirut, where they prevented an attempt to overthrow the government.

During his final years in office Eisenhower tried once more to slow down the arms race; it had taken an ominous turn with the launching of a Soviet sputnik, or earth orbiting satellite, in 1957, and the development of inter-continental ballistic missiles (ICBMs). In 1958 Eisenhower ordered the suspension of nuclear tests in the atmosphere, and invited Khrushchev to visit the United States in July 1959. At the end of the year he went on an eleven nation tour, whose itinerary included India, Turkey, Italy and France.

Hopes of progress towards *détente* at a second Summit Conference held in Paris in May 1960, however, were shattered. Khrushchev disclosed that an American U-2 spy plane on a reconnaissance flight over the Soviet Union had been shot down and its pilot, Gary Powers, captured. The Conference therefore ended in failure, with the outstanding issues of the day, the future of Germany and Berlin, and nuclear disarmament, unresolved.

Domestic issues: McCarthyism and the Civil Rights movement

Eisenhower became President at the height of a campaign led by Joseph McCarthy, Senator for Wisconsin, to root out all Communists who, it was widely believed, had infiltrated American society and government. McCarthyism was the product of many factors, including the onset of the Cold War, the communist victory in China, and Russia's development of the atomic bomb. It received a great impetus in January 1950 when a former state department official, Alger Hiss, was found guilty of perjury in a case involving the disclosure of state documents to communist agents in the 1930s. The following month Klaus Fuchs, a scientist who had worked in America during the war on the development of the atomic bomb, was tried and convicted in Britain for espionage. These two cases provoked an unreasoning fear of a great communist conspiracy in the United States.

McCarthy claimed that he had proof of many known Communists who held important posts in the government service, schools and universities. Although his allegations were never proved, both Truman and Eisenhower were compelled by the pressure of public opinion to investigate the backgrounds of thousands of government employees. As a result of this, many people's careers were ruined, despite the fact that very few security risks were discovered. McCarthy eventually overreached himself in late 1953 when he attacked the integrity of the US Army. The proceedings were televised, and McCarthy alienated millions of Americans by his conduct and accusations at the hearing.

The Civil Rights movement

McCarthyism was a temporary phenomenon, but the Civil Rights movement which developed during the 1950s was to make far-reaching changes in American society. Black people throughout the Deep South were second class citizens. The majority were deprived of their right to vote by a variety of devices such as literacy tests, and a regulation which disqualified from voting anyone whose grandfather had not been a voter. Negro children could not receive their education in all-white schools, and racial segregation was practised in nearly all public services, including transport, hotels and restaurants, theatres, parks and cemeteries. A National Association for the Advancement of Coloured People, was formed, having as its chief aims the equality of civil rights and an end to segregation. It made little progress until 1954 when the Supreme Court ruled that segregation of black and white children in separate schools was illegal.

In December 1955 Mrs Rosa Parks, a black seamstress who lived in the town of Montgomery, Alabama, was arrested when she refused to give up her seat in the front section of the bus reserved for white passengers. This incident sparked off a black boycott of the city buses, and brought into prominence a new Civil Rights leader, Rev. Martin Luther King. He inspired the black community to make the boycott effective, and after a campaign lasting eleven months the Supreme Court ruled that segregated seating on buses was unconstitutional.

In the following year the struggle was centred upon education. The all-white University of Alabama was forced by a court order to admit a female black student, Autherine Lucy. Her admission, however, was attended by riots which the university authorities seized upon as an excuse first to suspend her for causing a breach of the peace, and then to expel her for objecting to the suspension. Eventually the state Governor, George Wallace, dropped his opposition to the court order, and in 1957 black students were allowed to enrol at the university.

Meanwhile the township of Little Rock, in Arkansas, was in the headlines for the refusal of its school board to obey a federal order to abolish segregation in its high schools. On the pretext of keeping law and order, Governor Faubus used the state national guard to prevent black school children from enrolling. Eisenhower reluctantly used federal troops to force the school authorities to comply with the ruling, and nine black students began to attend an all-white high school under armed guard. Nevertheless, progress towards civil rights, despite the passage of a Civil Rights Act in 1957, was very slow; by 1960 few Southern states had accepted the idea of de-segregated education.

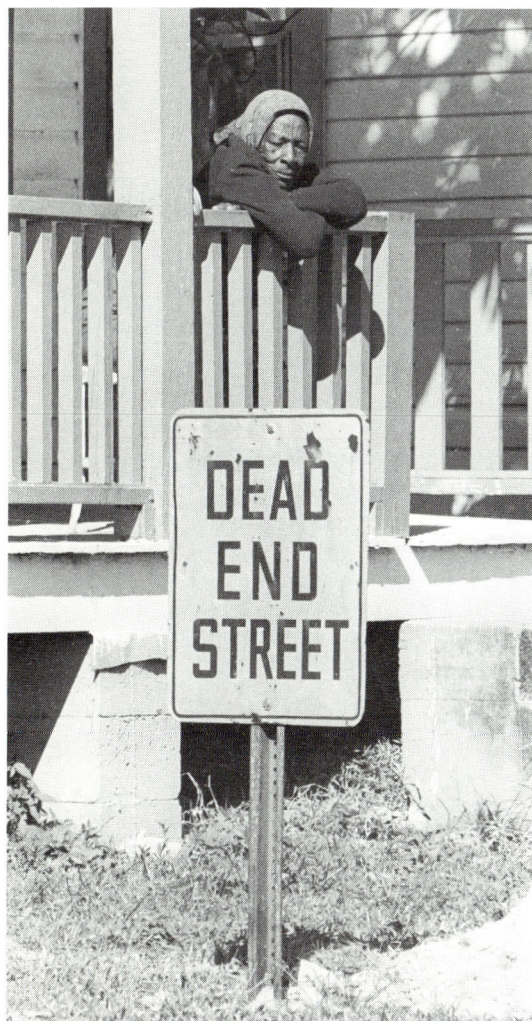

The Kennedy administration

John Fitzgerald Kennedy was born in Boston in 1917. When he was inaugurated as America's youngest President in January 1961 he seemed to symbolise the hopes of millions of Americans for 'a just peace and a better life', particularly for black people, whose votes had done so much to carry him to the White House. Among Kennedy's assets were his youthfulness, his energy and zest for life and his charm, which he exploited at press conferences and by carefully rehearsed television broadcasts to the nation.

Kennedy promised a new era in American politics. The problems of poverty were to be attacked by providing federal aid to depressed areas, increased social security payments and a housing and community development programme. Education and standards of medical care were to be improved, while increased spending on defence, and the Apollo space programme to put the first man on the moon, would help to revive the sluggish American economy. Black Americans hoped that he would also promote the cause of Civil Rights.

Kennedy wasted no time before choosing teams of experts to analyse urgent national problems. Key posts in the government were given to Dean Rusk, who became Secretary of State, and Robert McNamara, who became Secretary of Defence. The new administration quickly gained a reputation for decisiveness, but Kennedy later admitted that he did not realise how difficult would be the problems he faced, and how limited were his powers.

From the outset Kennedy assumed responsibility for foreign policy. He was greatly concerned over the lead which Soviet scientists appeared to have established in missile development, and the attractiveness of communism to Third World countries as a means of overcoming their economic problems. Kennedy believed that only firm action, combined with a determination to resist force with force, held out any hope for an enduring peace.

In June 1961 Kennedy met Khrushchev in Vienna, where the latter insisted that a settlement of the German problem could not be delayed much longer, and a confrontation developed over the future status of Berlin. Kennedy refused to be browbeaten, and insisted that the United States would keep its troops in West Berlin, even at the risk of thermonuclear war. The crisis subsided when the East German authorities began work on a wall which sealed off East Berlin from the Western sector. The Soviet Union therefore achieved its objective – two separate Germanys – without a peace treaty. After the wall had been completed the flood of refugees from East Germany was stopped, and Berlin ceased to be a centre of international tension when East Berlin was quietly incorporated into the German Democratic Republic in 1966.

Vietnam

By 1961 Vietcong successes in the Vietnamese civil war (see Chapter Thirteen) were threatening the survival of the American-sponsored government of South Vietnam. Kennedy regarded the conflict as part of the communist strategy of provoking wars of national liberation in order to achieve world domination. He was therefore determined to resist the communist threat to South Vietnam, and unwittingly committed the United States to a long war of attrition, which damaged its prestige and from which it was able to extricate itself only with great difficulty. This problem, however, belonged to the future. The attention of people everywhere was soon to be drawn to a Caribbean island, over which a nuclear confrontation developed and the peace of the world hung in the balance.

The Cuban missile crisis 1961–62

Soon after becoming President, Kennedy learned that a band of Cuban exiles was being secretly trained in Guatemala by the US Central Intelligence Agency (CIA) to invade Cuba and overthrow Fidel Castro's revolutionary government. Against the advice of his colleagues Kennedy allowed the preparations to proceeed, on the grounds that American troops would not be directly involved. It was to be a costly error.

In April 1961 the exiles landed at the Bay of Pigs, where Castro's forces were waiting, and within two days most of them had been killed or captured. The communist countries branded the United States as the aggressor, and the Soviet Union announced that it would give Cuba 'all necessary help in beating back the armed invader'.

During the next few months evidence of military aid and the presence of Soviet technicians in Cuba grew. On 14 October an American reconnaissance plane returned with photographic evidence that missile sites were being constructed on Cuban soil. Intermediate range ballistic missiles, each capable of carrying a nuclear warhead to many American cities, were also seen to be already in Cuba. They were the first Soviet missiles stationed outside the territory of the Soviet Union.

On 22 October 1962 Kennedy made a television broadcast, informing the American people that the purpose of the missiles:

can be none other than to provide a nuclear strike capability against the Western hemisphere. . . . American citizens have become adjusted to living daily on the bull's eye of Soviet missiles located inside the USSR or in submarines. But this swift, secret, and extraordinary build-up of communist missiles – in an area well known to have a special and historic relationship to the United States – is a deliberately provocative and unjustified change in the status quo *which cannot be accepted by this country if its courage and commitments are ever to be trusted again by either friend or foe.*

Kennedy imposed a naval blockade of Cuba and announced that Soviet ships carrying missiles to the island would be stopped and searched, if necessary by force. NATO air and ground forces were put on war alert. Kennedy also declared that any nuclear missile launched against the United States from Cuban territory would be met by a nuclear attack upon the Soviet Union.

Tension grew until 24 October, when the Soviet ships approaching Cuba first slowed down, and then altered course away from Cuba. Although the crisis was not yet over, for the missile sites were nearing completion, it was clear that neither side wanted war. On 26 October the Soviet Union agreed to remove its missiles from Cuba and to destroy the missile sites, and the United States promised that it would never attack the country.

Domestic matters

During Kennedy's administration the Civil Rights movement gathered momentum. In 1961 the Congress of Racial Equality sent 'freedom riders' into the southern states, and soon blacks could travel freely in the South without having to use separate waiting rooms and dining areas in interstate bus terminals. A campaign of 'sit-ins' at lunch counters plus marches and demonstrations in Birmingham, Alabama, eventually ended discrimination in the employment of shop assistants and segregation in the city's restaurants. In 1962 James Meredith, a black air force veteran, forced the University of Mississippi to open its doors to him and allow him to attend classes.

Kennedy, however, adopted a cautious attitude towards the Civil Rights issue. Federal agents were sent to the Deep South to help blacks to exercise their right to vote, and he extended the policy of appointing blacks to government posts. It was only in 1963 nonetheless, that he came down firmly in support of a Civil Rights Bill, which was eventually passed by Congress in 1964, several months after Kennedy's death.

The circumstances of Kennedy's assassination in Dallas, Texas, on 22 November 1963, helped to create the image of a brilliant, youthful President cut down in the prime of life. Although Kennedy's achievements in revitalising American society were modest, his death left as an open question what he might have achieved given the chance of a second term of office.

The Presidency of Lyndon Johnson

Lyndon Johnson had been overshadowed by Kennedy, but he was a shrewd politician with immense experience in dealing with Congress. He capitalised on the grief over Kennedy's assassination by an emotional appeal to Congress, in which he asked the elected representatives of the American people to pass the tax reforms and civil rights legislation which were already in the pipeline.

Congress agreed to the tax cuts readily enough when the government promised to prune its budget, but opposition to the Civil Rights Bill in the Senate was more difficult to overcome. Several southern senators indulged in filibustering tactics (making interminably long speeches in order to obstruct the passage of legislation), but eventually the Senate voted a closure on further debate, and Johnson signed the Civil Rights Act in June 1964. This prohibited segregation in restaurants, hotels and public places, and made racial or colour prejudice in schools and registration of voters a federal offence.

In November Lyndon Johnson won an overwhelming victory in the Presidential election over his Republican adversary, Barry Goldwater, whose opposition to the Civil Rights legislation frightened millions of voters. They were also disturbed by his apparent willingness to use nuclear weapons in order to combat the threat of international communism. Johnson refuted Goldwater's charges that he was 'soft on communism' by ordering air strikes against North Vietnamese naval bases, as a reprisal for a torpedo-boat attack upon an American destroyer which was carrying out electronic eavesdropping in the Gulf of Tongking.

The 'Great Society' programme

The Democrat landslide victory gave Johnson large majorities in both Houses of Congress, and enabled him to press ahead with measures to alleviate urgent social problems. Plans to improve standards of medical care of the elderly had already been delayed for several years. Three schemes were considered by Congress, before features of all three were incorporated in a Medicare Bill which became law in July 1965. Nineteen million people over the age of sixty-five benefited from its provisions, more generous than those of Kennedy's unsuccessful bill in 1962 which failed to pass Congress. Federal aid was given to education and summer camps were organised to provide holidays for deprived children. Minimum wages were raised, and measures taken to reduce unemployment, improve transport and replace slums through community housing schemes. But it was the continuation of the Civil Rights issue which caused most concern.

Civil Rights

In March 1965, Martin Luther King organised a march of thousands of demonstrators from the town of Selma, in Alabama, to the state capital, Montgomery. This was part of the campaign to win the vote for three million blacks disqualified by literacy tests. The televised scenes of violence as the local police assaulted and dispersed the marchers shocked the nation. George Wallace, the State Governor, was summoned to the White House, where he reluctantly agreed to guarantee the right to demonstrate peacefully, but when he returned home he claimed that he lacked the funds. Johnson therefore placed the Alabama National Guard under federal control, and the march from Selma to Montgomery took place without incident. Shortly afterwards Congress passed an act to ensure that blacks could vote regardless of any tests designed to deprive them of their right.

Despite the progress towards legal equality, black Americans were becoming increasingly alienated from the rest of society. In the cities the contrast between the affluent life-style of white Americans who lived in comfort in pleasant suburbs and the plight of millions of blacks who lived in slums, had created a potentially explosive situation. After 1965 many blacks deserted the moderate Civil Rights movement and joined extremist groups such as the Black Muslims. Their leaders, like Malcolm X and Stokely Carmichael, rejected the non-violent approach of Luther King and demanded 'Black Power'. By this they meant not integration, but separation. The assassination of Luther King in Memphis, Tennessee in April 1968, led to an orgy of violence and destruction in dozens of towns and cities. By then militant groups like the Black Panthers were openly advocating race war in order to destroy white supremacy.

The presidency of Richard Nixon

In the 1968 Presidential election Richard Nixon won forty-three per cent of the popular vote, compared with Hubert Humphrey's forty-two per cent. The narrowness of the victory reflected the deep divisions in American society, which was preoccupied with the growth of violence, the problem of race relations and the need to redefine American foreign policy in the light of the Vietnam war.

Nixon's achievements as President owed much to the ideas of Henry Kissinger, a Harvard professor whom he appointed National Security Adviser with the responsibility for coordinating United States foreign policy. Nixon recognised that with the rise of China, Europe and the Third World nations as power blocs in their own right, the United States could no longer influence world affairs as it had done during the 1950s. He thus sought *détente* with the USSR and friendship with China.

The end of the Vietnam war

Of all the problems Nixon inherited from the previous administration, the most pressing was the Vietnam war. President Johnson had escalated the conflict by bombing North Vietnam, but had failed to win victory; on the contrary, the Vietcong Tet offensive in 1968 seemed conclusive proof to the many opponents of the war that the United States had squandered lives and resources in a shameful bid to impose its will upon a foreign people.

Nixon was determined to extricate the United States from its involvement in the Vietnam war by gradually withdrawing American troops, whose role was to be taken over by the South Vietnamese army. This policy was known as Vietnamisation, and it marked the abandonment of containment. Nixon was not prepared to make a precipitous retreat, however, and the war dragged on until 1973, when all American troops were withdrawn from South Vietnam, despite the fact that North Vietnamese troops were permitted to stay. Nevertheless, the Vietnamese people were now able to decide their own future free from United States intervention.

The search for nuclear disarmament

For over a decade the USA and the USSR had been engaged in a nuclear arms race of frightening proportions. Both powers wished to prevent the spread of nuclear weapons to other countries, however, and this had enabled them to reach limited agreements. In 1963 they had signed a Test Ban treaty, which prohibited nuclear tests in the atmosphere and outer space, though underground tests were still permitted. Over one hundred countries signed this agreement, though France and China, which were close to becoming nuclear powers themselves, refused. In 1967 Latin America was declared to be a nuclear free zone.

In 1968 a treaty on the non-proliferation of nuclear weapons was signed by many states, but in a dangerous world not every country was willing to renounce possession of such powerful weapons. Thus a number of nations, including India, Israel, Egypt, Japan, South Africa, Brazil and Argentina, all approaching 'nuclear club membership', did not sign. In 1970 the superpowers agreed that they would not site nuclear weapons on the ocean floors.

Nixon abandoned America's insistence on nuclear supremacy, and recognised that the Soviet Union would not accept a position of permanent inferiority. He hoped that the two superpowers could agree to limit their nuclear weapons on the basis of equality. In 1969 the two governments began Strategic Arms Limitations Talks (SALT), but the difficulties of reaching an agreement which would also guarantee the complete safety of the two nations were enormous.

Eventually, in June 1973, Salt 1, an expression of aims rather than actual reductions of armaments, was agreed. Six years later, President Jimmy Carter and Leonid Brezhnev signed SALT 2 in Vienna, when the United States and the Soviet Union set modest limits to the growth of nuclear weapons up to 1985. In his statement to the Press, President Carter said:

The most powerful currents of history have often been the ones that swept nations to war. Today, the threat of nuclear holocaust still hangs over us as it has for more than thirty years. Our two nations are now armed with thousands of nuclear weapons, each capable of causing devastation beyond measure . . . The Strategic Arms Limitation Talks, which have gone on for nearly ten years without interruption, represent the realisation that a nuclear arms competition without shared rules, without verifiable limits, and without continuing dialogue, is an invitation to disaster . . . If we cannot control our power to destroy, we can neither guide our fate nor preserve our future.

The reconciliation with China

In July 1971 world opinion was surprised by Nixon's decision to visit China the following year. The United States also dropped its opposition to the admission of China to the United Nations, a move which led to the expulsion of Taiwan. Thus the long years of containment and confrontation with communist China came to an end, and the United States resumed its policy of friendship with China.

President Nixon and the Watergate scandal

Abroad Nixon's leadership ushered in an era of optimism and *détente*; at home, however, his opposition to the liberalism of the sixties, and his readiness to sacrifice principles to the political needs of the moment, were less praiseworthy features of his Presidency. By shifting on to the courts the responsibility for speeding up desegregation in schools, Nixon tried to avoid alienating southern voters. When the Supreme Court ruled in April 1971 that bussing of children was necessary in order to achieve a racial mix in many southern schools, Nixon managed to sidestep a controversial issue. The episode of the Pentagon Papers, which were 'leaked' to the newspapers in the summer of 1971 revealed the extensive measures taken by the government to conceal the truth about the Vietnam war. It was the Watergate scandal, however, which led to Nixon's resignation, and damaged the reputation of the United States government.

In the summer of 1972 the Democratic Campaign headquarters (the rival party to that of President Nixon) in the Watergate building in Washington were burgled by government agents, who were paid from President Nixon's campaign fund to keep their silence. When the truth emerged Nixon denied all knowledge of the affair, only to admit later that he had been aware of the cover up. After protracted legal proceedings, during which the President was forced to release transcripts of taped conversations relating to the Watergate affair, Nixon resigned in August 1974, when Vice-President Gerald Ford took his place. The Watergate affair, as a result of which some of Nixon's closest associates were gaoled, discredited the Presidency.

United States influence in world affairs since 1975

Both Gerald Ford and Jimmy Carter, elected President in November 1976, were anxious not to alienate Third World opinion. Relationships with South Africa were strained as both leaders warned its government that the United States would not intervene to save it from the consequences of its *apartheid* policy. After the death of a black leader Steve Biko while in the custody of South African police, the United States voted in favour of a UN embargo on the sale of arms to South Africa. The American government also pledged support for black majority rule in Rhodesia, and for an independent Namibia.

In his inaugural address President Carter affirmed that American foreign policy would embody the ideas of justice, equity and human rights, as well as the traditional issues of war and peace. Thus Carter defended the two Panama Canal treaties, which he signed in 1977, as a measure of international justice. The treaties, which were ratified in April 1978, made arrangements for the United States to hand over control of the canal to the Panamanian government in the year 2000. Carter also risked offending the Soviet Union by voicing his concern over the fate of Russian writers and scientists who spoke out against the harshness of their country's government.

Carter's chief anxieties, however, were over the Middle East crisis, and the search for a peace settlement following the 1973 Yom Kippur war. In 1977 Carter and Leonid Brezhnev, the Soviet leader, agreed to reconvene the Geneva peace

President Sadat and Prime Minister Begin in a rare moment of agreement. President Jimmy Carter looks on.

talks. Carter spoke of the legitimate rights of the Palestinians, as well as Israel's need to insure the security of its frontiers with its Arab neighbours, thus warning Menachem Begin, the Israeli Premier, that American support was not unconditional. Carter welcomed President Sadat's visit to address the Knesset, or Israeli parliament, in November 1977, and took the initiative in bringing the two leaders together at Camp David, Maryland, in September 1978. Their discussions led to the signing of a peace treaty between Egypt and Israel in 1979.

The Iranian revolution in 1979 posed fresh problems for the United States' government. The American Embassy in Teheran was seized in November by militant students demanding the return of the former Shah for judgement before they freed their hostages. President Carter halted shipments of arms to Iran and froze Iranian assets in the United States in a vain effort to secure their release.

None of these pressures seemed to have any effect on the Ayatollah's régime, whose action in holding to ransom the American citizens, and apparent refusal to negotiate except on terms of its own choosing, flew in the face of international opinion and posed a difficult diplomatic problem for the United States. President Carter's inability to impose a solution, despite being head of state of one of the most powerful nations on earth, was only too clear for all the world to see. Some observers derived a certain satisfaction over the United States' predicament, but the more far-sighted deplored the lack of respect for international law, upon which all nations, large and small, rich and poor, ultimately rely.

American foreign policy in the 1970s was characterised by a desire to solve world problems through negotiation rather than confrontation, and to seek a further relaxation of tension between the USA, USSR and China. Optimism that the world was a safer place than it had been in the 1960s, however, was tempered by the realisation that little progress had been made in slowing down the arms race.

In the late 1950s the two superpowers joined in a race to be the first nation to put a man on the moon. The Soviet *Sputnik V* orbited the earth in 1960 with two live dogs on board (which were safely recovered) and in the following year a Russian astronaut, Yuri Gagarin, became the first man to travel in space when he orbited the earth in the spaceship *Vostock* in 108 minutes. In 1962 John Glenn became the first American astronaut, while the Russian, Valentina Tereshkova, became the first woman in space when she circled the earth for three days.

Four years later the US *Surveyor I*, an unmanned spacecraft, landed on the moon and transmitted back to earth photographs of the lunar surface. In 1968 *Apollo VIII* with three American astronauts on board orbited the moon several times before returning safely to earth. Finally, on 20 July 1969 an American astronaut, Neil Armstrong, became the first man to walk on the moon, saying as he did so, 'I'm going to step off the lunar module now. That's one small step for a man, one giant leap for mankind.' What was only improbable science fiction in 1939 was fact only thirty years later, such was the speed of scientific and technological advance.

Yet in spite of the enormous increase in scientific knowledge and in man's mastery of the environment, it is very doubtful whether the world in 1979 was less free from suffering and misery than it was a generation before. It was certain that mankind's problems were vastly more complex and intractable, and that the survival of civilised life on earth, perhaps even of mankind itself, could no longer simply be taken for granted.

The dangers arose not only from mankind's capacity to destroy itself by nuclear or bacteriological warfare, but also from the world's population explosion, and a refusal by the Third World nations to accept that hunger and poverty should be their normal condition. The growing inequality between the wealthy industrialised nations and the under-developed Third World constituted the most important threat to world peace. It was a problem which could only be solved through international cooperation, and even then only with immense difficulty if man's environment was to be preserved. That would be the urgent task of governments and peoples in the latter part of the twentieth century.

The most important lesson we have learned from the astronauts is that the world is a single unit, a rather tiny place; that the conditions of life are incredibly fragile; and that human life is confined by its own requirements to a very small fraction of the earth's biosphere. The penalty of technological mastery of the earth is that, henceforth, there is no escape from the responsibility of planetary management. Man's future and man's environment must be conceived and managed wisely if he is to survive and prosper. Mankind cannot proceed, or even survive at all, as a divided and warring species.

We must hope that U Thant's words offer a blueprint for the progress of mankind, and not an epitaph.

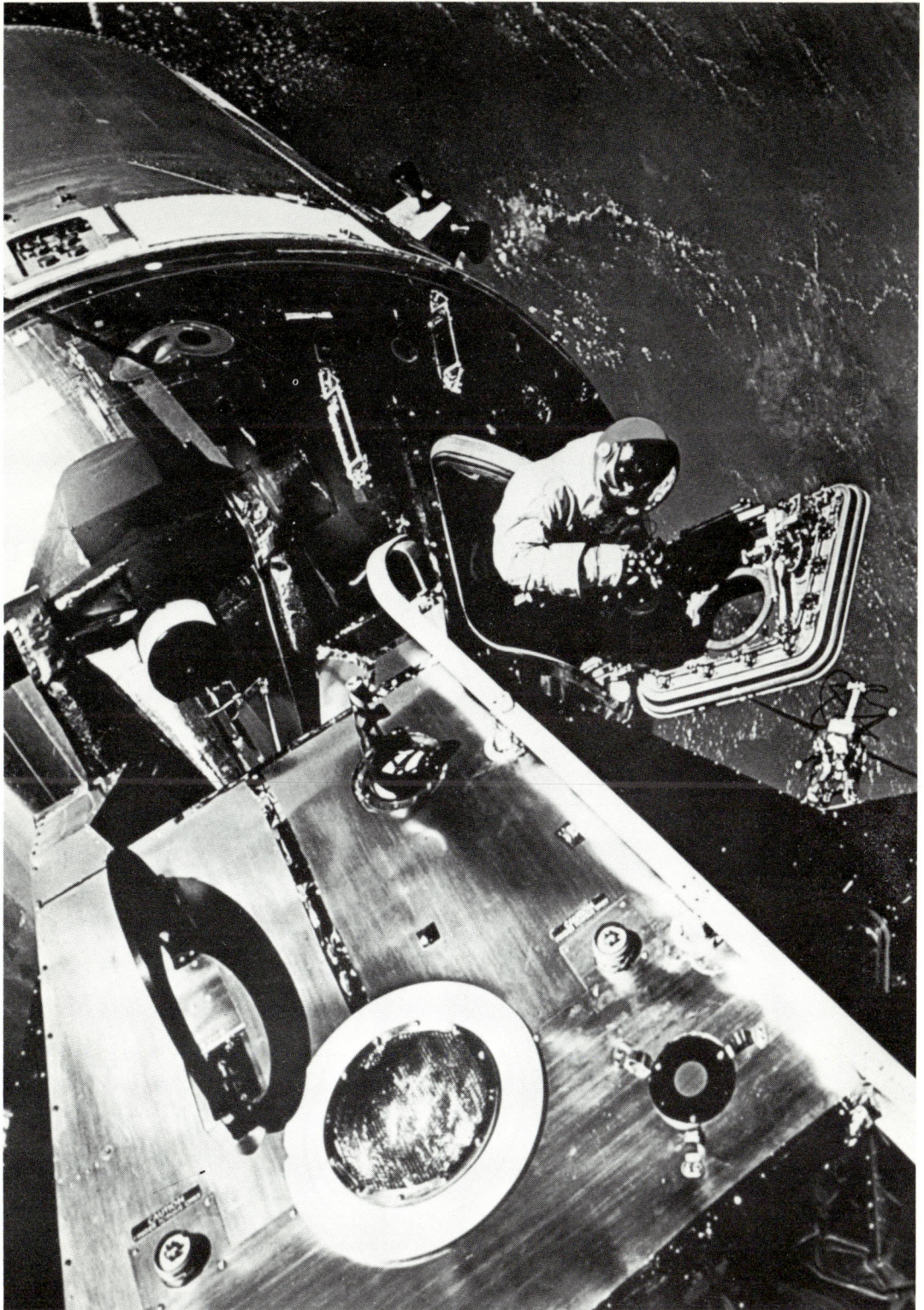

INDEX